BAD FAITH

ALSO BY NEIL J. KRESSEL

Mass Hate: The Global Rise of Genocide and Terror

Political Psychology

Stack and Sway: The New Science of Jury Consulting
(with Dorit F. Kressel)

NEIL J. KRESSEL

BAD FAITH

THE DANGER OF RELIGIOUS EXTREMISM

Prometheus Books
59 John Glenn Drive
Amherst, New York 14228–2119

Published 2007 by Prometheus Books

Inquiries should be addressed to
Prometheus Books
59 John Glenn Drive
Amherst, New York 14228–2119
VOICE: 716–691–0133, ext. 210
FAX: 716–691–0137
WWW.PROMETHEUSBOOKS.COM

11 10 09 08 07 5 4 3 2 1

Library of Congress Cataloging-in-Publication Data

Kressel, Neil Jeffrey.
Bad faith : the danger of religious extremism / by Neil J. Kressel.
p. cm.
Includes bibliographical references and index.
ISBN 978–1–59102–503–0
1. Religious fundamentalism. I. Title.

BL238.K74 2007
200.9'0511—dc22

2007011479

Printed in the United States of America on acid-free paper

To Leah, Noah, Hannah, and Sam

CONTENTS

Introduction: A Journey to the Heart of Religious Militancy 9

PART ONE: THE UNEXPECTED BATTLE OF THE TWENTY-FIRST CENTURY

Chapter 1: Who Exactly Is a Religious Extremist? 33
Chapter 2: Militant Islam: The Present Danger 55
Chapter 3: Killers in Every Faith: Christians and Jews 91

PART TWO: THE CAUSES OF MILITANT FAITH

Chapter 4: Dangerous Books? 139
Chapter 5: Vulnerable Minds and Sick Societies 199

PART THREE: FIGHTING EXTREMISM SENSIBLY

Chapter 6: A Battle on Many Fronts 235

Acknowledgments 267

Notes 269

Index 313

INTRODUCTION

A Journey to the Heart of Religious Militancy

When Cartoons Are Not a Laughing Matter

Several months prior to Hezbollah's war with Israel in 2006, Hassan Nasrallah told television audiences across the Arab world just what, in his opinion, had gone wrong with Islam. The problem, he explained, was too much moderation. According to the Hezbollah leader: "If any Muslim had carried out the [1989] fatwa of Imam Khomeini against the apostate Salman Rushdie [for writing his novel *The Satanic Verses*], those despicable people would not have dared to insult the Prophet [Muhammad]—not in Denmark, not in Norway, and not in France."[1]

Nasrallah spoke several months after the Danish newspaper *Jyllands-Posten* had published its controversial cartoons dealing with—and in some cases portraying—the Prophet Muhammad. In Nasrallah's view, boycotts, diplomatic efforts, and solidarity protests would not be enough: "If we tolerate this now, only God knows what they will do later." Leaving no doubt concerning the potential magnitude of his challenge, he added, "On this matter, we are not Lebanese, Syrians, Palestinians, Egyptians, Saudis, Malaysians, or Indonesians.

This is about the Prophet of the Muslims, the Prophet of 1.4 billion Muslims. I am certain that not only millions but hundreds of millions of Muslims are ready and willing to sacrifice their lives in order to defend the honor of their Prophet."[2]

Around the same time, Sheikh Yousef al-Qaradhawi of Qatar provided another glimpse into the heart and mind of a Muslim militant. In a widely televised sermon, he declared: "The nation must rage in anger." President of the International Association of Muslim Scholars and an influential guide for Islamist organizations across the globe, Qaradhawi explained his position: "It is told that [the famous Muslim cleric] Imam al-Shafi' said: 'Whoever was angered and did not rage is a jackass.' We are not a nation of jackasses. We are not jackasses for riding, but lions that roar. We are lions that zealously protect their dens, and avenge affronts to their sanctities. We are not a nation of jackasses. We are a nation that should rage for the sake of Allah, his Prophet, and his book. We are the nation of Muhammad, and we must never accept the degradation of our religion."[3]

Perhaps acting from similar sentiments, several Muslim leaders in early 2006 called for death to the cartoonists. In the Indian state of Uttar Pradesh, for example, a high-level government official, Haji Yaqoob Quereshi, offered to pay a sizable sum to anyone who killed one of the cartoonists. He also claimed that local women would donate gold jewelry equivalent to the weight of the assassin. When asked to rethink his offer of a reward in light of his political responsibilities, Quereshi stood firm, saying: "It is a matter of faith and deep love for the Prophet [Muhammad]."[4] The same week, an influential Pakistani cleric placed his own bounty on the cartoonists, this time proposing more than a million US dollars and a car—presumably in addition to divine rewards. He later told a reporter, "If the West can place a bounty on Osama bin Laden . . . , we can also announce a reward for killing the man [*sic*] who has caused this sacrilege of the holy prophet."[5]

In Yemen, one imam sermonized that "[a]nyone who insults the prophet must face the sword." Another Yemeni cleric declared, "The government must execute them." These religious leaders were speaking not about the cartoonists themselves or even their publishers but rather about several arrested Yemeni editors who had published selections of the cartoons with the clear intent of condemning them. One editor even put an X over each image.[6]

When an Islamic court in India issued a fatwa condemning the twelve cartoonists to death, religious leader Maulana Mufti Abul Irfan defended the decision. He claimed that the Koran clearly states that anyone who insults the Prophet deserves to be punished.[7] In Afghanistan, crowds chanted: "If they abuse the prophet of Islam again, we will all become al-Qaeda."[8]

But many other Muslims interpreted their faith very differently. For example, Salim Mansur, a Canadian Muslim, suggested that "since God in his infinite majesty neither compels, nor takes offence," it is reasonable to believe his followers should behave in a similar manner.[9] Mustafa Akyol, a Turkish Muslim writer based in Istanbul, said he understood the disgust of Muslims around the globe but that the Koran prescribed a clear and civilized response to mockery: simply do not sit with people until they cease blaspheming and commence talking about other matters.[10]

By the time the cartoon controversy wound down, businesses had lost millions, editors had been fired and jailed, artists were in hiding, government officials had stepped down, and bodies lay on the streets. Several death threats remained in effect, yet by the standards of our time, body counts were not high. Still, many sensed that the cartoon affair revealed much about the power of religious extremism in the contemporary world.

Though no one denied that the drawings themselves lay near the center of one of the biggest news stories of 2006, very few Western newspapers were willing to reprint them. Most commonly, papers claimed to refrain out of respect for religious belief or because journalistic manners precluded publishing something offensive to large numbers of readers.[11] There are good reasons to reject such rationalizations, however.

Some in the press suggested that Muslim prohibitions against showing images of their prophet are uniquely significant, often failing to note that, even within Islam, opinions differ greatly about the prohibition and that other religions have similar sensitivities that are commonly ignored.

Moreover, newspapers refused to reprint some of the Danish cartoons that did not actually portray Muhammad but were part of the original set published in *Jyllands-Posten*. Why, for example, did they not reprint the cartoon showing an artist who was apparently afraid to draw Muhammad, or the one that ridiculed the *Jyllands-Posten* drawings as a publicity stunt? These illustrations clearly made legitimate political points and they did not violate the prohibition against showing the image of Muhammad.

Some editors argued that the real problem lay in the insulting nature of the cartoons. And there can be little doubt that the drawings could be interpreted as disrespectful from the point of view of a religious Muslim. Yet, again, newspapers—and especially political cartoonists—have hardly been required to adhere to a strict "respect" standard in the past. A *New York Post* cartoonist, for example, has shown gas coming from the rear end of the Reverend Al Sharpton.[12] Yet the *Post* did not reprint any of the Danish cartoons. And remember how newspapers across the country reprinted images of "Piss Christ"—Andres Serrano's photograph of a crucifix with a representation of Jesus Christ submerged in a glass of the artist's own urine—on the grounds that it was art, arguably art, or at least newsworthy because some people had deemed it art.[13]

Some newspaper editors and publishers suggested that the Danish cartoons were juvenile and not worthy of republication. They objected, for example, that the most famous cartoon, the one with a bomb in Muhammad's turban, was ludicrous, as it made no sense to declare Muhammad a terrorist. However, a far more likely interpretation of the cartoon was the one offered by the cartoonist himself; the drawing was, he said, based on his belief that terrorism derived spiritual ammunition from Islam.[14]

More to the point, cartoonists have never been required to provide careful and wholly accurate arguments in the past, and the position implied by the drawing is at least a legitimate part of the debate. Back in 2002, Pulitzer Prize–winning cartoonist Doug Marlette had his own encounter with the Islam-sensitivity forces. He drew a cartoon showing, in his own words, "a man in Middle Eastern apparel at the wheel of a Ryder truck hauling a nuclear warhead. The caption read, 'What Would Mohammed Drive?'"[15] He claims the primary aim of his cartoon was to parody the "What Would Jesus Drive?" campaign in which Christian evangelicals sought to protest against gas-guzzling sport-utility vehicles. Whether or not this was truly Marlette's intention, one can certainly understand how some Muslims perceived their own faith as the target. In any event, he received more than twenty thousand e-mails demanding, as he put it, "an apology for misrepresenting the peace-loving religion of the Prophet Mohammed—or else." Some included very clear threats. Marlette published his response under the headline: "With All Due Respect, An Apology Is Not in Order."[16] He did, however, explain that his cartoon attacked only those "murderous fanatics" who distorted Islam. One might object to Marlette's cartoon, but his take on the First Amendment makes sense. He argues that it is "not just a passive shield of protection. In order to maintain our true, nationally defining diversity, it obligates journalists to be bold, writers to be full-throated and uninhibited, and those blunt instruments of the free press, cartoonists like me, not to self-censor. We must use it or lose it."[17]

Sensitivity, respect for the feelings of readers, and nuance may be standards that many religious leaders and some journalists desire, but they are not (and generally should not be) widely practiced journalistic norms—especially when they require censorship of material that everyone deems relevant, newsworthy, and vitally important. To this day, many people around the world have been unable to develop an informed position on the controversy because they have not seen the Danish cartoons. Worse, in some places, people now believe that far more objectionable cartoons—some involving bestiality, for example —were part of the original group published in Denmark.[18]

As columnist Jeff Jacoby aptly declared in the *Boston Globe*, "Rationalizations notwithstanding, the refusal of the US media to show the images at the heart of one of the most urgent stories of the day is not about restraint and good taste. It's about fear."[19] Editors and publishers worried about financial consequences, undesirable political reactions at home and around the globe, and, above all, physical attacks.

Perhaps not far from their consciousness were images of Theo Van Gogh, who had been assassinated in Holland for producing a film critical of Islam's treatment of women. Indeed, an Egyptian judge and author of books on political Islam seemed to get to the core of the matter. "I keep hearing, 'Why are liberals silent?'" remarked Said al-Ashmawy. "How can we write? Who is going to protect me? Who is going to publish me in the first place? With the Islamization of the society, the list of taboos has been increasing daily. You should not write about religion. You should not write about politics or women. Then what is left?"[20] Such fears, of course, are many times more justified for an Egyptian liberal than for a Western editor. But these days, they are relevant for anyone who may anger certain militant mullahs and imams.

The crime of the Danish editors and those who followed suit, according to the Jordanian parliament, was "striking at the sentiments of the Arabo-Muslim nation."[21] Similarly, a Pakistani leader notes after dutifully blaming troublemakers for the violence, that "[t]he people behind the cartoons are the biggest terrorists. The government of Denmark should have taken them under arrest. They have incited the emotions of Muslims around the world."[22] But if "inciting the emotions" of a religious group or "striking at their sentiments" becomes the standard, where does that leave the liberal democratic world, and where does it leave the democratic concept of a free press?

Some say in a very bad place. Lorenzo Vidino, a terrorism expert at Tufts University's Fletcher School of Law and Diplomacy, notes that

> the lack of support for the Danish newspaper by much of the Western media has shown we are willing to accept limits to free speech, if going beyond those limits provokes a clash with the most violent

> voices of the Muslim world. The key question is: where do we place that limit? How far must we compromise to respect other peoples' feelings? . . . Are we going to reach a point where no alcohol will be served in public places, as that could offend Muslims? By the same token, some Muslims are offended by mini-skirts and other revealing clothes. Are we going to implement a culturally sensitive dress code for Western women on our own turf?[23]

Another terrorism expert, Paul Marshall, offers a similar set of questions.

> If these countries succeed in exporting their repression on this issue, what will be the next step? Will governments be attacked if their media give internet links to cartoons of Mohammed, so that those who wish can see them? Will *South Park* be censored for the sake of international amity? Will there be attacks on publications featuring more positive images of Mohammed? Will U.S. embassies suffer violence if the Met[ropolitan Museum of Art] continues to allow images of Mohammed in their catalog online? Will the Met be attacked if it shows those paintings? If Americans overseas are threatened or held hostage until friezes [showing Muhammad] on the Supreme Court are sandblasted, what will we do?[24]

Vidino and Marshall use some hyperbole to make their point. But we are, nonetheless, left with the question: What next?

The cartoon controversy raises many issues:

- Are those who threatened to kill the cartoonists *religious* extremists? To what extent does their motivation derive from religious sources as opposed to political, economic, or psychological ones?
- How do we distinguish between intense piety and religious extremism?
- Is there a fundamental incompatibility between Islam—or at least some versions of Islam—and constitutional democracy?

- Can—and should—the West protect its system of free expression? How?
- Can—and should—the West devise and adhere to a strategy that prevents clashes with extremist Islam in the future?
- To what degree is "respect" for the religious beliefs of others a necessary or desirable part of Western civilization? What does such respect entail? To what extent does respect for religious belief trump freedom of expression?

After all, Muslim extremists may well have learned the lesson that if they are brutal enough, tough enough, and determined enough, they can intimidate the West, despite its empty professions of belief in freedom of expression.

National Review writer Jonah Goldberg objects when some news outlets speak of updating procedures (read: limiting the free press) to avoid offending "religious" sensibilities in the future. He protests that "[w]e're not talking about 'religion.' We're talking about a specific religion—Islam."[25] Discussing violence in Nigeria surrounding the 2002 Miss World contest, the sharp-tongued conservative columnist Ann Coulter makes a related point. She starts with the facts. Some Muslims had protested against the beauty pageant on the grounds that it promoted indecency and promiscuity. A local newspaper responded to their objections by stating that Muhammad, had he been there, would have selected a wife from among the contestants. Shortly thereafter, some Muslims initiated violent attacks against local Christians and churches. Some Christians retaliated by also committing violent acts, although Muslims bore responsibility for most of the bloodshed. Coulter's main objection is to the way Western journalists and commentators conceptualized the event. She writes,

> The *New York Times* can't bear to think that their little darlings—angry, violent Muslims—could be at fault in this melee. That makes no sense because Islam is a Religion of Peace. So the *Times* reviewed the facts, processed it through the PC prism, and spat out the headline: "Religious Violence in Nigeria Drives Out Miss World

> Event." According to the *Times*, "rampaging Muslims pouring out of mosques to kill Christians and torch churches resulted from the tinderbox of religious passions in the country." Islam is peaceful, but religion causes violence. Pay no attention to the fact that the most bloodthirsty cult in the 20th century was an atheistic sect known as communism. But that was not "true communism," just as Muslim terrorists are not practicing "true Islam."[26]

Coulter's words are controversial and incendiary, as she intends, and there is much room to argue with her interpretation of events, here and elsewhere. Yet she expresses what many in America, Europe, and elsewhere believe—that the problem is not one of "religious" extremism at all, only one of Muslim extremism.

Though in light of daily headlines it is easy to see how such a view might arise, that thinking is at its core historically shortsighted, theologically naive, and probably wrong even with regard to the present danger. In order to better comprehend this threat and others that might arise in the foreseeable future, we need to develop a broader perspective on the challenges we face.

THE CHALLENGE OF THE TWENTY-FIRST CENTURY

There is nothing new about religious extremism. Christianity, Judaism, Islam, and other world faiths have all inspired their share of evil deeds since time immemorial. Throughout history, many pious individuals have pondered their relationship with God only to end with a program of murder, misogyny, bigotry, or child abuse. Already religion has led some believers to contemplate the use of weapons of mass destruction to achieve their sacred goals. To say that such believers are misguided followers of a false religion does not get us very far. For we must be able to say which features render a faith dangerous and why so many people in so many times and places have been drawn to malevolent systems of belief when others were available.

It is not necessary to suggest scrapping religion altogether, though some have proposed this answer. Religion in its various forms seems to speak to what many consider a fundamental human need, so it is not apt to disappear any time soon. The problem is not religion but religious extremism. And, as events of our day have made abundantly clear, those of us—religious and secular—who cherish the accomplishments of a modern liberal democratic society can no longer afford to ignore the challenge posed by extremists. The dangers have grown even more intense and more pressing in a world where the Internet and broadcast technology can create instant global audiences often beyond the reach of the potentially moderating influences of government, traditional clergy, or anyone else.

The twenty-first century was not supposed to be an era of religious militancy. By the middle of the last century, most scholars expected religion across the globe to continue its evident decline, growing less and less relevant to world affairs, slipping—as Freud and many others predicted—into the dustbin of history or, at the very least, maintaining its long retreat from the public square. Yet as daily headlines attest, religion, for better or worse, is back.

And though the return of religion need not imply the return of militancy, many people now agree—not only on the basis of the September 11 attacks—that religious extremists pose a dangerous threat to humanity in the coming decades, perhaps the most dangerous threat. Unfortunately, that is just about where the agreement usually ends. We remain deeply divided and confused about the nature of religious extremism, how it differs from more traditional forms of piety, where it originates, and how we might best control its adverse effects.

The stakes are very high. The freedom to follow the religion of one's choice, or no religion at all, is one of Western civilization's greatest accomplishments and greatest treasures. Achieved over a period of centuries after all the alternatives proved worse, this freedom applies even when many of one's fellow citizens—or all of them—regard one's beliefs as incorrect, heretical, or misguided. And this is as it should be. Tolerance of religious diversity defines a healthy constitutional democracy every bit as much as free elections do, probably more. Yet a democratic society also guarantees the right to subject all beliefs, even religious beliefs, to critical examination, and this, of course, is the only way to understand what separates religion at its best from religion at its worst.

In the centuries before Western civilization evolved its tradition of tolerance, Europe was torn apart by an unending series of brutal and cruel wars based on what can, in retrospect, be regarded as relatively small differences within the Christian family of religions. We have in our own era observed in Bosnia, the Middle East, South Asia, and elsewhere a sampling of religion's continuing potential to inspire bloodshed.

If people in America and around the world do not find a way to control religious extremism while maintaining religious tolerance, the end of the twenty-first century may look less like the worldwide liberal democracy so widely envisioned at the conclusion of the Cold War and more like a global version of the era of religious wars in the sixteenth and seventeenth centuries. This will be made more terrible by the reach and destructive power of modern technology. Profound changes are needed in many areas and it is my desire to try to light a part of that path.

Those who wish to understand what separates constructive religious impulses from destructive ones face an unusually difficult task. In contemporary society, religion has been a most controversial topic, one frequently banned from polite conversation. This has never been truer than in the first few years of the twenty-first century, when the strictures of political correctness have made it nearly impossible to discuss differences among religious traditions with any degree of honesty.

Instead of serious and forthright analysis, we encounter a windstorm of bromides and obfuscation. Some, including President George W. Bush as well as many theologians, have argued that religiously motivated evil always represents a corruption of true religion, the core of which—as a tactical matter—they rarely identify with much specificity. Others have turned to the ever-popular explanation that the problem is not religion per se, but rather the other fellow's religion. Yet others—including Sam Harris in his recent best seller *The End of*

Faith—have suggested that religion itself, all religion, is the source of the problem. This answer is incomplete, given the many religious people who don't fall prey to extremism.[27] Ethical and reasonable people, whether religious, agnostic, or atheistic, will typically disdain and reject destructive violence perpetrated in the name of religious faith and ideology. Reality, as we shall see, does not lend itself to simple approaches.

Attempts to pinpoint the roots and origins of religious extremism have been equally off the mark. Many have portrayed religious militancy as a reaction to poverty, deprivation, frustration, or mistreatment. Some have sought its sources in insanity and psychopathology. None of these explanations fit the facts very well.

To get at the heart of religious extremism—our aim here—we must ask a series of questions that require us to make intellectual, moral, and psychological comparisons among and within religions. Such questions are often political and nearly always personal. For example:

- Are some religions, religious doctrines, and religious practices more apt to inspire hatred and extremism than others?
- How are the various manifestations of religious extremism similar, and how do they differ?
- Are people who commit evil acts in the name of their faith carrying out or corrupting the "true" message of their religion?
- Do coreligionists bear any responsibility for misdeeds carried out by fellow believers in the name of their religion?
- Which sorts of people are most prone to extremism?
- Which types of societies are most likely to become breeding grounds for extremists?
- Can (or should) anything be done to combat the various forms of religious extremism?
- What limits, if any, can (or should) be placed on religious practice in America and elsewhere?

Judge Michael W. McConnell, a constitutional law scholar, argues that we require "a sharp, and at times difficult, distinction between those practices of a religious-cultural minority that merely differ from our norms . . . and those practices that are genuinely inimical to our way of life, including most importantly our peace and security." Judge McConnell continues, "It does us no great harm—though it may sometimes be inconvenient—to accommodate religious difference. However, we cannot budge on the essentials."[28] George Washington made a similar point when he suggested that the "delicacy and tenderness" with which we should treat the religious scruples of all men must be tempered only by "a due regard for the protection and essential interests of the nation."[29] One principal goal here is to identify when religious extremists cross the line from different to dangerous.

Another objective is to identify the warning signs of religion that is about to run amok. To that end, theories from many sources help get to the heart of the distinction between constructive and destructive religious practices. The English writer G. K. Chesterton suggested that perhaps the quickest test of a particular religion is "whether you can joke about it."[30] Though not altogether without merit, it is easy to imagine circumstances under which this simple criterion fails.

William James, the founder of modern psychology and the pragmatist school of philosophy, was in general a friend of religion. Though he formulated his ideas at the end of the nineteenth century, his views remain remarkably on-target regarding some realities today. For James, most of the bigotries and atrocities commonly blamed on religion are, in actuality, "chargeable to religion's wicked intellectual partner, the spirit of dogmatic dominion, the passion for laying down the law in the form of an absolutely closed-in theoretic system."[31] Some other offenses associated with religion, for instance, religious antisemitism, James links to a basic human tendency to hate people and things that are foreign and different. In both instances, it is not the religion per se that deserves the blame.

Still, there is one crime associated with religion for which the great psychologist and philosopher cannot produce a ready acquittal—

and that is fanaticism. This occurs, James says, "when an intensely loyal and narrow mind is once grasped by the feeling that a certain superhuman person is worthy of its exclusive devotion."[32] When this happens, "[v]ocabularies are exhausted and languages altered in the attempt to praise him enough; death is looked on as gain if it . . . [attracts] his gainful notice; and the personal attitude of being his devotee becomes what one might almost call a new and exalted kind of professional specialty."[33] The worst trouble starts because "[t]he slightest affront or neglect [of the worshiped one] must be resented, the deity's enemies must be put to shame."[34] In people who have narrow minds and strong willpower, this urge to protect the deity and attack those who offend his name can become "an engrossing preoccupation."[35] And the result can be—as our era is painfully aware—crusades and massacres "for no other reason than to remove a fancied slight upon the God."[36]

This century-old theorizing—written at a time when nobody in the West was thinking about Islamic extremism—can perhaps shed some light on the mentality of Nasrallah, Qaradhawi, and others who were enraged by the 2005 publication of cartoons in Denmark depicting Muhammad. More generally, James calls attention to the thought processes of those practitioners of all religions who seek to punish and destroy the purveyors of blasphemy. For James, much of the problem can be avoided if theologies represent God as less intent on preserving and ensuring his own honor and glory.

As James knew, the danger intensifies greatly when destructive religious beliefs mix with particular personality types. Since James opened up the psychology of religion, many of the twentieth century's leading psychologists have offered their insights into the origins of destructive faith, including Sigmund Freud, Carl Jung, Erich Fromm, Gordon Allport, Abraham Maslow, and Viktor Frankl.[37] In addition, dozens of scientific researchers have compiled a storehouse of data on how religion functions.[38] Much of this work nowadays attracts only specialists in the field, but buried amid dusty tomes and seldom-touched scientific journals lie important clues to our current predicament. Research suggests that we must look not only at the content of a person's religious beliefs but also at how such beliefs work in concert with, or in opposition to, a person's psychological makeup and social and political circumstances.

Perhaps the best recent attempt to understand how religion goes astray comes from Charles Kimball, a liberal Baptist minister. Untrained in psychology and the social sciences, he has a strong theological education and has spent years trying to understand the religious world of the Middle East. He rests his important 2002 book, *When Religion Becomes Evil*, on the assertion that "[w]hatever religious people may say about their love of God or the mandates of their religion, when their behavior toward others is violent or destructive, when it causes suffering among their neighbors, you can be sure the religion has been corrupted and reform is desperately needed."[39] In light of religion's frequently dysfunctional role in world history, opponents of religion may reasonably object that he too readily exonerates the forces of mainstream—or uncorrupted—religion. When one dismisses all evil associated with religion as a "corruption," one may be engaging in mere semantics. Nonetheless, Kimball's approach is constructive.

Kimball suggests that we should look out whenever believers claim to possess complete, unchanging, and absolute truths. Beware also, he warns, of charismatic religious leaders who demand blind obedience, because, in his view, openness to honest inquiry and freedom of individual thinking are necessary even in the realm of religion. He also sees trouble when people and groups claim that they possess a mandate from God to start making big political changes. And he understandably worries when valid religious ends are seen to justify any means.

Kimball's list is a good place to start, but it is incomplete and leaves much room for debate. For one thing, when he argues that "authentic religion encourages questions and reflection at all levels," his definition excludes nearly all of what most people deem to be religious matters.[40] In addition, despite his vast experience in the Middle East, his views of that region and Islam seem dangerously dominated by wishful thinking.

It is worth noting that, in a recent survey, three-quarters of Americans agreed that there are many religious paths to eternal life, some through religions other than one's own.[41] An understanding of religious extremism would be incomplete were it to omit an explanation of how so many religious Americans and others around the world have come to accept a degree of moderation that would, no doubt, have struck many of their ancestors as heretical.

A Plan for Understanding and Combating the Religious Extremist

Journalists and other writers have produced fascinating and informative profiles of particular extremists and groups of extremists. But such an approach cannot carry us to the crux of what makes a creed extremist, or answer the question of when, how, and why such creeds succeed in capturing the human spirit. Moreover, they cannot show the conditions under which the individual so energized will proceed to behave destructively. For this, we must draw on modern psychology, history, and other social sciences. And we must take care not to confuse the social, political, and psychological forces sustaining belief in general with those that spark extremist ideology and behavior.

The first chapter tackles the thorny matter of how to define religious militancy and identify religious extremists. Chapter 2 assesses extremism in the world of Islam, exploring how Muslim religious beliefs can interact with politics, life circumstances, personal psychology, and a variety of social forces to create militant and terrorist tendencies. Chapter 3 turns to extremism in Christianity and Judaism. The goal here is to examine how and why religious evil has waxed and waned in these faiths over the centuries.

The next two chapters deal directly with the causes of militant faith. Chapter 4 looks at sacred texts and asks how holy books might be implicated in the genesis of extremist behavior. Equally important, chapter 4 probes how religions have dealt sometimes effectively and sometimes ineffectively with their "troubling" source materials. Chapter 5 starts by looking to modern psychology for insights into the extremist mindset; to do so, it considers the psychological origins and consequences of nonextreme religious belief and proceeds to identify when and how the religious impulse goes awry. Next, this chapter seeks to identify which societies are most likely to experience the worst manifestations of religious extremism—and when.

The last part of the book considers how we might best protect against the forces of religious militancy. One way is for believers to reform themselves. Chapter 6 provides a consumer's guide to religious belief, identifying which belief systems can be constructive and which tend toward destructiveness and extremism. Finally, this chapter considers how we might best draw on the arsenal of weapons available to combat the forces of extremism in their various manifestations.

A FRAME OF REFERENCE

Bad Faith relies heavily on the social sciences, but this is not, in the final analysis, a work *of* social science. Like any book that deals with religion, this one reflects the author's biases and beliefs. No one comes to this topic value-free or agenda-free. By way of example, one well-known writer on religious extremism is a former nun whose new habits are more spiritual than Catholic, and who possesses a far-reaching sympathy for Islam. Another is a politically and theologically liberal Baptist minister, also deeply sympathetic to the Islamic tradition. Yet another is a committed atheist, disapproving of religion in more or less every sense. And three social scientists who have coauthored a recent and important study are all former Christian fundamentalists who retain substantial respect for that which they have abandoned.[42]

As for me, I am a licensed psychologist, a Jew, a political moderate, a great believer in the American constitutional tradition, a strong supporter of the separation of church and state, and a skeptic concerning nearly all matters religious, especially those involving mysticism, God, and the afterlife. As a teenager, for several years, I was somewhat more religious than I am now. Then, as a young adult, I moved away from Jewish practice. These days, I maintain considerable respect for many of the forms and traditions associated with Jewish observance, though, in truth, I rarely believe the words associated with such observances in anything approximating a literal sense. My strongest identification is with Judaism in an ethnic, historical, and sociological sense.

I have spent many years researching genocide, terrorism, and antisemitism and I should acknowledge that I am revolted by the incredible clamor of anti-Jewish hatred that has been spewed under the guise of Christianity, mainly in the past, and Islam, mainly in the present.

I am deeply disappointed by the failure of many religious leaders in all traditions to speak out sharply and clearly against extremists who share their faith and I have little sympathy for those whom I deem extremist within Judaism. I agree with Nobel Peace Prize–winner and Holocaust survivor Elie Wiesel, who notes that "[o]ne can encounter fanaticism in the framework of all monotheistic religions—Christian, Jewish, Moslem—and extremism in any form revolts me. I turn away from persons who declare that they know better than anyone else the only true road to God. If they try to force me to follow their road, I fight them. Whatever the fanatic's religion, I wish to be his adversary, his opponent."[43]

But I am also convinced that the religious impulse sometimes operates benignly and constructively, and that, as communism and Nazism attest, irreligion is no guarantee of moderation. Moreover, as a psychologist, I have observed that religion can at times—though not always—help people to deal with the inescapable and sometimes terrifying challenges of life. I am sure that faith is not the only path to psychological adjustment, and often it is not the best. But the religious life with certain qualifications seems to me a viable one for many. I think the liberal priest, sociologist, and engaging mystery writer Andrew Greeley is on target when he suggests that, while everyone need not have "a religion, much less the sacred, much less a church," there is "in the human condition a built-in strain toward evolving an ultimate meaning system and making it sacred."[44]

There is no universally meaningful moral or psychological distinction between secularism and religion, between believers and freethinkers, though one frequently hears that the line is all-important. The most significant distinction lies between reasonable and unreasonable people on both sides of that line.[45]

All (or nearly all) religions, East and West, can provide fertile ground for the growth of close-mindedness, hatred, bigotry, and violence. All of the major creeds possess the potential to impede social, psychological, political, and intellectual development. And the seeds of such pathological religion lie sprinkled dangerously throughout the very sacred texts that believers often regard as error-free. What's more, I agree with political scientist Charles Liebman, who writes that "a propensity to religious extremism . . . is entirely consistent with basic religious tenets and authentic religious orientations. It is religious moderation or religious liberalism, the willingness of religious adherents to accommodate themselves to their environment, to adapt their behavioral and belief patterns to prevailing cultural norms, to make peace with the world, that requires explanation."[46] In other words, events and conditions sometimes discourage the development of extremism. We need to understand how and why this happens.

In this sense, I do not see much advantage in the original core beliefs or sacred texts of any of the three Abrahamic religions: Judaism, Christianity, or Islam. Indeed, the natural tendency of all three—at least as a matter of original theory—is to overturn, transform, or exit from existing modes of life. And this transformative energy is too easily applied to evil ends. For many believers, now and in the past, the morality of a religion matters far less than its promise of union with God and a rewarding afterlife. When a psychic and spiritual sensation is what the believer seeks, rationality can very quickly disappear or become irrelevant.

And when religion leads to evil, it makes little sense to say that the believer has misconstrued the truth of the whole enterprise. The enterprise itself is a mixed bag. All of the good that inarguably has flowed from religion—think, for example, of the massive faith-based relief efforts for tsunami victims in 2005—depends on believers interpreting their religious traditions constructively. And this, in turn, depends on spiritual leaders making morally and intellectually responsible choices in an appropriate social and political environment.

Here lies the problem in much of contemporary Islam. Numerous well-known scholars of religion—Gilles Kepel, Karen Armstrong, Martin E. Marty, and R. Scott Appleby, to name a few—have made the useful point that virtually every religion on earth has had its "fundamentalists" at various times and that, in the past few decades, such fundamentalism has been on the rise.[47] But much is lost by trying to squeeze, as they do, very different manifestations of religion into so-called global trends. What's more, it makes little sense to speak, as some do, about "the varied strains of bin Ladenism—Muslim, Christian and Jewish alike."[48] The fundamentalist believers about whom scholars speak adhere to widely divergent perspectives. They do not exist in comparable percentages in each religion, and the consequences they have produced are worlds apart. One needs a remarkable ability to turn one's gaze from reality not to notice that, for more than a few Muslims, religion has been transformed from a traditional faith into an ideology of hate, far less progressive than it was ten centuries back. Some roots of this development can be traced to the origins of the faith, but most lie in recent history.

When imams, priests, ministers, and rabbis say truth lies within the text, they seem to me to be telling a half-truth. The holy words may often seem clear enough, but in every major faith religious leaders have managed to interpret black to mean white, yes to mean no, and never to mean sometimes. What's more, none of the faiths stem from a credible and independently verifiable early history. Thus, believers may endlessly re-create the models of Moses, Jesus, Muhammad, and others to fit the perceived needs of the moment. Religious reality is made, rather than found. And, using modern social science, we can identify the conditions and circumstances under which it will be made in the totalitarian mold. Sometimes the roots lie in economics, sometimes in politics, sometimes in personal despair. But it is never enough to examine the ideas. One must evaluate the context in which those ideas reside.

Though devotees of moderation and toleration must consider ways to respond when religion becomes an ideology of hate, they must act carefully and with respect for benign religion, not least because one reason for the rise of contemporary religious extremism has been the perception among believers that their ways are under attack from progressive forces.

Without doubt, religion can be one useful source of guidance, morality, and psychological adjustment for many. But, in light of its destructive potential, it should never be the sole, unfettered, and unchecked source. The astronomer Galileo had it right; when confronted by an unyielding authoritarian religion, he contended that he did not feel obliged to believe "that the same God who has endowed us with senses, reason, and intellect has intended us to forego their use."[49]

What is needed is not the abandonment of religion but rather a social, psychological, theological, and political system of checks and balances, a way to shout, "Whoa!" when faith starts galloping down the wrong path. As I see it, the responsibility for implementing these checks and balances lies first with believers of every faith.

Part One

THE UNEXPECTED BATTLE OF THE TWENTY-FIRST CENTURY

CHAPTER 1

WHO EXACTLY IS A RELIGIOUS EXTREMIST?

FROM PIETY TO MILITANCY

It would seem sensible to start by defining religious extremism and identifying exactly to whom we refer when we speak of religious extremists. Yet this is no simple matter.

It takes little reflection, after all, to conclude that Osama bin Laden's religious views are extreme in the sense that they have inspired great evil. But what, for example, are we to make of the beliefs of Sheikh Abdur-Rahman al-Sudais, an imam of Islam's holiest mosque in Mecca, whom the BBC depicts as a brave worker for community cohesion and an advocate of peaceable relations with nonbelievers?[1] The imam has indeed condemned the September 11 attack and some other terrorist acts, but he endorses Palestinian suicide bombers and refers to Jews as "pigs and apes."[2] Does he, on the basis of such beliefs alone, merit the label "extremist"?

Closer to home, speaking in 2003 about the religious beliefs of President George W. Bush, former vice president Al Gore offered the opinion that "[i]t's the American version of the same fundamentalist impulse that we see in Saudi Arabia, in Kashmir, in religions around the world."[3] Following the president's 2004 reelection, *New York Times* columnist Thomas Friedman charged Bush and "Christian fundamentalist supporters" with using "religious energy to promote divisions and intolerance at home and abroad."[4] Yet even some nonbelievers might agree with Christian columnist Gregory Rummo, who charges slander when the Religious Right in the United States is denounced, as it has been by some liberals, as "the American Taliban."[5]

The extremist tag has also been applied to Jewish ultra-Orthodox Hassidim and those from other faiths who embrace beliefs that strike most outsiders as outmoded, unsubstantiated, and strange, and who perform myriad religious rituals throughout the day. Some of these believers may have relatively little interest or involvement in affairs outside of their own respective communities of faith and may live their lives—as much as possible—apart from others in the modern world. Does the infusion of religion into every waking moment of one's day and the failure to interact with outsiders merit the extremist label, even in the absence of destructive activities?

And what about the nineteenth-century English Catholic leader John Henry Cardinal Newman—the namesake of American Catholic campus organizations—who famously maintained that "[t]he Catholic Church holds it better for the sun and moon to drop from heaven, for the earth to fail, and for all the many millions on it to die of starvation in extremest agony, as far as temporal affliction goes, than that one soul, I will not say, should be lost, but should commit one single venial sin, should tell one wilful untruth, or should steal one poor farthing without excuse."[6] It would be hard to deem such an outlook moderate, yet, by most behavioral standards, the cardinal lived his life well and free from fanatic activities. Does he qualify as an extremist?

It depends, of course, on how we define our terms. If our objective is to understand the circumstances under which religion becomes a force for evil, defining religious extremism usefully remains a difficult task. To begin to understand, let us look closely at some religious believers whose belief systems might be deemed extreme.

APOCALYPTIC CHRISTIANS: EXTREMIST OR NOT?

"If I [had] invented the story, you're right, I'd be terribly arrogant," explained Dr. Tim LaHaye to a newspaper reporter. "But I didn't invent the story."[7] In his late seventies at the time of the interview, LaHaye acknowledged that he and coauthor Jerry Jenkins had invented part of their fabulously successful end-of-time tale—but not the important part. That aspect of the *Left Behind* series was dictated by divine scripture, and the critical events described in their twelve novels, they believe, are destined to occur in reality, as certainly as the sun will rise, or, as their books insist, more certainly.

They admit that details like times and dates remain unknown. But LaHaye, Jenkins, and, no doubt, many of their readers—who bought well over forty million copies of the books—fully expect the Rapture, and sooner than you think. The Rapture has different meanings for different Christians. But according to LaHaye and others in what is known as the premillennial school, the Rapture is an event that occurs just prior to the last seven years of the world as we know it. God takes all true Christians from earth to heaven and transforms them into immortal beings. Afterward, everyone else is left behind to face the grueling Tribulation—a period of horrible wars, persecutions, and misery—until Jesus finally arrives in the Second Coming to rescue those who have passed the test. Various events in world affairs—typically involving Israel, the Middle East, the former Soviet Union, and the United Nations—signal the onset of the prophesied era, but LaHaye sees the Rapture as an especially critical and irrefutable sign.

Indeed, in the first chapter of the first book of the *Left Behind* series, published in 1995, all the truly good people of the world dematerialize into thin air, as if they had been transported by a futuristic Star Trek device, to borrow one of the images chosen by the authors themselves.[8]

Simultaneously across the planet, the sinners left behind are suitably surprised as their saintlier companions leave neat little piles of clothes where a few moments earlier flesh-and-blood human beings had been going about their business. Pregnant sinners suddenly become pounds lighter as their unborn fetuses are whisked off to God knows where. All of the people who disappear are sincere and enthusiastic Christians, but those believers who have practiced their Christianity in moderation or professed it with a grain of salt—even when they are quite likable—must face the terrible music along with everyone else.

By the twelfth volume of the series, published in 2004, Jesus returns—but not until the world has been rent asunder through battles with evil forces led by the secretary-general of the United Nations, aka the Antichrist.[9] The return of Christ is marked by a gory scene of blood and entrails in which all the world's non-Christians are thrown into an everlasting holocaust. One critical reviewer calls this event "ethnic cleansing celebrated as the height of piety" and suggests that "[i]f a Muslim were to write an Islamic version of . . . [this book] and publish it in Saudi Arabia, jubilantly describing a massacre of millions of non-Muslims by God, we would have a fit."[10]

Despite the popularity of the *Left Behind* series, many aspects of its core theology are not accepted by mainstream Christian denominations.[11] For example, most Christians reject belief in a Rapture event that occurs well before the Second Coming of Christ; they see these events as more or less simultaneous. Some Christians don't believe in the Rapture at all. Many regard the menu-like detailing of predictions about the end of the world in the book of Revelation as symbolism, perhaps a code more directly relating to the predicament of early Christians living under Roman persecution. Some liberal Christians do not accept any literal interpretation of the Second Coming. And some evangelical Christians object that the view expressed in the *Left Behind* series permits relatives and friends of Christians to be saved *after* the Rapture, thereby sending the dangerous message that one can sin now and get redeemed later.[12]

Still, some Christians who disagree with LaHaye on eschatology disagree more with his critics. One, for example, rejects the "ethnic cleansing" charge, saying that "seeing belief in God's wrath as 'intolerance' shows the loss of a sense of sin. . . . Sinners cannot stand before the Holy God without being destroyed."[13] According to this fairly common belief, sinners must repent and the particularities of one's religious affiliation matter very much. But ethnicity and race are not the relevant variables.

Hence, apocalyptic thinkers are not speaking of "ethnic" cleansing, but they are speaking, in some sense, of a malignant cleansing. And they are adamant about one thing: liberal Christians and just about everyone else with beliefs different from theirs will not be saved. In their defense, however, it should be noted that God, not human beings, is the punishing agent. This is a significant point, putting apocalyptic Christians in a very different category from those who believe that they themselves must carry out God's verdict.

How, one wonders, is the sensible person to enter into these discussions? For LaHaye, who spent three decades writing self-help books and ministering to believers at a San Diego church, finding truth may indeed require a bit of effort. But the pathway is obvious. His 1989 book *Finding the Will of God in a Crazy Mixed-Up World* advises people on all sorts of tricky personal matters.[14] For example, should an unfaithful husband who sinned—only once—be required to tell his wife and seek her forgiveness? What should a good Christian woman do if she learns that her husband is a "porno freak"? Should a man merge his printing company with another firm? For all these issues, LaHaye tells us, crystal-clear guidance can be found in the Bible.

He reports that "God has given us a sixty-six volume road map that provides not only guidelines and principles enabling us to make correct choices in life but also examples of real-life people—some who obeyed those guidelines and succeeded; others who rejected them and failed."[15] He further explains: "Happy is the Christian who understands that human wisdom is limited, unscriptural—and wrong. Admittedly, it may seem very attractive, but if we contemplate a major decision and muse inwardly, 'It seems right to me,' we'll be wrong every time."[16]

To prove his point (needless to say), LaHaye cites scripture, in this instance, Paul warning the people of his day: "The natural man does not receive the things of the Spirit of God . . . nor can he know them, because they are spiritually discerned."[17] LaHaye does not worry much that people, even very learned ones, may perceive the same lines of scripture very differently and that some parts of the Bible may seemingly conflict with other parts. Instead, he advises those in need of guidance to pray, seek the Holy Spirit, and surrender in advance to the will of God. To those who wonder whether the plan will work, he explains: "[R]emember this, the Spirit of God will never lead you to violate His Word—for He wrote it! God is not the author of confusion."[18]

And when the attacks of 9/11 occurred, Dr. LaHaye was not for a moment confused. He noted that, by the end of the day, the phones of prophecy scholars were ringing off their hooks with reporters seeking Christian interpretation. But he did not perceive in that day's events any direct prophetic significance, beyond showing, in accordance with prophecy, that we live in "increasingly perilous times."[19] The attacks, he suggested, might have *indirectly* set in motion some end-of-time happenings. But they were not acts of God. And, for believers, the path was—as usual—clear. They must stand up and be counted on a day when "on the one hand we have the unity forces of Antichrist forming even before he arrives on the scene, and on the other hand we have the forces of Islam."[20] Christians, Dr. LaHaye insists, cannot cooperate with either group. He writes: "From now until the rapture will be a time for the real Christians to stand firm in their faith! Jesus is not just 'the way, the truth, and the life'; He is the ONLY way, truth, and life."[21]

This perspective does not leave much room for interfaith cooperation. Regarding Islam, LaHaye explains: "We should not be deceived by the well publicized belief in 'Allah' as though the Muslim and Arab world truly believe in God. The god they believe in is definitely NOT the God of the Bible, either in the Old or New Testaments. Not only do they practice the unbiblical concept of advancing their beliefs by the sword, they also do not acknowledge Jesus as the Son of God and the Messiah or savior of the world."[22]

In the post-9/11 environment, various Christians—who may or

may not share LaHaye's view of the Rapture and Second Coming—have similarly used scripture, alone or in conjunction with other sources of truth, to buttress their belief in the superiority of Christianity, sometimes in ways that have attracted considerable media attention. At a time when most Christian leaders were speaking of encouraging moderate trends within Islam, a not-insignificant minority offered a more assertive solution to America's predicament: convert the Muslims.

Thus, the Reverend Franklin Graham, Billy Graham's son, shocked many in the mass media—but perhaps fewer in his audiences—when he declared Islam to be "a very evil and wicked religion." The Reverend Jerry Falwell, founder of the Moral Majority, called Muhammad a "terrorist," and the Reverend Jerry Vines, former head of the Southern Baptist Convention, described him as a "demon-possessed pedophile."[23]

Speaking about the war against terror and Saddam Hussein at a time when the American government was trying to gain support in the Muslim world, General William "Jerry" Boykin—a prominent military leader involved in the effort—declared that "[t]he enemy will only be defeated if we come against them in the name of Jesus."[24] He also recounted a tale of an encounter with a Muslim Somali warlord and explained his source of strength: "I knew my God was a real God, and his was an idol." The general further explained that "my God was bigger than his God."[25] When the inevitable media stir followed each of these comments, the speakers dutifully offered some partial apology or clarification.[26] But few observers doubted where they stood.

LaHaye, Graham, Falwell, Vines, and Boykin all have run afoul of mainstream Christian establishments, and all are regarded by some to different degrees as religious extremists. A few observers go a step further, arguing that even President Bush, driven by Christian faith and possessed of a powerful tendency to see the world in terms of good and evil, is—despite his public respect for all mainstream religions—a religious extremist. Quite a few secular intellectuals and even some liberal theologians see truth in the characterization of the Religious

Right in the United States as "the American Taliban," and many argue that as America fights Islamic religious extremism and intolerance abroad, it must also address Christian extremism at home.

They would point out that Tim LaHaye, for example, was one of the inspirations behind the Moral Majority and that he is not a thoughtful conservative but rather an off-the-charts right-winger. He is strongly antiabortion and antichoice, and though he befriends Jews and the state of Israel, he does so only because of their presumed role in bringing on the end-of-time events so central to his theology. He opposes homosexuality and any extension of gay rights. He has little respect for separation of church and state, asserting a central role for religion in the public square.

There is, for LaHaye, not a shred of doubt about the fundamental superiority of his brand of Christianity over all others and no room for any countervailing influences. What's more, he prophesies about the end of time in incredible detail and based on a scriptural mentality that seems impervious to logic, scientific argument, or the possibility of alternative interpretations. Some might also object that his "Christian" counseling goes against the tenets of modern psychology and keeps needy people from getting the help they patently require. Instead, his methods, some might argue, approach quackery, as when he advises the use of "fleeces," direct and specific requests for providential signs from God, to help make key life decisions. (For example, let a blue bird fly by if I am supposed to marry this man.)

On the other hand, one might point out that Dr. LaHaye's theology has not inspired violent acts and that he speaks with 100 percent clarity about the need to work within the democratic system. Referring to those who have bombed abortion clinics, he states: "Such activity is wrong; it violates the law and endangers precious lives. The energy of such people should be aimed at registering more Christians to vote and working on behalf of candidates who share their moral values so that unjust laws can be changed legally."[27] Far from being a bomb thrower, LaHaye has made a fetish of following the status quo. He writes: "God's will calls for Christians to be obedient to government authorities, laws, even employers, as long as their requirements don't cause us to violate the higher law of God."[28]

LaHaye's beliefs about the Rapture, the years of Tribulation, and the Second Coming of Christ concern a future time and cannot be proven false. Though he provides no convincing evidence to the nonbeliever, the deep needs to which he ministers—needs concerning such transcendent issues as understanding how the world might end, thinking about the possibility of an afterlife, and wondering about the ultimate rewarding of good and punishing of evil—are fairly widespread, if not nearly universal. While different ways of addressing these matters may appeal more to modern, scientific minds—and some of LaHaye's perspectives may seem strange—it is sometimes difficult to demonstrate that other views about life's ultimate issues rest on a much firmer foundation. The very psychiatrists who would object to Dr. LaHaye's techniques might be hard-pressed to back up their own tactics with rock-solid scientific evidence. So it may make more sense to classify LaHaye as very religious, opinionated, unscientific, and politically well to the right of center, but not as a *dangerous* extremist. He has not advocated violence against any groups.

According to syndicated evangelical columnist Gregory Rummo, there is a galaxy of difference between fundamentalist Christians and the Taliban. He says the latter are misanthropic, misogynistic, antimodern, anti-Christian, antisemitic, terroristic, jihadistic, and suicidal.[29] In contrast, Christian evangelicals, according to Rummo, typically support democracy, religious tolerance, and peace. In his view, they do this all the more so because of their religious faith.

Logically, people prefer their own belief systems. In this sense, the claim by many evangelical Christians that their faith possesses distinct heavenly advantages is hardly unique. And Rummo's point about the difference between Christian evangelicals and the Taliban is to some degree correct. But he is wrong in his assessment of the role of religious faith in sustaining support for democracy and religious tolerance. As Charles Kimball has suggested, "A strong case can be made . . . that the history of Christianity contains considerably more violence and destruction than that of most other major religions."[30] Still, in recent years, relatively little violence has been perpetrated directly in the name of evangelical Christianity.

To cut through the confusion in defining and identifying religious extremists, one might turn to William James, who—in an invocation of New Testament scripture—asserted that religions should be judged *not by their roots, but by their fruits*.[31] But which fruits are best to cultivate, and how we are to evaluate religions that produce both sweet *and* bitter fruits? Whether the belief systems proposed by LaHaye, other Christian evangelicals, moderate Christians, believers from other faiths, or even nonbelievers promote desirable or undesirable outcomes is a matter to which this book devotes much attention. But first, we examine the question of how to identify extremism in the context of Islam.

The Boundaries of Moderate Islam

In recent years, observers from a variety of political, religious, and ethnic backgrounds have objected that discussions of terrorism and religious extremism turn too quickly to the Islamic case and then, almost automatically, become mindless and unjustified indictments of one of the world's great faiths. For example, British author William Dalrymple writes: "The massacre of more than 7,000 Muslims at Srebrenica in 1995 never led to a stream of articles in the press about the violent tendencies of Christianity. Yet every act of al-Qaeda terrorism brings to the surface a great raft of criticism of Islam as a religion, and dark mutterings about the sympathies of British Muslims."[32] Others have noted that few blamed Christianity when Timothy McVeigh and Terry Nichols bombed the Murrah Federal Building in Oklahoma City in 1995. Similarly, Judaism, Hinduism, Buddhism, and other religions seldom take much heat in the American press when their extremist adherents carry out evil acts. Old habits die hard, some maintain, and Islam has been unfairly singled out for criticism in Western media because of its fourteenth-century history of conflict with Christianity—the principal religion of the Western world.

Karen Armstrong argues that "[t]he US is the true home of religious extremism."[33] and that "[d]uring the 20th century, a militant piety, often called 'fundamentalism,' had erupted in every major religious tradition. It was a widespread rebellion against secular modernity. Wherever a Western-style society was established, a religious counterculture grew up alongside it, determined to drag God or religion from the peripheral position to which they had been relegated back to centre stage."[34] In her perspective, "[r]eligion itself was hijacked and discredited on 11 September, and it must now be reclaimed by a compassionate offensive which shows that religion can make a difference to a world torn apart by hatred and fear."[35]

To some extent, Armstrong is correct. Adherents of many religious traditions felt challenged by the September 11 attacks, and religious extremism is not unique in any meaningful sense to Islam. Yet it is undeniably in the world of Islam where—*these days*—manifestations of religious hatred and terror have been most frequent, most pronounced, most apparent, most consequential, most popular, and most supported by mainstream clerics. To deny this, as Armstrong and other ecumenically minded writers sometimes do, is to deny reality. Moreover, Islamic extremists themselves adamantly insist that their motivation is religious in nature. We would do well to take this claim seriously.

Though many reasonable and tolerant Islamic voices are heard—especially in the West—immoderation coexists throughout the Muslim world and shows up in many forms. Extremists, however they are defined, number far more than a handful and far less than the entire Muslim population. A key—and largely unanswered—question is just how deeply extremism in its various forms has penetrated different Muslim societies across the globe. Equally important, what social, political, and economic forces lend them support; what countervailing visions of Islam stand the best chance of competing successfully; and to what extent have Islamic history, traditions, and sacred texts contributed to the current wave of extremism? Finally, what, if anything, can be done by those outside the faith to support and empower moderates within?

As with Dr. LaHaye and the Christian case, we quickly encounter the difficult matter of how to identify moderates and determine which beliefs and actions distinguish them from extreme coreligionists. Let us return to the case of a prominent Muslim leader mentioned at the beginning of this chapter, Sheikh Abdur-Rahman al-Sudais.

In June 2004, Sheikh al-Sudais flew to London to inaugurate a large new Islamic cultural center. Several weeks after the September 11 attacks, the sheikh had declared: "It would be a great calamity when the followers of this phenomenon [terrorism] use religion as a camouflage, because true Islam stands innocent from all that. Its teachings stand aloft from people who believe in violence as a course of action and sabotage as a method and bloodshed as a way of reform."[36] And in autumn 2003, the sheikh had urged British Muslims "all to be nice to your neighbours whether Muslim or non-Muslim as the Prophet taught."[37] He further insisted that "Muslims have nothing to do with terrorism or killing innocent people."[38] Thus, it was not altogether surprising when the BBC felt justified in describing the sheikh in sympathetic terms.[39] At the dedication of the London Islamic Cultural Center, the network took note of the religious leader's message that "Muslims should exemplify the true image of Islam in their interaction with other communities and dispel any misconceptions portrayed in some parts of the media."[40] The Associated Press reported al-Sudais's participation in the event under the headline "Saudi Imam Urges British Muslims to Promote Peace."[41] On the basis of such coverage, one might conclude that this prominent and influential sheikh was just the sort of moderate whom the West ought to support. After all, the online encyclopedia Wikipedia calls him "one of the most widely respected Imams in the Muslim world."[42]

But al-Sudais has another, less ecumenical side, one that does not often find its way into English-language media. Just months before his London message, he had sermonized from his home pulpit that Jews are "killers of prophets and the scum of the earth."[43] The sheikh had explained to followers that "Allah had hurled his curses and indignation on them and made them monkeys and pigs and worshipers of tyrants."[44] In this sermon, al-Sudais proceeded to describe Jews as "a continuous lineage of meanness, cunning, obstinacy, tyranny, evil, and corruption."[45] It was not a new theme for the imam, who in November 2002 had called upon Allah to annihilate the Jews. He further advised Arabs to abandon all peace initiatives with the Jews.[46]

Sheikh al-Sudais's animus toward Jews becomes even more intense when the Jews he's referring to are Israelis. Around the same time he was leading prayers in London and being hailed by the BBC, the sheikh had praised Palestinian suicide bombers in glowing terms on Saudi television, saying: "You have revived the hopes of this nation through your blessed jihad. . . . With Allah's help, one of two good things will be awarded you: either victory or martyrdom. Our hearts are with you; our prayers are dedicated to you. The Islamic nation will not spare money or effort in support of your cause, which is the supreme Muslim cause."[47]

Additional aspects of the sheikh's worldview may trouble many Americans and others in the West. In February 2004, he lamented that Iraq "bleeds and that the occupant has ransacked it and raped its riches," and he called on Muslims everywhere to unite "to defeat all their occupiers and oppressors," presumably referring to the US forces in Iraq.[48] Though Sheikh al-Sudais's deepest anger erupts against Jews, he has—on occasion—spoken against Hindus and Christians as well.[49]

Like Franklin Graham and Tim LaHaye, Sheikh al-Sudais believes his own faith is unquestionably superior to all others. He explains that "[t]oday, Western civilization is nothing more than the product of its encounter with our Islamic civilization in Andalusia [medieval Spain] and other places. The reason for [Western civilization's] bankruptcy is its reliance on the materialistic approach, and its detachment from religion and values."[50] He was particularly enraged by one very popular Western-inspired broadcast—the *Star Academy* reality show—which had become the rage of Arab television. The program is an Arab version of the American show *Big Brother*. Young Arab men and women live for months in the same house in Lebanon, though they sleep in separate quarters.[51] Programs such as these al-Sudais dubs "weapons of mass destruction that kill values and virtue," saying they promote vice and debauchery.[52]

Some who hear the whole story about al-Sudais might conclude that he is a less-than-perfect poster boy for Islamic moderation, but that he nonetheless possesses moderate tendencies worth encouraging. After all, though he is a foe of globalization, he does not reject modernity altogether. Instead, he suggests that "[t]he collaboration between originality and modernisation [*sic*] does not contradict Islam. We should take from modernisation what benefits our society from a religious perspective and leave what contradicts our values."[53]

More important, and despite his support for terrorism against Israelis, Sheikh al-Sudais sometimes speaks unequivocally against other manifestations of terrorism, as he did, for example, following the April 2004 bombing of the security service headquarters in Riyadh, Saudi Arabia. He then called on all Muslims to help the police locate the perpetrators of the attack.[54] And when the first phase of the Iraq war was winding down in early April 2003, al-Sudais spoke of a Muslim "defeat," but also said in a televised sermon that "[t]he bloodshed in Iraq and Palestine must stop immediately. . . . The killing of civilians, destruction of property, looting, and robberies must all be stopped."[55]

Thus, those who perceive Sheikh al-Sudais as an influential Islamic moderate are not entirely wrong, but he is certainly not the sort of moderate whom the United States would choose to empower if it had other real choices. It is also true that those who seem more truly "moderate" to Western ears are often unable to command much support in the Muslim Middle East. Thus, in the search for powerful moderates, the West is sometimes tempted to support religious leaders who reflect many of the tendencies observed in al-Sudais.

Such moderates endorse a general vision of Islam as a religion of peace. They typically condemn the September 11 attacks and disassociate themselves from Osama bin Laden with regard to means, if not ends. Their interpretation of the religious requirement of jihad does not translate into a direct call for violent conflict with the West. They are open-minded about technology and generally are willing to work with the West when common interests exist, though—despite occasional lip service to democratic principles—they typically regard Western culture as despicable and morally corrupt. From a Western standpoint, they show little respect for the rights of women or homosexuals. Separation of church and state is, for them, an entirely alien concept, and few show much spirit for interfaith cooperation, at least in the sense that we often experience it in the United States. Though in principle such Islamist moderates accept Jews and Christians as "peoples of the Book," in practice most are deeply antisemitic and show little respect for Christianity. Some view Hinduism with disdain. Most reject the possibility of peaceful coexistence with Israel and view Israel or Zionism as the root of many of the world's problems.

In short, such religious leaders can be classified as moderate only in contrast to others who are even more extreme. But it is a grave error to conclude from this state of affairs that Islam cannot sustain moderate and progressive alternatives to the extremists. All religious traditions, including Christianity and Judaism, can be used to sustain a broad range of positions and ideologies.

Consider in a bit more detail al-Sudais's description of Jews as "pigs and apes." Not too long ago, an interviewer on an Arabic TV broadcast, *The Muslim Woman Magazine*, queried a three-and-a-half-year-old guest on the matter of Jews. The purportedly unrehearsed little girl announced that she did not like them and, upon further probing, explained that they were "apes and pigs." Asked for the source of this insight, the youngster responded, "Our God . . . in the Koran." No rebuke, correction, or clarification was offered and, at the conclusion of the segment, the obviously pleased adult interviewer declared: "No [parents] could wish for Allah to give them a more believing girl than she. . . . May Allah bless her, her father and mother. The next generation of children must be true Muslims." (This exchange took place on Iqraa, a joint Saudi-Egyptian satellite network that purportedly aims to highlight a "true and tolerant picture of Islam," to refute "the accusations directed against Islam," and to open "channels of cultural connection with the cultures of other nations.")[56]

Sheikh Tantawi, the influential top cleric from Egypt's prestigious Al-Azhar University, would concur with the little girl. So would Sheikh Madhi, the imam of Gaza City's main mosque; Salim 'Azzouz, a columnist for a major Egyptian daily; Muhammad 'Abd al-Sattar, the Syrian deputy minister of religious endowment; and many other Muslim leaders.[57]

But the Koranic verses to which the little girl and the learned sheikhs refer are ambiguous. In several places, the Koran does indeed state that some Jews were transmogrified into animals. One section refers specifically to Jews who broke the Sabbath, saying: "You shall be changed into detested apes" (2:65). Another section appears to refer to Jews and Christians, stating: "People of the Book, do you hate us for any reason other than that we believe in Allah and in what has been revealed to us and to others before us, and that most of you are evil-doers? . . . Shall I tell you who will receive the worse reward from Allah? Those on whom Allah had laid his curse and with whom he has been angry, transforming them into apes and swine" (5:60). Thus, the Koran clearly seems to suggest that *some* Jews were turned into pigs and apes as a form of punishment for perceived transgressions. But, that being said, whether to embrace such statements as a literal message relevant for today is a choice of present-day Muslims.[58]

The Islamic religious tradition provides the extremist with abundant source material. But most major religious traditions contain messages that may, without much creativity, be interpreted hatefully. And theologians in every tradition, including Islam, have found ways to modify, reinterpret, counterbalance, or otherwise incapacitate such verses.

Thus, to understand the rise of extremism in Islam, we must understand how and why a religion that once sustained great scientific and cultural advances and at times considerable tolerance for diversity of many sorts has been transformed by some of its adherents into an extremist ideology. To do so, we need to understand how extremists built a hostile worldview around sacred concepts, which have also, even frequently, been understood differently. The same text may yield a dozen very different forms of Islam, all going by a common name. And the same is true for Christianity, Judaism, and other faiths.

KNOWING EXTREMISM WHEN WE SEE IT

Religious extremists broadcast their beliefs in many ways, but they rarely label themselves as dangerous militants.

One way we might identify pathological religion is similar to the way the doctor identifies psychiatric abnormality in the patient.[59] In that context, no single dimension separates the normal from the pathological, and the difference between health and illness is a matter of degree. To make a clinical judgment about whether a person is mentally ill, the psychiatrist or psychologist typically asks three questions. First, to what extent do the thoughts and deeds of the patient deviate from what is typically expected and observed in one's culture? Second, to what extent do these thoughts and deeds cause the person to experience misery and distress? Third, to what extent do they interfere with his or her efforts to maintain a successful life in the realm of work, love, and day-to-day living? If a patient comes across as extremely abnormal on any one of these dimensions—say, unhappiness—he or she might be deemed ill, even if everything falls well within the normal range for the other dimensions.

The approach of the psychiatric diagnostician can help us to assess some of the ways that religion can lead to trouble, particularly from the standpoint of individual suffering. But all three of the diagnostic dimensions fall short in their ability to diagnose manifestations of religious extremism. For one thing, when a lifestyle is assessed against the expectations of a culture, there remains the problem of an entire culture embracing tenets of militancy. When a whole society is ill, the sane individual appears deviant. In addition, psychiatrists by inclination and training are focused on their patients' happiness and interpret happiness as a sign of well-being; yet it is certainly possible, if not common, that the most extreme and dangerous religious beliefs render their adherents happy, or even ecstatic. One imagines, admittedly without conclusive evidence, suicide bombers feeling very content in their last moments as they visualize their imminent greeting in heaven. Another problem with the psychiatric approach is that some religious views that prove highly dysfunctional for society might actually aid individuals in their efforts to get along better with their families, peers, and associates.

Indeed, the appeal of extremism may be precisely the same as the attraction of more moderate religious beliefs, in meeting previously unmet needs, sometimes spiritual, sometimes emotional, and sometimes social. Along similar lines, believers may turn to extremism because they find—or expect to find—that militant religion provides rewards and satisfactions that exceed those associated with available alternatives.

Determining whether beliefs are empirically supported, logical or cogent in the eyes of nonbelievers does not get us far in distinguishing between religious extremists and religious moderates. Recent surveys, after all, show that more than one-third of Americans (38 percent) are convinced that the Bible is the literal word of God.[60] This percentage rises to 51 percent in the South, and to 56 percent among African Americans. Forty-five percent of Americans (not just Roman Catholic Americans) judge the pope (John Paul II, at the time) infallible when he teaches formally on matters of faith, such as the divinity of Christ.[61] A much larger segment of the American public (79 percent in 2004) believes that Jesus Christ was born of a virgin without a human father.[62] And still more, 89 percent in 1998, have no trouble accepting the notion that Jesus Christ rose from the dead after dying on the cross.[63] Such beliefs are not scientifically or logically provable; whether they are true or false is not the point. What matters here is that they are so common that they cannot be relied upon to distinguish extremists from moderates.

Moreover, one must avoid confusing the religious extremist with someone who is just extremely religious. There are many ways in which manifestations of religiosity can be intense without necessarily having dangerous ramifications. Consider, for example, a woman described in psychologist William James's classic *The Varieties of Religious Experience*. This woman had been raised without any significant exposure to Christian doctrine. At some point, Christian friends introduced her to the faith and brought her to a point where God's plan for salvation seemed immediately apparent to her. She explained: "The very instant I heard my Father's cry calling unto me, my heart bounded in recognition. I ran, I stretched forth my arms, I cried aloud, 'Here, here I am, my Father . . .' Since then, I have had direct answers to prayer—so significant as to be almost like talking with God and hearing his answer. The idea of God's reality has never left me for one moment."[64] On the basis of this self-report, one might conclude that this woman is extremely religious. Her outlook may strike many nonbelievers as far from sensible. But nothing in her declaration would lead us to define her as a threat. If God tells her to kill someone, she might indeed become dangerous. But to predict such a scenario based on her religiosity alone is unwarranted. One might guess that she believes fervently in an afterlife where rewards and punishments will be more intense than they are in this world, and that such beliefs might lead her to engage in extreme behaviors. But this, too, is mere hypothesis, not something logically based on the woman's intensely felt religious experience.

Many writers have attempted to define phenomena related to religious extremism. Originally, fundamentalism was a specific conservative movement within the Protestant Church in the United States; its adherents opposed modern theology and the secularization of society, advocating in their place certain biblical doctrines. Recently, however, the fundamentalist label has also been applied to believers in other religions. One team of psychological researchers—Ralph W. Hood Jr., Peter C. Hill, W. Paul Williamson—explained that "[w]hat distinguishes fundamentalism from other religious profiles is its particular approach toward understanding religion, which elevates the role of the sacred text to a position of supreme authority and subordinates all other potential sources of knowledge and meaning."[65] Along with many writers, they note that such positions have typically been adopted as part of a defensive reaction to modernism. They also note that some have attempted to draw a line between fundamentalism and evangelicalism on the grounds that adherents to the former have far greater hostility toward mainstream society.[66]

Scholars and theologians have vigorously debated the usefulness of the term *fundamentalist* in discussions of religious extremism. Some support its use, arguing that

> [w]hatever the background religion in question, fundamentalists claim that their religion is absolutely true, that it owes nothing to any human culture, that we must all return to a "true" form of this religion in order for society to be "right" and "moral," that the only "true" form of this religion is what they claim is the "original" form—untainted by human culture—and that true believers are obligated to fight against corrupting influences from the broader culture. . . . Religious fundamentalists frequently have more in common with fundamentalists from other religions than they do with more liberal adherents of the same religion.[67]

Other writers see the use of the term *religious fundamentalism* as conceptual legerdemain. In an article titled "Fundamentalism Isn't the Problem," Kenneth Minogue objects that "'fundamentalism' is an all-purpose expression denigrating the peoples of the Book (as the Muslims call them). Anyone who takes the Bible (either Testament) or the Koran seriously falls under the terminological lash of terrorism-inducing fundamentalism. How is it that millions of harmless American Christians, or orthodox Jews, living pretty blameless lives, come to be incorporated under such a denigratory slogan?"[68] He then offers an answer, claiming that especially for American liberals, "it is an irresistible rhetorical triumph to be able to package all the people of whom you disapprove in one nauseous bundle."[69]

In any event, Professors Hood, Hill, and Williamson present an approach that allows us to proceed. For them, the most important point is: "Although it is true that some fundamentalists may be militant, it ought not to be their defining characteristic, lest we foreclose the interesting empirical issue of exploring under what conditions they may or may not be militant."[70] This is sound advice. Fundamentalists, whether Christian, Muslim, Jewish, or another variety, are not, by definition, dangerous militants. What we require is an analysis of the circumstances under which some fundamentalists become dangerous religious extremists.

In seeking a useful definition of religious extremism, we must return to William James's insistence that religions should be judged not by their roots but by their fruits. Along these lines, theologian Charles Kimball suggests that "[w]hatever religious people may say about their love of God or the mandates of their religion, when their behavior toward others is violent and destructive, when it causes suffering among their neighbors, you can be sure the religion has been corrupted and reform is desperately needed."[71] Thus, the definition of religious extremism should start by considering the impact of religious beliefs, rather than their content.

Religious extremists can be defined as those persons who—for reasons they themselves deem religious—commit, promote, or support purposely hurtful, violent, or destructive acts toward those who don't practice their faith. The proposed definition requires judgment at several levels. *How much* support for destructive behavior is required for the supporter to be considered an extremist? *How hurtful* must acts be? Do angry, hurtful speeches count as violent acts? Do they count if they incite violent action? And what of those individuals who are not themselves extremists but who fail to condemn cobelievers who are? Perhaps such persons are best classified as extremist fellow travelers. Of course, religious people, like nonreligious ones, may justify certain hostile acts based on generally accepted principles of self-defense, but such justifications must be convincing without reference to religion.

When the fruits of a religion frequently include attacks on the life, liberty, and happiness of nonbelievers or those who don't practice the faith, the religion can be reliably classified as extremist. When a set of religious beliefs is incidentally hurtful to some individual or group, the classification is trickier. Moreover, when the fruits of a religion include impediments to the health, happiness, and development of believers who are allowed to leave freely if they so choose, the religious system should be dubbed dysfunctional but not labeled as religious extremism. Faith that leads one to harm only oneself is also dysfunctional, but it belongs in a separate category and poses a different type of challenge. For example, religious beliefs may lead people to conclude that they are eternally damned and may thereby destroy any chances of their leading personally fulfilling lives. But this would not qualify as religious extremism as we have defined it here.

Anger toward nonbelievers may be a precursor of religious extremism, but it is not, in itself, a defining characteristic. Most important, a useful definition of extremist religion should rest not on the strangeness or perceived irrationality of a creed but rather on whether its consequences are destructive. This definition of religious extremism is not perfect. But it does provide a place to begin.

CHAPTER 2

MILITANT ISLAM: THE PRESENT DANGER

A COMMITTED FAMILY

The Koran says: "And say not of those who are slain in the way of Allah: 'They are dead.' Nay, they are living, Though ye perceive (it) not" (2:154).[1]

Salah Ghandour would probably have been very proud of his young widow, Maha, the mother of his children. She not only accepted his decision to become a "martyr" for Islam but actively supported it. Indeed, she recalls, "From when I just married him, I expected his martyrdom at any minute. When we had three children, I told him he was taking his time. I didn't expect to live with him for five years."[2] In recounting this conversation, she did not seem especially coldhearted. She grinned warmly, as if recalling a little family joke.

One can never be certain from a distance, but they may even have been a happy family. Footage shows Salah playing cheerfully with his kids. "Of course, I miss him and remember his words," she explains. But she remains completely supportive of his mission. "Unless women sacrificed their husbands and brothers, this land [presumably southern Lebanon] would never have been liberated. Praise Allah, our homeland was liberated by the blood of the martyrs and the efforts of the mujahideen [Muslim holy warriors], some of which are still fighting the [j]ihad to this day."

Fortunately, Maha has found a way to continue to share her life with her husband. Salah's sponsor, the Hezbollah terrorist organization, filmed his operation and broadcast it on its al-Manar TV network. In a way, the video brings Salah back to his family. "Sometimes it saddens me," Maha says, "but I love to watch him." And their children love it too. Salah's son points to the television screen and announces, "This is the operation that Daddy carried out. . . . This is the car Daddy blew up." His younger sister chimes in, "This is the place of the operation in which he was gone."

We know about the Ghandour family from a 2005 television special "The Culture of Martyrdom," which aired on Al Arabiya TV in Dubai, a small emirate often touted as a Western ally. Though this program never mentions the word *terrorist* and can reasonably be denounced as biased, it does provide some unusually telling insights into the minds of some Islamic extremists. According to the ostensibly objective reporter, the targeting of Israeli civilians has gained the support of "most Muslim clerics." One such cleric, the influential Sheikh Qaradhawi, issued a televised fatwa on Al Jazeera giving religious support to such operations.[3] And Hezbollah leader Hassan Nasrallah announced that "[t]he martyrdom operations are the shortest way to Allah. They are the most exalted and magnificent way of martyrdom in this generation. . . . They can take away our cannons, our tanks and our planes. But they cannot take away our spirit, which yearns for Allah."[4]

The religious leaders make two important assertions to justify the suicidal attacks. First of all, the operations do not really target civilians because Israeli society has become militarized and, in effect, all Israelis have therefore become legitimate targets. More important, anticipating the traditional Islamic injunction against suicide, the leaders explain that the forbidden suicide is killing oneself "for personal reasons," something altogether different from "martyrdom operations," where one dies "for a greater cause." Such actions are "a part of the war movement."

The Al Arabiya broadcast includes footage of an open-air rally where the speaker demands, "What is your goal?" The crowd yells, "Allah." The speaker asks, "What is your constitution?" The crowd replies, "The Koran." The speaker: "Who is your leader?" The crowd: "The Prophet Muhammad." The speaker, "What is your path?" "The crowd: "Jihad." The speaker: "What is your greatest desire?" The crowd: "Death for the sake of Allah."

The Al Arabiya special, and this rally in particular, highlight how religion pervades the mindset of at least some extremists. Religious leaders are prominent, the perceived will of Allah is central, and militant fighters are widely portrayed as religious martyrs. Even Maha's focus on regaining land and the specific targeting of Israel, which suggests that political and nationalistic motives are also involved, is stated in religious terms, as she praises Allah for the martyrs' sacrifice. And, given the social recognition and approval heaped on "martyrs" and their families, one cannot help but wonder whether, at some level, Salah acted to earn the respect of his wife and bring esteem upon his family members, as well as to fulfill his religious destiny.

In this regard, it is worth noting the commentary on suicide bombers offered in 2002 by Dr. 'Adel Sadeq, chairman of the Arab Psychiatrists Association and head of the department of psychiatry at Ain Shams University in Cairo. Sadeq, who strongly sympathizes with suicide bombers, suggests that

> [w]hen the [suicide bomber] dies a martyr's death, he attains the height of bliss. As a professional psychiatrist, I say that the height of bliss comes with the end of the countdown: ten, nine, eight, seven, six, five, four, three, two, one. And then, you press the button to blow yourself up. When the martyr reaches "one," and then "boom," he explodes, and senses himself flying, because he knows for certain that he is not dead. It is a transition to another, more beautiful world, because he knows very well that within seconds he will see the light of the Creator.[5]

Putting aside questions about the state of the mental health profession in Egypt, one can see how, for the believer, such thoughts might provide powerful motivation, perhaps powerful enough to overcome basic survival instincts.

The Worried West

According to an important study conducted in 2005, 25 percent of the people in Pakistan—a country with a population of 166 million—now support "suicide bombings and other acts of violence in defense of Islam."[6] For the researchers who conducted the poll, this was actually good news, because a year earlier, the figure had been 41 percent. Throughout the Muslim world, appallingly large numbers of people now see terrorism "in defense of Islam" as acceptable: 39 percent of the population in Lebanon, 15 percent in Indonesia, 13 percent in Morocco, and 57 percent in Jordan (sometimes billed as our closest Arab ally in the Middle East). Even in Turkey, a member of NATO, 14 percent see some good in terrorism when carried out in the name of Islam.

Many of the pro-terrorist survey respondents were probably thinking about Jews or Israelis as the principal targets of the militants' attacks in the name of Islam, though the study did not specify. One might justifiably make this inference partly on the basis of the deep and widespread hostility toward Jews that the researchers found in the Arab world and—to a somewhat lesser extent—in non-Arab parts of the Muslim world.[7] In Jordan, for example, 99 percent of the public hold very unfavorable opinions about Jews. Moroccans, Indonesians, Pakistanis, and Turks are also overwhelmingly anti-Jewish.[8] (And it's not that other Muslim countries are necessarily more sympathetic; it's just that they weren't included in the study.)

The populations of these countries also view Christians unfavorably.[9] And support for terrorism remains high when Americans and other Westerners *in Iraq* are identified as the targets. In some Muslim countries, support for terrorism in this instance even increases substantially over levels of support for terrorism "in defense of Islam," where the intended target is not specified. Thus, more than half of the people in Morocco approve of suicide bombings directed against Americans and other Westerners in Iraq, and nearly one-quarter of the population in Turkey agrees.[10]

Support in the Muslim world for Osama bin Laden has been high in the years since September 11, 2001, although support varies from country to country and sometimes fluctuates from time to time. In 2005, 60 percent of Jordanians expressed "a lot of" or "some" confidence that Osama bin Laden would "do the right thing regarding world affairs." In Pakistan, where the terrorist leader was believed to be hiding, more than half of the public supported him.[11]

Notwithstanding these statistics, it should also be noted that in some Muslim-majority countries, sizable segments of the public typically express grave concern about threats emanating from extremists. And this, of course, makes sense, as the most frequent victims of Muslim militants are other Muslims. When asked whether Islamic extremism poses a threat to their countries, 73 percent of Moroccans said yes. Around half of those surveyed in Pakistan (52 percent), Turkey (47 percent), and Indonesia (45 percent) responded similarly.[12] All in all, however, there can be little doubt that support for Islamic militancy, even in its most violent manifestations, extends far beyond a handful of radical Muslims.

One way to document the impact of Islamic militancy on day-to-day life in Western countries is to examine an American newspaper on any given day. May 10, 2006, was chosen for no particular reason.

The front page of the *New York Times* on that date reports on a letter from President Mahmoud Ahmadinejad of the Islamic Republic of Iran to President Bush, which, among other things, hints at some vague conspiracy behind the September 11 attacks.[13] Adopting a paternalistic tone, the letter also urges the United States to abandon its secular, liberal democratic ways in favor of a turn to religion, even Christian religion. Pundits debated whether or not the Iranian president's missive contained any hidden clues about Iran's nuclear intentions, a matter of heightened concern during recent months.

The same *New York Times* front page presents recent polls showing very low approval ratings for President Bush, in large part because of widespread dissatisfaction with his handling of the war in Iraq. Also on page one, we learn of Shiite and Sunni Muslim militias battling each other in Baghdad.

But that's just the beginning of the day's coverage of Islam-related affairs. The *Times* that day further reports that

- The United States has softened its position on aid to the Palestinians, which was suspended following the ascension to power of the Islamic extremist Hamas group.
- A (presumably Sunni) suicide bomber has killed seventeen people in a public market in a Shiite neighborhood in northern Iraq.
- Saudi Arabia, Pakistan, and several other countries cited by human rights groups for frequent infractions of basic rights have been elected to a new, "improved" United Nations Human Rights Council. This new council was deemed better because of rules discouraging election of countries such as Libya and the Sudan, which had previously used their position to thwart investigations into their own nations' untoward goings-on.
- Egyptian security forces have shot a man whom they think masterminded five suicide bombings in the Sinai during the past year and a half.
- James Elshafay, a Staten Island New Yorker, has testified that he plotted to bomb a subway station in part because someone with whom he conspired had obtained a fatwa authorizing the act from an imam; the article notes that Elshafay has been diagnosed with schizophrenia.
- Some parents and community advocates have urged New York City Schools chancellor Joel Klein to close down the city schools in observance of two Islamic holidays, Id al-Fitr and Id al-Adha.

- A group of Riverdale, New York, rabbis have protested that a panel discussing the Israeli-Palestinian conflict at the private, prestigious Fieldston School was biased against Israel.
- A plan for building a financial district in Riyadh, Saudi Arabia, might have trouble finding employees because the kingdom follows strict Islamic laws regarding women.

The letters to the editor page that day is dominated by a discussion of how to attribute responsibility for Gaza's plight, with some blaming Hamas extremists themselves, some Israel, and some the United States. On the op-ed page, an advertisement touts the accomplishments of Israel's Technion (the Israel Institute of Technology) in fighting terrorism; it cites a new device that could detect triacetone triperoxide, a moldable sugarlike explosive that was used by the London subway bombers. And another advertisement on the entertainment page calls attention to a new movie about the passengers of United Flight 93, the airliner that was hijacked by terrorists and crashed in Pennsylvania on September 11, 2001.

The lengthy (and incomplete) list demonstrates the extent to which lives in New York and throughout the West have been influenced by the rise of Islamic extremism and by a greater attention to Islam in general that is, in part, a consequence of this rise—and, of course, of September 11.

Americans are still coming to terms with the situation. When the Cold War ended in the late 1980s, only a handful of prescient observers identified Islamic extremism as a central threat to Western interests. The Ayatollah Khomeini had indeed created a hostile regime in Iran, Hezbollah had shown its muscle in Lebanon, and Hamas was on the rise. Muslim militants had already carried out terrorist attacks, and our mujahideen allies in Afghanistan had started to turn on us. But to many observers, Islamic extremism still seemed a relic of the past, possibly a small bump on the road to worldwide liberal democracy, possibly a small but serious problem worthy of attention, but hardly something that threatened the day-to-day quality of life of people living in the United States.

Nowadays, of course, few Americans or Europeans doubt the magnitude of the challenge from extremist Islam. But the American public has yet to form a clear and stable impression of Islamic militancy. Numerous pollsters have attempted to learn just what Americans think and feel about these matters. The story that emerges is complex and nuanced. Americans certainly worry they will experience more terrorism. Thus, in August 2005—four years after the World Trade Center came down—45 percent of adult Americans still judged it very likely that "Islamic extremists will carry out major terrorist attacks against U.S. . . . cities, buildings, or national landmarks in the near future."[14] An additional 37 percent saw such attacks as "somewhat likely" in the near future. Only about one American in seven saw such attacks as "not too likely" or "not at all likely."

The public in the United States remains willing to distinguish between mainstream Islam and the extremists. Thus, several months after the September 11 attacks, Americans (71 percent) overwhelmingly agreed with President Bush that "suicide bombings and other violence by some followers of Islam . . . represent a perversion of Islam by extremists."[15] Only 16 percent saw such violence as reflecting "an important part of Islam's teachings." More recently, in July 2005, a majority (60 percent) continued to see such attacks as part of a conflict with only a small, radical group of Muslims. But a fairly large minority (29 percent) saw terrorist attacks as part of a major conflict between Islam and the West.[16] Interestingly, Americans are less likely than other Westerners to judge Muslims "fanatical." According to a 2006 poll, only 43 percent of Americans thought so, compared with 48 percent of people living in Great Britain, 50 percent in France, 78 percent in Germany, and 83 percent in Spain.[17]

When we probe attitudes toward Islam a bit more deeply, we find that American opinions are divided on whether mainstream Islam teaches "respect for the beliefs of non-Muslims." About a third say yes (31 percent), a bit more say no (43 percent), and about one-quarter (26 percent) have no opinion, according to one 2003 poll.[18] When asked to compare Islam to other religions, 39 percent of Americans said

Islam produced more violent extremists, while only a small number (4 percent) said fewer; on the other hand, 40 percent said "about the same."[19] When asked to compare Islam to the respondent's own religion, a solid majority saw it as a very different kind of faith, but a nontrivial minority saw it as having a lot in common with their own religion.[20] All in all, in April 2006, only a tiny segment of the American people (2 percent) described their impression of Islam as very favorable, and only a relatively small group (17 percent) reported a somewhat favorable impression.[21] Nearly a third said they hadn't heard enough to make up their minds, but almost half had formed a somewhat unfavorable or very unfavorable impression.

On one matter, most Americans were unequivocally critical of mainstream Islam. Nearly three out of four Americans (73 percent) thought the leaders of mainstream Islam were not doing enough to prevent Muslim extremists from carrying out terrorist deeds.[22] Only 13 percent expressed satisfaction with their efforts.

But perhaps most telling of all, 68 percent of Americans admit they know "not very much" or "nothing at all" about the Muslim religion and its practices.[23] Although more than half (56 percent) of Americans claim they know more about Islam now than they did at the time of the September 11 attacks, only 51 percent can name the Koran as the Islamic equivalent to the Bible.[24] Whatever people in the United States may say about how much they understand, one might reasonably conclude that knowledge about Islam for many Americans does not run very deep, even after years of intense media coverage.

Thus, when typical Americans make judgments about the role of Islamic faith in bringing about extremist practices, it is likely that most are extrapolating from general principles, attitudes, and values, rather than reporting fact-based inferences and deductions. People in the United States are without doubt very concerned about the problem of Islamic extremism, and they may read about and discuss the matter more than other topics in current events. But the average American's perceptions of Islam are poorly informed, unclear, and—probably—vacillating.

According to the statistics, the American public splits on the matter of the extent to which the religion of Islam deserves blame for deeds carried out in its name. However, it may make more sense to think of the American public as sizable masses of people who are uninformed or undecided, rather than to imagine two clear-thinking, opposed camps. In large part, this is because assessing the true spirit of a religious system with more than a billion adherents and no central leadership is an impossibly difficult task rendered even more complex by the lack of clear and unbiased sources in the English language. Political scientists have long known that most people possess extremely limited knowledge of world affairs and invest very little time in rectifying the deficiency. But even for those who follow the news closely, there is no easy way to get at the real nature of the Islamic faith.

The Many Faces of Islam

As part of his sermon one Friday in August 2004, the Palestinian sheikh Abu Muhammad al-Maqdisi told his followers, "Cutting off heads is a part of our religion. Indeed, by God, slaughtering Allah's enemies is part of our religion. It should be done in accordance with the interests of the Islamic nation."[25] In an article titled "The Infidels Will Be Obliterated," the cleric Seif al-Din al-Ansari writes that "Allah made annihilating the infidels one of his steadfast decrees. According to the [divine] natural law of alternating fortunes, Allah said [Allah will] obliterate the infidels. . . . It inevitably follows that this wisdom . . . has become the way according to which life is lived. . . . The [Koran] mentions this decree frequently, to the point that it makes you feel that it is a truth of supreme importance."[26] In another context, Sheikh Nasser ibn Hamed, an al Qaeda–affiliated Saudi cleric, considers the permissibility of using weapons of mass destruction to bring about the will of Allah. He first cites several Koranic verses that generally authorize retribution in kind, proportionate to transgressions that have been committed against the Muslims. The sheikh then concludes that, considering what the Americans have done, "If a bomb was dropped on them . . . that would annihilate 10 million and burn their lands to the same extent that they burned the Muslim lands—this is permissible, with no need to mention any other proof. Yet if we want to annihilate a greater number, we need further evidence."[27] The reader somehow senses that finding such evidence would not prove an insurmountable burden for this cleric.

But just when some in the West might be poised to pronounce Islam a form of madness and hatred cloaked in theological garb, we must come to terms with yet another, very different face of the faithful. A young woman, Asma Gull Hasan, smiles warmly from the cover of her 2004 book *Why I Am a Muslim*. She wears denim and a black blouse. Her neckline forms a tasteful V, not revealing but also not what many would expect from the author of a work touting the virtues of an Islamic life. She is not wearing a veil. Even before opening the book, it is hard not to like her.

A graduate of Wellesley College and New York University School of Law, she declares: "What Islam is really about is so different from the many misconceptions—about women, about other religions, about even the concept of *jihad*. Islam does not preach violent aggression against one's 'enemies.'"[28] She then asks, "Do you honestly think I would be a Muslim if that were true?"[29]

Hasan contends that "[i]n fact, the [Koran] and the core values of American society are strikingly similar."[30] Citing "some scholars," she even suggests that "the ideas of democracy and equality presented in the [Koran] are so strikingly similar to the foundational ideas in the U.S. Constitution."[31] Certainly her heart is in the right place when she proclaims: "Today, America comes the closest to fulfilling the ideal state as described in the [Koran], where one is free from tyranny and democracy reigns."[32]

Asma Hasan's book is a personal one, and her goal is not to assess the orthodoxy or relative popularity of her interpretation of the faith. Yet others who have written for American audiences likewise have suggested that Islam—at its core—provides little fuel for the extremists. Like Hasan, Imam Feisal Abdul Rauf sees America as a pretty good country, one that embodies the principles that Islamic law requires of a government.[33] The head of an American mosque not far from Ground Zero, Rauf sees himself as "a kind of marriage counselor," one whose role is not to condemn one side or the other. Instead, he says his aim is to tell Muslims, Christians, and Jews what each must do in order for everyone to get along. In other words, his commendable aim is to mend the relationship between the United States and the Muslim world.

Rauf perceives with clarity some of the pathologies evident in the ideology that extremists like bin Laden call Islam. But he does not attribute any of these dysfunctional tendencies to "true" Islam. Partly, and not trivially, he ascribes blame to the United States for falling short of its own principles by supporting corrupt dictatorships in order to benefit short-term, selfish interests. As for the essence of Islam: he sees this as supportive of a pluralistic, free, democratic, and mainly capitalistic society. The real cause of violence by religious extremists, Rauf argues, is not religion. Instead, he looks to sociology, economics, and politics for the answers.

In doing so, he echoes the most common view among American scholars of Islam. John Esposito, in his recent guide *What Everyone Needs to Know about Islam: Answers to Frequently Asked Questions from One of America's Leading Experts*, defends and absolves Islam in effect at every turn. Speaking of the extremists, he argues that "[t]hey attempt to impose their ideological brand of Islam and 'hijack' Islamic doctrines such as jihad, claiming to be defending true Islam, to legitimate their illegitimate use of violence and acts of terrorism."[34] He poses the question "Do Muslims support extremist and terrorist groups?"[35] And then, instead of attempting an answer based on assessments of contemporary Muslim attitudes, he centers his response on a philosophical point: "Determining who qualifies as a terrorist continues to be difficult."[36] By declaring the extremists' viewpoint "illegitimate," Esposito arrogates to himself the right to choose among competing explanations offered by Muslim scholars.

In any event, he, Rauf, Hasan, and many other writers for Western audiences since September 11 have erred by "downplaying or disregarding Islam's more contentious teachings."[37] There is a tendency, as one reviewer of Rauf's book notes, to paint "with a broad brush, leaving disturbing details safely blank."[38] The most troubling Koranic passages—for example, those that seem on their face to be misogynistic or supportive of the murder of infidels—quite simply, are omitted. Thus, Western readers are sometimes left with images of Islam and the Koran that are incomplete and, consequently, incorrect. Most Muslims believe that the Koran was sent to Muhammad chapter by chapter and word for word. That, after all, is why no translations are deemed adequate and why we in the West ignore the details of the sacred texts at our own risk.

For a variety of reasons, English-language sources tend to convey an incomplete picture of the Islamic faith, skewed in favor of moderate interpretations. For one thing, those writers who live in the West and wish to communicate to Western audiences tend to be more moderate. For another thing, many liberals—including the ones who dominate publishing—want to view Islam through "all religions are basically the same" lenses; in these troubling times, some are willing to sacrifice accuracy in order to avoid throwing grease on the flames. Mostly, however, there is the problem of "doublespeak." One Muslim writer who straddles the fence between moderation and extremism, Tariq Ramadan, even hints at how he uses the technique: "I must speak in a way that is appropriate for the ear hearing me . . . yet faithful to the religious sources of authority. . . . We must know how to speak to those who do not share our history."[39] Or, to put the matter a bit differently, very few Muslim spokespeople—whether moderate, mainstream, or extremist—see much value in telling Western audiences the whole story. (This, by the way, is why the Middle East Media Research Institute, MEMRI, which provides translations from generally unseen Arabic and Farsi sources, is such a vital resource.) However, to convey the whole story of any religion to those without the background is a tall order.

If one examines sources in which some Muslims are speaking to other Muslims, another face of contemporary Islam emerges. Unfortunately, this one has inspired much bloodshed over the past few decades. According to many extremist scholars, their followers, and vast groups of fellow travelers, the traditional sources of the Islamic faith—the Koran, the Sunna, the hadiths—provide crystal-clear justification for the entire program of militancy—a program that people like Asma Hasan and Imam Rauf would consider un-Islamic. Thus, many Muslims now believe that their religion teaches them that

- They are required to carry out a violent holy war (jihad) against infidels.
- Nonviolent alternatives will not fulfill this responsibility adequately in the present era.
- Death in the jihad procures for the martyr a blessed place in the afterlife.
- Suicide bombing is a perfectly acceptable way of becoming a martyr.
- Most current Muslim leaders are not true Muslims and most can be regarded as apostates.
- No one is permitted to convert out of Islam.
- Apostates should be put to death.
- Separation of church and state is a dangerous doctrine.
- The sharia, Islamic law, must be put in place first in Muslim lands and, ultimately, everywhere.
- Muslims may not be friends with non-Muslims.
- Jews and Christians deserve protection as second-class citizens (*dhimmis*) under the law, but only if they accept the rule of the Muslims and pay a special tax.
- Hindus and others outside the Abrahamic tradition are not entitled to this protected status.
- The penalty for blasphemy against God or his prophet is death.
- Adulterers should be punished by whippings or stonings.
- Feminism and tolerance for homosexuality are dangerous Western imports not sanctioned or acceptable under Islam.

- Religions other than Islam must not be tolerated on the Arabian Peninsula.

In each instance, Islamist clerics are able to cite chapter and verse—if not from the Koran, from the hadiths—that at least arguably might be taken to support their contentions. Hadiths are sayings attributed to the Prophet and hence carry a high level of authority when they are believed to be authentic.

Yet nearly all beliefs held by the extremists can also be plausibly refuted using religious texts and methods. If we visit one popular Web site, www.understanding-islam.org, we begin to appreciate a bit more how the debate shapes up for believers. The Web site is especially useful because the authors speak primarily Muslim-to-Muslim, but the language is English. Run by Moiz Amjad, a Pakistani scholar, this Web site exudes neither the warm decency of Asma Hasan nor the dyspeptic anger of the most dangerous terrorist groups. Affiliated with the Al-Mawrid Institute of Islamic Science in Karachi, the approach championed by the "Understanding Islam" scholars is defined not by their politics but rather by their willingness to reopen the process of interpreting the original, sacred Islamic sources "in a time when blind acquiescence is in vogue."[40] They assert that ongoing reinterpretation is key because, while the sacred sources are perfect, human error can never be eliminated.

In principle, such an approach might be liberalizing, radicalizing, or destabilizing. When asked whether the death penalty for apostasy is too barbaric, for example, the author suggests that "[s]aying that a particular punishment is too barbaric or otherwise, [*sic*] is basically giving a value judgment about that punishment. If that punishment is fixed by Allah or any of His prophets, it is the belief of all Muslims that then that punishment, whether severe or soft, serves justice."[41] Along similar lines, Amjad explains: "'Fanaticism' and 'Moderation' are not terms of the [sharia]. These terms are coined and used to refer to the various attitudes relating to religion. . . . Rather than calling someone 'Moderate' or 'Fanatic,' I would suggest that the views propounded by the individual or group should be scrutinized and analyzed on the basis of the [Koran]. If the view is understood to be based on the correct interpretation of the [Koran], then it should be taken as 'correct'—whether the world labels it to be 'moderate' or 'fanatical.'"[42] Thus, a combination of a serious attitude toward the authority of the sacred texts and a willingness to engage in reinterpretation might lead to unpredictable places. And so it often does, in the case of the Al-Mawrid Institute and its affiliates. The ultimate outcome has been, on balance (but not always), to reject the most extreme readings of the faith.

For example, someone submits a question to the Web site about the advisability of using the death penalty, but this time in reference to those who have abandoned Islam. According to the posted reply, this penalty has its roots in a non-Koranic saying (hadith) ascribed to Muhammad: "Whoever changes his Religion, kill him." And when the Koran itself mentions apostasy, it, too, suggests that a terrible punishment will follow, but—and this is the critical point—it will follow *in the hereafter*. Moreover, the Koran does state clearly that "[t]here is absolutely no compulsion in religion." Finally, the Koran more generally disallows the death penalty except under certain specified conditions, none of which deal with apostasy. With all these considerations, the scholars conclude that "either the saying [prescribing death for apostasy] has been wrongly ascribed to the Prophet . . . , as it is clearly contradictory to the [Koran] and the Prophet . . . could not have said anything contradictory to the [Koran], or that the saying ascribed to the Prophet . . . relates not to apostates, but to a particular and specific people."[43]

Of these two options, the author of the response prefers the latter. He then explains that the Koran generally regards the direct addressees of Muhammad as an exception to the rule against compulsion in matters of faith. Here, the author summarizes: "In short, the [Koran] says that it is the unalterable law of God that when He sends His messenger in a people, these particular people are left with no option, but to accept His message or to face the punishment of death and sometimes complete annihilation."[44] (Note that Jews and Christians are exempted from this requirement if they agree to Islamic rule and special taxation.) By this logic, then, the only apostates who would face the death penalty would be those who had been among the direct addressees of Muhammad. Of course, no such people are alive today, and, consequently, Muslims may not execute those who have left the fold, even though this appears to contradict a sacred hadith. Yet another purported saying of Muhammad in support of killing apostates is rejected outright on the grounds that its authenticity is in doubt.[45] Perhaps not by the most enlightened road, in this instance the religious scholar does get to the right place.

The Al-Mawrid approach comes down squarely against the inclusion of terrorist violence under the duty of jihad. Just after September 11, when someone objected on the Web site that Muslims who do not support jihad in Kashmir and Afghanistan are really abandoning part of the faith, Moiz Amjad replied: "[T]hose Muslim scholars, who consider *Jihad* to be allowed only after the fulfillment of certain conditions and under specific circumstances, do not consider any such aggression of the Muslims, which does not satisfy these conditions to be *Jihad* and, therefore, do not approve of the Muslim's participation in it. On the other hand, those who do not consider any prerequisite conditions for *Jihad*, have the tendency of labeling every aggression of the Muslims, irrespective of its moral implications, as '*Jihad*.'"[46]

According to the Al-Mawrid scholars, much of what passes for militant jihad in the contemporary world does not fit the requisite religious conditions for several reasons:

- Only states can launch a jihad.
- There are no grounds to argue that most governments in the Muslim world (and for this Pakistan-based group, especially the one in Pakistan) are in violation of Islamic law.
- Muslim states must be obeyed even when their leaders are corrupt.
- Individuals cannot fight evil by using force outside of established social, legal, and political authority—except under specified conditions.

- These specified conditions for rebellion against the state have not been met.
- No individual can declare another to be an apostate.
- The argument that terrorist aggression is self-defense is baseless.
- It is against Islam to lynch non-Muslim citizens of a Muslim state for blasphemy.[47]

Using similar logic, the Al-Mawrid approach offers a shred of hope—but perhaps only a shred—with regard to the pervasive anti-semitism in the Muslim world. Jerusalem is seen as the rightful possession of the Muslims not for reasons based on recent history or contemporary politics; the conclusion is that the Jews lost their rights because they, starting in biblical days, were not loyal to their God or observant of their religion.[48] Responding to a question about whether God dislikes the Jews most because they are always trying to harm the Muslims, the Web site suggests that "[w]hatever animosity there is between some Muslims and some Jews has no impact on how God observes us and judges us. Each individual will be held accountable for their wrongs whether they harm a Muslim or a non-Muslim." The Koran speaks of punishments meted out against the Jews. Here, the Web site suggests: "God's wrath upon the Jews was because of their rank transgression against God, their egregious disobedience and their atrocious murders of god's prophets. This, of course, is related to those Jews who did such a thing and [it] cannot be assumed that this blankets the entirety of all Jews who lived after the advent of the Prophet. . . . One needs to be careful not to use such specific instances of religious guidance for political or personal agendas."[49]

On some matters, however, there are few traces of any progressive approach whatsoever. Flogging and stoning are, for example, upheld as legitimate (though not required) penalties for sex outside of marriage.[50] But the logic the Web site scholars use and their attitude toward source materials reveal much about the all-important and rather large region that lies between Western-style moderate Muslims and the extremists. Many variations of Islam exist within this region. And because the Al-Mawrid scholars speak the same language as the worst extremists, or at least a dialect of that language, they might be in a position to reach the extremists where others cannot.

This, indeed, has crossed their minds. One protégé, Asif Iftikhar, explains:

> Often, criminals are of two kinds: there are those who know that the wrong they do is wrong—and there are those who think—who actually believe—that their deeds are virtuous. When those of the latter category have a religious basis for their activities, they can rarely be dissuaded by legal and penal measures alone, for bearing chastisement is in itself sublime to them—something that gives them a cause to rejoice in being "persecuted for righteousness' sake"—something that only adds to their commitment. The best defence against these people is an attack on the religious foundation their leaders use to convince them. A fortiori, legal and penal measures must be accompanied by propagation of counter arguments. For this purpose, arguments developed on the basis of superficial study won't do. No one is easily convinced into becoming a murderer on religious grounds and no one is easily dissuaded once so convinced.[51]

Of course, there are problems with this approach. As we have seen, the Al-Mawrid Muslims—and others who use similar methods—sometimes end up in places that many in the West cannot accept. Most troubling, the psychological, social, and political forces that bind extremists to their ideology may be so powerful that they resist and repel any attempts at counterargument, no matter how cogent and no matter how deeply rooted in their own traditions.

Later, we will return to the matter of how we might best combat extremist interpretations of Islam. But first we must understand why it is that so many Muslims in recent years have located in their faith the very foundations of extremism that other Muslims have pronounced entirely nonexistent.

The Road to Muslim Extremism I: Creating an Ideology

A century ago, Islam had the same Koran, the same Prophet Muhammad, the same stories about the founding of the faith, and the same religious and legal traditions. Yet there were no suicide bombers like Salah Ghandour, no incendiary leaders like Hassan Nasrallah, no militant sheikhs like Yousef al-Qaradhawi, and no murderous conglomerates like Hamas and al Qaeda. And that there were not should give pause to all those who claim that Islam is, necessarily, a violent and destructive faith. To attribute today's problems to the essence of the religion is to commit a grave error of oversimplification. Islam is a grand tradition that has proven itself capable of sustaining many different cultures, philosophies, approaches to life, and political arrangements. Some of these Islamic civilizations have stood out as impressive when judged against the standards of their times, others have manifested a business-as-usual approach for their eras, and still others have been repressive, even nightmarish.

As a consequence of the relatively recent extremist war against apostasy, many true liberals in the Muslim world have been forced to lay low. And, partly as a result of this, the visions of various extremist ideologues over the past half-century have gained enormous support in many parts of the Muslim world with devastating consequences. The challenge, then, is, as renowned Middle Eastern historian Bernard Lewis has noted, to identify what has gone wrong and when.[52]

Since September 11, and to a lesser extent before, many authors have probed the history of Islam and the Arabs in search of the roots of extremism. There are many places to look, and a comprehensive explanation should not shortchange any of them. Yet we must exercise caution when we look for origins of the present in the distant past, for instance, in the seventh, eighth, and ninth centuries, when Islam was in its childhood. For such distant history generally becomes relevant only when it has been activated or reactivated in the minds of men and women. Sometimes the most telling explanations come from the very recent past. And sometimes it makes more sense to look directly at the immediate circumstances of the al Qaeda, Hezbollah, and Hamas militants themselves.

One good place to start is with the story of Sayyid Qutb, an Egyptian writer who has been described as "the intellectual hero of every one of the groups that eventually went into Al Qaeda, their Karl Marx . . . their guide."[53] Others have called him the Lenin of the movement, because he laid out in writing "What Is to Be Done."[54] Back in 1964, Qutb wrote: "Mankind today is on the brink of a precipice, not because of the danger of complete annihilation which is hanging over its head—this being just a symptom and not the real disease—but because humanity is devoid of those vital values which are necessary not only for its healthy development but also for its real progress. Even the Western world realises that Western civilization is unable to present any healthy values for the guidance of mankind. It knows that it does not possess anything which will satisfy its own conscience and justify its existence."[55] These words, the opening to Qutb's most famous work, *Milestones*, might have been written by preachers in many faiths who saw in their religion the key to spiritual renewal. For Qutb, there was only one path to revival and one road to salvation, that specified by the Koran. *Milestones* was intended as a guidebook for an Islamic vanguard whose task it was to usher in a religious utopia. There is little doubt that Osama bin Laden, Ayman al-Zawahiri, and their followers to this day see themselves as part of Qutb's vanguard. Indeed, bin Laden himself studied under Qutb's brother.

Sayyid Qutb was born in Egypt in 1906. The product of a Western-style education, he spent his early adult years as a teacher, novelist, literary critic, and functionary in Egypt's Ministry of Education. From 1948 to 1950, he studied in Colorado for a master's degree in education. Some time between the late 1930s and the early 1950s, Qutb lost confidence in secular approaches to reform and became a radical Islamist. Just why this happened remains a matter of debate, but many scholars think his years in the United States at the very least contributed to this change.

In *Milestones*, Qutb recounts some of the things he did not like about 1940s America:

> Look at these concepts of the Trinity, Original Sin, Sacrifice and Redemption, which are agreeable neither to reason nor to conscience. Look at this capitalism with its monopolies, its usury and whatever else is unjust in it; at this individual freedom, devoid of human sympathy and responsibility for relatives except under the force of law; at this materialistic attitude which deadens the spirit; at this behavior, like animals, which you call "Free mixing of the sexes"; at this vulgarity which you call "emancipation of women"; at these unfair and cumbersome laws of marriage and divorce, which are contrary to the demands of practical life; and at Islam, with its logic, beauty, humanity and happiness.[56]

But *Milestones* was written many years after Qutb's return to Egypt, and some biographers have suggested that his conversion to Islamism was well under way prior to his American journey. When Qutb returned to Egypt, he at first made common cause with Gamal Abdel Nasser's secular revolution. Soon after Nasser achieved success and assumed the reins of government, he parted ways with Qutb and other Islamists. Nasser's dictatorial ways confirmed for Qutb that only Islam holding the reins of power could provide a meaningful answer to the problems of Egypt and the world. As Qutb spoke out in ways deemed dangerous by Nasser, the regime imprisoned him from 1956 to 1964. He was apparently tortured. It was during these years that he wrote his best-known and most influential works, including *Milestones* and a thirty-volume commentary on the Koran, *In the Shade of the Koran*. Nasser released him briefly in 1964, then rearrested him on charges of plotting the overthrow of the state. That he wished in some sense to do so was manifestly obvious from the text of *Milestones*. Whether he actually engaged in active plotting was another matter. In any event, Nasser executed him by hanging in 1966, thus giving the Islamists one of their earliest and most revered martyrs. Qutb had the opportunity to flee or beg for a pardon; instead, he chose to stay and face his sentence, a move that added considerably to his legend.

But the Islamist movement has had many martyrs, and it is as a theorist that Qutb made his greatest mark. In traditional Islam, the concept of "*jahiliyyah*" refers to the state of lowly and abhorrent ignorance that existed in the world before Muhammad. What Qutb did, with great consequence, was to extend this notion to cover all non-Islamic governments, including in his era all the nations in the Muslim world. To say that the Muslim countries were in a state of *jahiliyyah* then permitted Qutb to conclude that all true Muslims living in such countries were obligated, as a matter of faith, to participate in a revolution against their governments.

A few of Qutb's remarks about *jahiliyyah* tell us much about the seemingly unbridgeable gap that currently exists between the extremists and Muslims like Asma Hasan. Qutb's ideology does not permit compromise. In his words:

- "Islam cannot accept any mixing with Jahiliyyah, either in its concept or in the modes of living which are derived from this concept. Either Islam will remain, or Jahiliyyah: Islam cannot accept or agree to a situation which is half-Islam and half-Jahiliyyah."
- "The foremost duty of Islam in this world is to depose Jahiliyyah from the leadership of man, and to take the leadership into its own hands and enforce the particular [Islamic] way of life."
- "Indeed, people are not Muslims, as they proclaim to be, as long as they live the life of Jahiliyyah. . . . Today, the task of the Call is to return these ignorant people of Islam and make them into Muslims all over again."
- "A person who feels the need of defense, justification and apology is not capable of presenting Islam to people. Indeed, he is a person who lives the life of Jahiliyyah, hollow and full of contradictions, defects and evils, and intends to provide justification for the Jahiliyyah he is in. These are offenders against Islam."[57]

Thus, Western thought processes, like all the other trappings of life in the West, were taboo. For Qutb and his followers, the Muslims who used them had started to lose faith. Qutb's use of the *jahiliyyah* label condemns Muslims like Asma Gull Hasan and Imam Feisal Abdul Rauf as surely as it condemns American leaders like President Bush. It has provided justification for attacks on many Muslim leaders, including Egyptian president Anwar Sadat.

At a time when much of the Arab world was putting its hopes in a secular pan-Arabist movement, Qutb called for the formation of an Islamic vanguard that would begin to set a revolution in motion. The devoted few in this group were going to replace the legal codes of all societies with the Islamic law, or sharia. To accomplish this objective, persuasion would be one tool, but not the critical one. Jihad was the indispensable key, and by this concept, Qutb explains with great clarity, he does not mean mere defense. Arguments to the contrary are "nothing but a product of a mind defeated by the present difficult conditions and by the attacks of the treacherous orientalists [Western scholars] on the Islamic jihad."[58]

Qutb acknowledges the traditional Islamic rule, noted above, that there is no compulsion in matters of faith. But here, he argues that people must be free to choose their religion, and they cannot do this in non-Islamic societies. Hence, jihad must put in place a society based on the sharia. Then, and only then, according to Qutb, people will be free to choose their religion. He explains:

> It is not the intention of Islam to force its beliefs on people, but Islam is not merely "belief." As we have pointed out, Islam is a declaration of the freedom of man from servitude to other men. Thus it strives from the beginning to abolish all those systems and governments which are based on the rule of man over men and the servitude of one human being to another. When Islam releases people from this political pressure and presents to them its spiritual message, appealing to their reason, it gives them complete freedom to accept or not to accept its beliefs. However, this freedom does not mean that they can make their desires their gods, or that they can choose to remain in the servitude of other human beings, making some men lords over others. Whatever system is to be established in the world ought to be on the authority of God, deriving its laws from Him

> alone. Then every individual is free, under the protection of this universal system, to adopt any belief he wishes to adopt.[59]

Needless to say, this notion of freedom of belief is rather distant from the American one.

In fact, as the writer Paul Berman has noted, the entire vision would "plainly . . . require a total dictatorship." By claiming not to rely on man-made laws, Qutb's system "[would] have to rely, instead, on theocrats who would interpret God's law to the masses." In this sense, Berman correctly notes, the final outcome of Qutb's Islamism would not be very far from the outcome of "the other grand totalitarian revolutionary projects of the 20th century, the projects of the Nazis, the Fascists and the Communists."[60] Contemporary Iran is a good example of this.

It is worth making a few other points about Qutb's philosophy. Though he regarded the Jews with great hostility, he did not focus his attentions on the Arab-Israeli conflict. Similarly, despite his dislike of the United States, he did not seem preoccupied with America. His greatest concern was to prevent Muslims from being consumed by the appeal and allure of the West. He did criticize America and democratic governments for their inconsistencies, but he did not want America to be less hypocritical and truer to its ideals. He wanted to replace the patently false American way with the true Islamic way.

Sayyid Qutb was, without doubt, a creative writer who did more than merely parrot the words of those who came before him, and his intellectual influence remains to this day unequaled among the Islamists. Witness, for example, the words of one fan on the Web site of the Canadian Young Muslims, an organization that claims to be working toward the spiritual, intellectual, moral, and social revival of Islamic youth through education, personal development, community involvement, and activism. Here, Zafar Bangash speaks of Qutb as a "man of impeccable Islamic credentials" who made "an immense contribution to Muslim political thought" and was "an Islamic intellectual and leader of rare insight and integrity," one who "lives in the hearts of millions of Muslims worldwide."[61]

But Qutb was only one among many intellectual sources of contemporary Islamic extremism, some of whom came earlier, some later. Nearly all of these writers reacted to the effects of European colonialism and, more significantly, the disturbing message that accompanied it: Far from achieving the ordained and expected world domination, Muslims were no longer calling the shots on their own turf. By the nineteenth century, it was clear to most Muslims that the West had triumphed militarily over the Islamic world.[62]

The Muslims' defeat was an unacceptable culmination of a millennium of conflict between Christianity and Islam. Because they constituted part of the frequently recounted religious tradition, no one had forgotten the early successes of Muslim armies crossing the Middle East, North Africa, and Spain. These victories had hardened in the collective consciousness of Muslims a sense that Islam would always be in the ascendant. Despite major setbacks suffered at the hands of the Crusaders and, more importantly, the Mongols, the rise of the Ottoman Empire and the fall of Christian Constantinople in 1453 had once again reinforced the Islamic sense of destiny. As late as the sixteenth century, Islamic Ottoman armies threatened Vienna and the very survival of much of Christian European civilization. Greece, Hungary, and many southern Slavic domains remained in Muslim hands for some time afterward.

But by the nineteenth century, Britain and France began exercising direct or indirect control over several Islamic countries. The early victories of Islam had been interpreted as evidence of the ultimate truth of the faith. Now defeat brought an era of soul searching, no doubt made more wrenching by the arrogance of the colonialists.

Although many reformers settled upon a secular path to modernization, one that in key ways mimicked the West, others developed an array of strategies seeking to synthesize Islam with what they perceived to be the best in Western science and modern civilization. These Islamic modernists are the intellectual forerunners of today's extremists, though some did not themselves advocate radicalism of any sort. Jamal al-Din al-Afghani (1838–1897) argued that Muslims needed to appropriate Western science, technology, and constitutionalism, all of which he saw as sources of power. Such power would then be used to fight and ultimately defeat the imperialists. His contemporary Muhammad 'Abduh (1849–1905) favored social, educational, and legal reforms. For instance, he interpreted the Koran in a manner that permitted some improvement in the status of women. Together, Afghani and 'Abduh bequeathed to modern Islamists several central notions: (1) that all worthy Western ideas can be found in the Koran and the hadith, if only these are read properly; (2) that Islam itself bears no responsibility for the problems experienced by Muslims in modern times; and (3) that things will get better only when Muslims return to the pious ways of the Prophet Muhammad and his companions.[63]

'Abduh was less defiant in his approach to the West than Afghani, and a few modernists, like Sir Sayyid Ahmad Khan (1817–1898), did not see rejection of the West as a necessary condition for the modernization or revitalization of the Islamic community. One of Abduh's followers, Sheikh 'Ali 'Abd al-Raziq, called for many moderate reforms and even suggested that the link between religion and politics might not be critical for Islam in modern times; instead, he interpreted it as something particular to the era of Muhammad himself. An Indian Muslim, Muhammad Iqbal (1875–1938), saw Islam as passing through a reformation similar to the Protestant Reformation in Europe. Islam, as he saw it, provided an indigenous foundation for parliamentary democracy.

However, the ways of the more extreme disciples of 'Abduh and Afghani proved appealing to many. The Syrian cleric Rashid Ridha (1865–1935) emphasized political aims and included among his disciples the pro-Nazi mufti of Jerusalem, Hajj Amin al-Husseini, and the terrorist 'Izz al-Din al-Qassam, for whom a Hamas unit and the Qassam missiles fired at Israel are named.

Most contemporary manifestations of Islamic extremism can trace their earliest organizational roots to two movements: the Jamaat-i-Islami founded in India in 1941 by Mawlana Abul Aala Mawdudi (1903–1979) and the Muslim Brotherhood, established in Egypt by

Hassan al-Bana (1906–1949) in 1928. These organizations spread many of the messages we have already discussed, though—within the lifetimes of their leaders—they never gained much worldly power. The Muslim Brotherhood was, however, the organizational home of Sayyid Qutb on his return to Egypt from America. At present, it has achieved a degree of electoral success in Egypt, though some extremists believe that in order to do so it has moderated to a degree. The Muslim Brotherhood and its offshoots also played a role in the education and training of bin Laden's lieutenant Ayman al-Zawahiri and many other terrorists. The Brotherhood has provided a network of social services and, for its followers, an alternative to what they see as the corrupt government in Egypt. It should be noted, however, that part of what they label corruption is the Egyptian government's willingness to do business with the United States and Israel.

At least two other traditions fed into the development of extremist ideology in contemporary Islam. As far back as the mid-eighteenth century, the Muslim scholar Muhammad ibn 'Abd al-Wahhab, based in Arabia years prior to the rise of colonialism in the Middle East, issued a call for a return to the pious ways of the forefathers, based on strict adherence to the Koran and the hadith.[64] He objected to a variety of innovations and, particularly, imports from the non-Islamic world. His alliance with Muhammad ibn Saud, the founder of the House of Saud, gave his ideas a longevity they otherwise would not have had. In the twentieth century, Saudi leaders clung to the Wahhabi ways mainly as a means of establishing and reinforcing the legitimacy of their rule. By so doing, however, they fed and promoted a doctrine that had much (but not everything) in common with the extremism of Qutb, the Muslim Brotherhood, and their offshoots. Thus, the Saudis strongly supported the Taliban, which provided a home for bin Laden, even though bin Laden regarded the Saudi leadership as partners with the satanic Americans. The Saudis, as a consequence of their commitment to Wahhabi Islam, also pumped a great deal of money into a variety of radicalizing organizations.

Meanwhile, in the world of Shiite Islam, the Ayatollah Khomeini had developed a parallel movement, based on Islam, as the answer to the disruptions to traditional life caused by the shah of Iran.[65] Khomeini provided a modernist solution that appealed to many who were disturbed by the shah's personal excesses as well as his attempts to push modernization of Iran forward at a feverish pace. Khomeini's 1979 rise to power in Iran led many to conclude that an Islamic government had an important place in modern times. It also established hostility to compromise and anti-Americanism as principles that went hand in hand with the call for a return to Islamic fundamentals. Today, this extremist tradition continues in Iran and its Hezbollah protégé and may be on the rise elsewhere in the Middle East.

THE ROAD TO MUSLIM EXTREMISM II: FAILED SOCIETIES, INDOCTRINATION, PERCEIVED SUCCESS

The biggest question is not why Sayyid Qutb and others developed their extremist take on Islam, but why their ideas have proved appealing to so many. In part, the answer lies in the message itself. Islam is a powerful, multifaceted, story-laden, at times poetic, philosophically developed, time-honored system that has proven equal to countless challenges in the past. Thus, many Muslims find comfort in relying on it in an era of great uncertainty and rapid change. Moreover, leaders like Sayyid Qutb and others have intelligently and fluently identified real feelings and needs in the Muslim population, and to a lesser extent in the wider non-Muslim population as well—feelings and needs that have not been adequately addressed by others.

And once one makes a decision to turn to the texts, one finds messages that readily lend themselves to extremist interpretation, even if such interpretation is, as moderates insist, misinterpretation. The words themselves then take on tremendous power.

However, the extreme hostility toward Americans, Jews, and other infidels requires a deeper level of explanation. Here we must examine how some Muslims have reacted psychologically to their contemporary predicament and how some have been, in effect, indoctrinated by their religious leadership. And we must see how the history of Islamic extremism since the 1970s and the West's reaction to it has confirmed, in the eyes of many extremists, that theirs has been a path sanctified by God.

The story of political, economic, and social decline in the Arab and Muslim states would fill volumes.[66] It is partly a tale of long-term social, intellectual, theological, and political failure dating back centuries, but, most importantly, it is a recounting of *recent* failures across the Arab world during the past six decades. Many people in most—but not all—Muslim and Arab countries experience considerable disappointment, anger, shame, disgust, helplessness, hopelessness, and a range of other negative feelings about their own situations. In some cases, these emotions derive from general perceptions of the unenviable state into which their subgroup, nation, or religion has fallen. The contrast with the powerful heights achieved by classic Islam only intensifies the sense that something is amiss in the world order. And the success of previously underdeveloped states in East Asia and elsewhere, some lacking equivalent natural resources, has sent a message that some of the problem is internal.

Similarly distressing for many Arabs and Muslims is the fact that a series of military defeats in 1948, 1956, 1967, 1973, and 1982 were suffered at the hands of Jews, the very same people whom the religious and cultural tradition taught were profoundly inferior, even powerless. That others, besides the Jews, have prospered beyond the Muslims in intellectual, financial, and military arenas has not been much easier to take. Historically, the defeat in the 1967 Six Days' War was most important. Gamal Abdel Nasser and the pan-Arabists had staked everything on their expectation of a victory and then they lost—miserably. It was apparent to everyone inside and outside the Arab world that pan-Arabist secular dictatorships had brought nothing good to their populations. And no better secular alternatives appeared in the offing.

How blows to the collective ego are translated into individual frustration, despair, discontent, and anger is a complex matter. For some, diffuse hostility may stem from their own, more immediate economic, social, spiritual, or familial difficulties. As the mass media broadcast images of life across the globe, the experience of relative deprivation may increase. Individuals not sharing in the immense oil wealth of some parts of the Muslim world may feel especially wronged. In addition, many in the region bear animosity toward their political leaders and their state, which they perceive—rightly or wrongly—as the source of their problems.

In this context, we gain a clearer understanding of the psychological function of anti-Americanism, anti-Christianity, anti-Westernism, Jew hatred, and hostility toward Israel. For many in the Arab and Muslim world, Israel has become a central element in a collective obsessional delusion, and America has become inextricably tied to Israel. Sometimes Israel is seen as the tool of America. Sometimes America is seen as the tool of Israel. But both, together, are frequently seen as the source of all evil.

With no shortage of injustices close to home in countries such as Pakistan, Indonesia, Sudan, Libya, Saudi Arabia, and elsewhere, one wonders how so many people find so much energy to devote to a conflict so far away. Even if Israel were conducting itself as unjustly as its detractors maintain, it remains to be explained why its particular infractions should loom so large in Muslim and Arab public consciousness. America as a world power can at least plausibly be implicated in many events around the world. But this is not the case for Israel. Part of the explanation is that hostility toward the Jewish state is what Bernard Lewis calls a licensed grievance: "[T]he only one that can be freely and safely expressed in those Muslim countries where the media are either wholly owned or strictly overseen by the government. Indeed, Israel serves as a useful stand-in for complaints about the economic privation and political repression under which most Muslim peoples live, and as a way of deflecting the resulting anger."[67] Anti-American hostility can play a similar safety-valve role, though—sometimes—governments view antagonizing the United States as a costlier approach. But when all else fails, a bit of anti-Israel or anti-American sloganeering can sometimes get the troops back in line.

People naturally have a self-serving bias that they use when they explain life's ups and downs.[68] While they take credit for accomplishments, they assign blame for failures to others. Elsewhere, I have argued that "[e]xperiences of real injustice lie at the heart of some destructive impulses, but a sense of inequity need not arise out of any actual persecution, nor from the deeds of the eventual targets [of such destructive impulses]."[69] Europe, America, and Israel have not been blameless, but they have received more blame for causing the problems of the Muslim world than they deserve.

The differences in attitudes and opinions held by people hailing from the same culture can be explained, in part, by the extent to which the prevailing ideology squares with individual needs and cognitive strategies.[70] Receptivity to the message of hate depends also on exposure to socialization agents promoting hatred, exposure to alternative viewpoints, and the extent to which one's own experiences match, or seem to match, the tenets of the ideology.

Throughout the Arab and Muslim world, many mosques, schools, governments, newspapers, and broadcast media are spreading elements of the extremist message. Children learn from these sources what their cultures deem to be true and meritorious. Kuwait, for example, is a place where extremism has not achieved great success. Yet even there, the schools are sending discouraging messages. As Shamlan Yousef al-'Issa, a political scientist at Kuwait University, reports:

> The official government institutions—that is, the elementary, middle, and high schools, and even the vocational institutes and the universities—are spreading religious thought by means of children's books full of lessons about *Jihad* in Islam, and of repeated calls to expel foreigners from the lands of the Arab Gulf countries. . . . The *Jihad*-waging youth in the Gulf . . . attended the state schools in Riyadh and Kuwait, and also the public universities. . . . What does the Kuwaiti government expect when its students' textbooks are full of calls to *Jihad*?[71]

In Saudi Arabia, things are worse. Saudi children in grades 1 through 10 are told that Jews and Christians are the enemies of Islam, that Jews are a wicked nation characterized by bribery, slyness, deception, and aggressiveness, and that prohibitions against terror do not apply to cases that fall under the categories of jihad and martyrdom. Students are further taught that "the Jews' disappearance is . . . desired" and that "Palestine in its entirety should be liberated by force and purified of its Zionist filth."[72]

In Pakistan, madrassas (Islamic religious schools) teach millions of schoolchildren a version of Islam that is deeply hostile to the West.[73] An article in the *New York Times* describes the situation: "[S]tudents ranging in age from 7 or 8 to men over 20 are taught a strict interpretation of the Koran, including the duty of all Muslims to rise up in jihad. . . . There are no magazines or newspapers except those deemed acceptable by the elders. The outside world is closed to them, and many of the students seem puzzled when asked if they mind that." One teacher explains: "There is no practical training of terrorists here. . . . We prepare them for the jihad mentally." Presumably, they get the rest of their training elsewhere.

Hamas, the Muslim Brotherhood, and other extremist organizations have long specialized in providing healthcare and a variety of other social services. They are then in a position to deliver their messages while they are doing good deeds and thereby gaining legitimacy. The combination can be powerful. Above all, the extremists and their fellow travelers communicate their values by the honor they bestow on the "martyrs" and their families.[74]

Against the backdrop of Muslim failures in the modern era, the extremists have achieved a measure of success. Khomeini's revolution bloodied America's nose in the late 1970s and has thus far escaped significant retaliation. The Islamic government in Iran has convinced many Muslims that a revival of historic traditions, far from being a fantasy, is possible, and—in the minds of some—inevitable. The victory of the Afghans over their Soviet masters has further hammered home the message that Islam can best the superpowers by virtue of its intensity and moral energy. Hezbollah was able to attack and drive out American forces from Lebanon in the 1980s and, two decades later, outperformed most expectations in its 2006 war against Israel. The nonreligious Palestine Liberation Organization (PLO) managed to transform itself from a minor group into an international player with tremendous influence mostly by carrying out successful terrorist attacks, or so it appeared to many Muslims. If secular attacks brought such success, they reasoned, how much more could be accomplished in a holy war blessed by God? Even the reaction to the September 11 attacks reinforced a sense of protected destiny in the minds of many extremists. The United States committed all its wealth and might to the battle against al Qaeda, and yet bin Laden and al-Zawahiri remain at large. This seemed to indicate a level of divine involvement. When Americans could not defeat Islamist insurgents in Iraq, the extremists again took heart that theirs was a blessed cause. Never before in modern times have Islamic concerns loomed so large on the worldwide public agenda, and, not unreasonably, many see Qutb's revolution doing rather well. Such beliefs are perhaps illusory, but they give many Muslims more to believe in than they have had for some time.

Noble Rebels, Adoring Fans

Mohammed Atta, one of the September 11 pilots and a leader of the plot, forever changed how we in the West view Islamic extremists and suicide bombers. Once they were widely imagined to be intellectually and materially impoverished, barely postadolescent, desperate, helpless, and clinically unstable. But Atta held a degree in architectural engineering and had worked as an urban planner for several years. The son of an attorney, he received an additional degree in city engineering in Hamburg, Germany. At the university there, people described him as very intelligent, reasonably pleasant, and a fine speaker of German. Coming from a somewhat religious background, he appears to have immersed himself ever more deeply in the ideology of Islamic extremism. He became progressively more hostile to Jews and America, and more and more committed to his own personal participation in the jihad.[75]

Atta may have moved in this direction as an act of expiation to alleviate guilt that he felt. Daniel Benjamin and Steven Simon, two leading scholars of Islamic terrorism, conclude that "Atta was a man flagellating himself. At some point, how and when are not clear, he had a brush with temptation; perhaps he felt he had succumbed. Whatever touched him, he identified with the West. It might have been as simple as a personal desire to be a part of the West that caused him to feel contaminated. His repulsion was powerful, and he felt somehow humiliated."[76] This explanation makes sense, though it is hard to prove. All of the anti-Western jihadists denounce the West loudly with words drawn from their sacred texts, yet their biographies reveal far more ambivalence. Perhaps this is why they often decry Western sexual mores most powerfully; it is precisely this aspect of Western culture that may be most threatening.

In any case, the new image of the Muslim militant is that of a well-informed, competent rebel against the modern. Poverty and deprivation play little if any role, and many terrorists are drawn from families of privilege; many have had disproportionate exposure to Western ways. Inside, some may be reacting to an allure they personally feel within Western culture, one that clashes with values acquired during their upbringing. To describe such perpetrators of atrocities, even terrible atrocities, as insane gets us nowhere. Instead, they are best seen as proponents of an extremist religious ideology, one that has been culled from an ancient religious tradition and transmogrified over the past half century.

Thus Salah Ghandour, too, saw himself as part of a noble cause whose time had come. His cause seems incomprehensible to those of us who have been raised in the West. But it was not incomprehensible to him or to many of those with whom he associated on a daily basis. Leaders and followers, educated and uneducated, happy and unhappy, stable and unstable—many like Salah had absorbed the ideology of extremism. Osama bin Laden, the bombers of the USS *Cole*, Zaccarias Moussaioui, the "dirty bomb" bomber, the shoe bomber, Hassan Nasrallah, and Yousef al-Qaradhawi all come at Islam from different angles. They are drawn to their tasks in the movement for the usual variety of motives that characterize human behavior. Some seek a feeling of personal fulfillment, some seek to escape guilt, some seek respect or fame, some seek intellectual accomplishment, and some seek social support. Some are a little insane. But all draw on an ideology that provides them with direction and purpose. They are not merely evil people who are operating under the cover of Islam. They are people who have embraced a fairly widespread—and perhaps deeply flawed—variant of Islam that contains much hatred and anger and that condones and promotes violent acts in its name.

Thus far, fairly small numbers of Muslims—Qutb's revolutionary vanguard—have been willing to sacrifice their lives in order to further the war against the infidels. But, as Bernard Lewis has noted, "Islam is not only a matter of faith and practice; it is also an identity and a loyalty—for many, an identity and a loyalty that transcend all others."[77] Thus, when they perceive Islam itself to be engaged in a worldwide struggle, very large masses—hundreds of millions—have, as a matter of tribal loyalty, been willing to give moral support to Qutb's vanguard. One question is how much damage the vanguard can do on its own. A second question, at least as important, is what can be done to keep the wavering millions from finding common cause with Islam's most deadly elements.

CHAPTER 3

Killers in Every Faith: Christians and Jews

The Army of God—Christian Terrorists

The young Massachusetts doctor cannot reveal her name. She now performs as many as ten abortions a day, twice a week. This doctor finds many different aspects of obstetrics and gynecology gratifying, and laments that so much of her time is spent terminating pregnancies. But only a few physicians in her area will perform abortions, and she typically ends up performing many, even though, when she started medical school, she didn't want to do any. Back then, she already agreed that a woman should have the right to get an abortion, but she did not want to get involved because her upbringing and religious background made her feel conflicted.[1]

In contrast, she now believes abortion rights are an important component of American civil rights and that physicians have a moral obligation to make them available, even if at considerable risk to themselves. Her change of heart came partly from experiences during her medical training, including one occasion when she had to counsel an eleven-year-old girl. The doctor recalls: "[I]t soon became obvious that she had no understanding of sex—she didn't really understand that she'd even had it, or that it had any connection to her pregnancy. We literally had to teach this girl about what it means to have sex. . . . I remember thinking: In a world where people don't want kids to learn about these things, how can you not give them the choice to terminate a pregnancy? Even if she had chosen to continue the pregnancy and opt for adoption, what would that have done to her own childhood?"[2] The doctor claims that she has the utmost respect for "life" and that when she ends it—which, she agrees, is what she does—it is for good reasons. Sometimes she saves a woman's life; sometimes she improves the lives of the other children in a family. Sometimes there are other reasons she deems satisfactory. One thing is for sure: This doctor is deeply committed to her cause.

She is, in short, someone who members of some of the antiabortion extremist groups would deem one of the worst people on earth—satanic, heartless, brutal, and on a par with the likes of Josef Mengele and the Auschwitz doctors. In the view of some fanatics, killing the young doctor would be an act of unparalleled goodness, a godly deed that would procure a lofty place in the world to come.

Thus, physicians who provide abortions are at risk. So are all those who work with them and near them. And so are the patients who visit their offices and clinics. Since 1991, there have been seven murders and seventeen attempted murders of abortion providers and their associates. There have been 300 reported death threats, 84 incidents of assault and battery, 99 acts of arson, 967 cases of vandalism, 367 bomb threats, and 15 bombings. On 482 occasions, antiabortion activists have stalked doctors, staff members, or patients. Minor disruptions are more frequent. For example, more than eleven thousand harassing phone calls and letters have been received by abortion providers and clinics.[3] As columnist Anna Quindlen has remarked, "Reading over even thumbnail sketches of what has happened to clinics and clinic owners since abortion became legal makes any sane person wonder how dedicated or stubborn an individual would have to be to continue."[4]

Dr. Barnett Slepian was one such stubborn and dedicated physician, and on October 23, 1998, a member of the Army of God, an extremist group, finally delivered his "just deserts." Slepian had returned from synagogue with his wife and four sons. While standing in the kitchen of his home, surrounded by his family, he was shot dead by sniper James Kopp, who liked to call himself "Atomic Dog." Kopp immediately became a legendary figure among antiabortion extremists, his image only enhanced by widespread awareness that he was also suspected in the earlier shootings of several other abortion providers.

The Army of God Web site still triumphantly displays a photograph of Dr. Slepian amid wavy yellow and orange flames. The caption proclaims: "Slepian now burning in hell fire where he belongs."[5] The Web site also shows Kopp's smiling, clean-cut face beaming above the doctor's tombstone. The caption under the photograph of the tombstone announces: "I will not be intimidated! Babykilling Abortionist Barnett Slepian."

The Army of God obviously does not speak to pro-choice audiences; the message targets more moderate opponents of abortion who reject Kopp's militancy. A question is posed to "those who denounced the one who saved many innocent lives from a painful death at the hands of this abortionist": "Pro-lifers which do you prefer: Live babies or live babykilling abortionist? Dead babies or dead babykilling abortionist?"[6] In case anything is left unclear, there is also a very graphic and gruesome photograph of a dead fetus (or baby) with his detached head beside him.

What motivated James Kopp? Clearly, he shows no remorse and acknowledges that he would kill again if abortions were still being performed when (and if) he got out of prison. He declares: "I hope that my younger brothers and sisters in the movement know that we can still cut some holes in the fences of the death camps and let a few babies crawl to safety. We can still derail a few trains."[7] The comparison to those who resisted Hitler and the Holocaust is one frequently invoked by antiabortion activists. Kopp feels certain that he is part of a just moral crusade. He further insists that his goal was to stop the doctor from conducting future abortions, and not to punish him for past ones. But the bullet took a crazy ricochet, he claims from the jailhouse: "The truth is not that I regret shooting Doctor Slepian. I regret that he died . . . I aimed at his shoulder."[8] Though this distinction between prevention and punishment is sometimes made by other antiabortion militants as well, it is hard to have confidence in their sincerity.

A college graduate and once a professional trumpeter, Kopp—unlike the majority of violent antiabortion extremists—is Roman Catholic. He arrived at his commitment to a strategy of murder gradually. At one point in the 1980s, he headed an organization that operated a "crisis pregnancy center." Under this ambiguous name, advisers at the center and others like it did—and continue to do—whatever they could to dissuade pregnant women from having abortions. Kopp also lived and worked for a short while at Mother Teresa's organization in New York City.

He engaged in clinic protests in the mid-1980s and became associated with two extremist groups, Operation Rescue and Lambs of Christ. Kopp soon became well known among antiabortion extremists. One major protest in 1988 led to his arrest and jailing along with other militants, including Shelley Shannon (who later shot Dr. George Tiller), John Arena (who later committed a butyric acid attack against an abortion clinic), and others. It was around this time, most likely, that Kopp acquired his "Atomic Dog" nom de guerre and when he helped organize the Army of God and write part of its manual.[9] This manual offers various strategies for disrupting abortion clinics but maintains that violence toward abortion providers is likely to be the best way to stop abortions. Although Kopp was arrested several times over the years, there was a period during which he apparently kept a low profile and may have been carrying out his earlier physician shootings.

Kopp's stepmother provides an interesting angle on his motivation. While attending college, he apparently had a girlfriend with whom he was in love. She told him she wanted to end the relationship and proceeded to have an abortion, informing Kopp that the aborted child was his. Kopp's father recalls that this event sparked his interest in the antiabortion movement. But Kopp himself tells the story a bit differently. In his version, the girlfriend did visit the abortion clinic but learned that she was not, in fact, pregnant. Kopp says he first became attracted to the antiabortion cause when he visited a morgue and saw a fetus that had been aborted due to birth defects.[10] If events transpired in accord with the stepmother's recollection, the abortion of his own child may have produced great guilt, perhaps at the unconscious level, and Kopp may have sought to alleviate this guilt through activism. Even if Kopp's version is true, the event may have been psychologically significant.

Catholicism has been a central part of Kopp's life, and no doubt the church's teachings contributed to his view that abortion is murder. A priest, Father Norman Weslin, heads the radically antiabortion Lambs of Christ, for which Kopp was once a chief strategist. In 1992, Weslin said: "Unless you understand that this is a colossal war between Jesus Christ and Satan, you don't understand what we are doing."[11] Weslin continues his activism to this day and was arrested as recently as May 2006, at age seventy-five, for blocking the entrance to a clinic.[12] To my knowledge, he has not spoken publicly about his association with Kopp. Still, no readily identifiable religious experiences set Kopp on the path to his extremism position. He was already militant when he met Weslin. We may yet learn more about his motivation, but Kopp does not seem to have been converted to the cause by contact with Catholic religious leaders or by his particular take on Catholic theology. Still, he drew moral support from Catholic and non-Catholic extremist clerics who are on the fringe of the Right to Life movement.

Kopp is one of a handful who have perpetrated major crimes against abortion providers. Just weeks after the 9/11 attack, and while the country reeled from unsolved anthrax assaults, Clayton Waagner mailed white powder and threatening letters to hundreds of abortion clinics across the country. Though the powder was not really anthrax, he deemed his act successful and it was perceived to be so by many antiabortion militants. According to Waagner's logic, he disrupted about twenty thousand scheduled abortions and, since many of those women would not reschedule, he believes he saved thousands of the unborn. In what appears to be a frank conversation with another antiabortion activist, he insists that he would have used real anthrax had he possessed it.[13] He also claimed, after mailing the letters and while on the run, that he had a list of people who worked at abortion clinics, along with their addresses and other identifying personal information. If these people didn't immediately quit working at their clinics—and if they did not provide proof by following instructions on an antiabortion Web site—he was going to kill them all.

Another fanatic, Eric Robert Rudolph, bombed an abortion clinic in Birmingham, Alabama, and in the process killed an off-duty police officer. Rudolph also carried out several other attacks, including one targeting a gay bar and the notorious bombing at the 1996 Atlanta Olympics. Perhaps the best known in the violent antiabortion world is Paul Hill, executed in 2003 for the shooting murder of Dr. John Britton and his volunteer clinic escort, James Barrett, in Pensacola, Florida. It is worth taking a moment to examine the motivations and mindsets of these criminal activists—all of whom are loosely associated with the underground Army of God.

Clayton Waagner proudly declared in an Internet posting in June 2001, several months prior to mailing the fake anthrax letters, that "the government of the most powerful country in the world considers me a terrorist. . . . They're right. I am a terrorist. To be sure, I'm a terrorist to a very narrow group of people, but a terrorist just the same. As a terrorist to the abortionist, what I need to do is evoke terror. Thus the reason for this letter. I wish to warn them that I'm coming."[14] He had considered following in the footsteps of previous activists and shooting physicians, Waagner later explains, but he ultimately rejected the idea. He had gone so far as to climb roofs and target doctors entering clinics. But he couldn't pull the trigger, he says, because he didn't want to hurt innocent passersby. And then, after the September 11 attacks, he claims to have abandoned the plan to shoot abortion providers altogether, asserting that he "[loves] America as much as anyone else."[15] So, he says, he settled on terrorizing abortion providers without actually killing them.

Waagner, like others imprisoned for antiabortion violence, has become a folk hero to the militant fringe of the Right to Life movement. In keeping with the role, he has written numerous articles and a book, *Fighting the American Holocaust*.[16] He was arrested for various crimes in 1999; it is not clear whether all of his earlier criminal activity was related to his antiabortion mission, though he claims to have been plotting attacks against abortion providers. When he escaped from a high-security prison in February 2001, he called it a "miracle of the Lord." He further reported that he "felt like Jonah on the way to Nineveh: the Jail was my whale, but it would spit me out to go where God had sent me," that is, to stalk physicians, launch the fake anthrax assault, and threaten clinic employees. Later, in prison, Waagner claims to have received a direct message from God. The message concerned the execution of Paul Hill and was more clearly prophetic and divine than anything Waagner had experienced before.

God now wanted a bit of moderation and commanded believers not to seek revenge for the death of Hill. The prophecy is reprinted word for word and reads, in part: "You who are known must seek My Will within My Revealed Word, Those who are known must fight for the innocent, but not with the weapons of man. You must trust Me, not the desires of your heart. Trust Me. My Justice will be served to those who murder My innocent children by the hands of warriors who are not known."[17] Waagner proceeds to offer an exegesis developed during months "seriously seeking the Lord through . . . prayer, fasting and meditation."[18] He advises: "This may be a bitter pill for some of you. Some of you are no doubt thinking about an action, and some may even consider following Paul's courageous example by laying down your life for the pre-born. Though I might think this is a great idea, God feels otherwise. It seems He would rather you who are known do no illegal actions . . . but that you seek His will in His revealed Word. (I feel confident this is the Bible)."

Waagner evidently enjoys the position of leadership and influence he has assumed within the antiabortion fringe. Though in prison, he squabbles with other activists and issues opinions on pending matters. In a dispute with his former ally Neal Horsley, he rebukes and disavows Horsley for the latter's anti–United States government attitudes, especially when he brought the movement for the unborn into disrepute by threatening to burn an American flag. Waagner wants activists to stay focused on the abortion issue. Several of those who have interviewed Waagner note his intelligence.[19] Unlike Kopp, he was not known among abortion activists in the years before he committed his most notorious acts. He speaks of God and religion frequently, but his interpretation is personal rather than institutional. He is not a disciple of any cleric. He believes that God and, to a lesser extent, the Bible communicate with him more or less directly and he provides interpretations for others.

Eric Robert Rudolph comes to his antiabortion activism from a different ideology than most antiabortion militants. As one writer explains, he has had "a long association with the radical Christian Identity movement, which asserts that North American whites are the direct descendants of the lost tribes of Israel, God's chosen people."[20] The Christian Identity movement is rejected by nearly all Christian groups as un-Christian and heretical. It is racist, antisemitic, even neo-Nazi, and deeply hostile to the United States government. It may have provided part of the inspiration for Timothy McVeigh to bomb the Murrah Federal Building in Oklahoma City. Interestingly, Rudolph's focus on antiabortion and antigay issues is a bit idiosyncratic for Christian Identity followers. These themes usually constitute part of the movement but are almost never the central preoccupation.[21] Rudolph's decision to target the 1996 Atlanta Olympics also would not have been easily predictable from Christian Identity theology.[22] Militants inspired by this outlook have perpetrated numerous acts of terrorism, but—Rudolph notwithstanding—they do not appear to be a driving force behind antiabortion violence.

Paul Hill is the only man ever executed for crimes against abortion providers and, among the extremists, he is an unrivalled candidate for canonization. The day before receiving his lethal injection, Hill told reporters, "I expect a great reward in heaven."[23] He rejected and disavowed threats made against Florida's governor and the state attorney general, Charlie Crist, saying: "I think those bullets should be pointed in the direction of abortion providers."[24] His final words were in stark contrast with God's will, at least as it was later interpreted by Waagner. Hill said: "If you believe abortion is a lethal force, you should oppose the force and do what you have to to stop it. May God help you to protect the unborn as you would want [them?] to be protected."[25]

Hill explains how he came to kill Dr. Britton in several articles and his book *Mix My Blood with the Blood of the Unborn*.[26] The Army of God makes these materials readily available, always picturing Hill with a warm, avuncular grin. Once a Presbyterian minister, religion means everything to Hill. He claims to have turned from his ministry because of a doctrinal difference regarding infant communion, though he claims the decision was easy to make because his preaching career was unsuccessful. He then joined a Reformed Presbyterian church that agreed with him on the doctrinal issue and became very involved in pro-life activism. When another activist shot Dr. David Gunn, Hill called the *Phil Donahue Show* and compared the act to killing a doctor in a Nazi death camp. Soon after, he appeared on ABC's *Nightline* to justify yet another violent attack on an abortion provider.

Hill cites scripture frequently but not compulsively. None of his scriptural references or detailed arguments deal directly with the morality of abortion or its legalization. He rather assumes that readers will share his views on this core issue. Instead, he marshals his efforts and whatever text he can find to support the idea that when the government requires sin, people must disobey and follow the will of God. Hill also compares his murderous tasks to those performed by several biblical role models. The book of Esther teaches him that very violent defensive force can prevent "a calamity of immense proportions."[27] The Jews in this book carry out a preemptive attack on their enemies and, in the end, all is well. When Hill played with his children prior to embarking on his mission of murder, he reflected on how deeply they would suffer in the aftermath of his deed. Then he thought of Abraham offering his son to God. In the story, God prevented Abraham from going through with the sacrifice, but Hill gives no indication that he expected this to happen; nonetheless, the comparison works for him. Also, Hill speaks of Christians overturning "the tables in abortion clinics, and . . . [chasing] everyone from the premises—much as Christ cleansed the temple."[28]

But his ultimate argument is similar to that of nearly all anti-abortion militants. As he puts it, "If mass rape or enslavement should be resisted with the immediate means necessary, should not mass murder be resisted with similar means?"[29] The hardest part of the decision did not concern the moral correctness of murdering Dr. Britton. Instead, the question was whether this imperative outweighed his responsibility to his family. Here, he concluded: "I would be leaving my home, children, and wife but I felt that God had given me all I had so I could return it to him. . . . I was also assured, from God's word, that he would be a Father to my children and sustain my wife. . . . I was not standing for my own ideas, but God's truths—the same truths that have stopped blood baths and similar atrocities throughout history. Who was I to stand in God's way."[30]

Comments such as these suggest that religious thoughts, feelings, and experiences propel most violent antiabortion activists, and sometimes provide their central inspiration. Far from being impulsive or insane, these extremists contemplate and calculate their terror as a means of achieving what they consider to be a religiously certified objective. Several violent activists equate abortion with murder because they learned precisely this as young Catholics and Protestants. Christian clerics, of course, figure prominently in the Right to Life movement, and some priests and ministers from mainstream denominations still in good standing (e.g., Father Weslin) have spearheaded antiabortion protest movements that employ questionable tactics. One even finds some fringe Christian clergy associated with the Army of God. The Web sites and writings of the antiabortion extremists overflow with biblical quotations and allusions. And at least a few activists believe they have been directly commanded by God to carry out their attacks. Thus, we might use the term "Christian terrorist" to describe Paul Hill, Clayton Waagner, James Kopp, and others who committed violent acts against abortion providers and their staffs, even though these criminals generally inhabit a religious domain quite far from the mainstream.

To portray the antiabortion killers as "unhinged zealots," "domestic crackpots," or "a homicidal collection of loose screws" misses an important aspect of their motivation.[31] These people are extremists, not lunatics. They do not comprise a tight organization, but this is because—for tactical reasons—they favor a leaderless, loose structure. They thereby avoid doctrinal disputes and, more importantly, cannot reveal plans they don't know. And they can't be readily prosecuted for conspiracy. Still, it makes little sense to treat Christianity as an unindicted coconspirator in the crimes of Army of God extremists.

For a variety of reasons, many from across the political spectrum have drawn comparisons with Islamic extremism. After describing Eric Robert Rudolph as "Osama Bin Rudolph," Arsalan Tariq Iftikhar, a spokesperson for the Council on American-Islamic Relations, writes: "In essence, Rudolph's actions were just as 'Christian' as Osama bin Laden's actions were 'Muslim.' Furthermore, just as there are those in the world who may support bin Laden's actions against America, so too are there those within our own borders who encourage Christian militants like Rudolph."[32]

Others have offered different sorts of comparisons. An editorial in the *Toronto Sun* suggests that "[w]e do not [i.e., should not] blame Christianity when lunatics proclaiming themselves as Christians shoot abortion doctors and bomb abortion clinics. And we do not blame Islam for terrorism."[33] Janan Najeeb, director of the Muslim Women's Coalition of Milwaukee, argues that "you can't say the people who bomb abortion clinics represent the Christian faith. Every single faith is going to have extremist elements. No one faith has a monopoly on that."[34] Professor Jamal Badawi of St. Mary's University says: "Christians do not associate the actions of abortion clinic bombers with their faith. Likewise, Jews do not associate the militancy of the [West Bank] settlers with Judaism. Outsiders, due to either lack of knowledge or inherent bias, are not always as enlightened. To some, terrorism committed by Muslims seems part of their faith. However, closer scrutiny reveals that such heinous actions are often misrepresentations of core teachings."[35] And columnist Anna Quindlen claims, "There's no real ideological difference between these people [i.e., violent antiabortion extremists] and the people who flew planes into the World Trade Center."[36] Since September 11, discussions of antiabortion terrorists have frequently referred to Muslim terrorists, and vice versa. The two forms of evil share common features, but there are also very important differences.

In each instance, individuals become convinced that the cause matters more than their families and their own personal contentment. Though they typically arrive at their calling gradually, they all come to a point when they feel compelled to act. Muslim terrorists and antiabortion terrorists alike believe that their own reading of religious law trumps any secular law. Most rest their case on some strain of a "justifiable homicide" argument, suggesting that not killing is an even greater evil than killing. And sacred books are often quoted in support of that reading. In most instances, an extremist spiritual leader is found who condones their intended act, and a larger religious subgroup supports their ends while rejecting their means. Both types of terrorists express hostility toward modern liberal society. Though some may feel guilt over past misbehaviors or perceived misbehaviors, they all believe they have found a stairway to spiritual purity and heavenly reward. Few appear to regret their deeds after the fact. The psychological experiences of both sorts of militant are, indeed, similar, though it is—I think—going too far to say that the killers are birds of a feather.

The two evils take place in very different worlds, and this leads to differences that overwhelm the similarities. First of all, the antiabortion activists focus mainly on one issue. A few have become involved in antigay activities, and several have comprehensive worldviews with other elements of extremism. But most care overwhelmingly about the abortion issue. That is the locus of their mission. Had there never been a 1973 *Roe v. Wade* decision, it is conceivable that some would have found other issues. But little evidence directly supports this position. The antiabortion terrorists have not used suicide bombings and only a handful have put themselves in situations where capture and imprisonment seemed a certainty. In addition, as terrorists go, they have to date been concerned with using the minimum force they deem sufficient to achieve their ends and have avoided actions that might have resulted in casualties of those they deem innocent.

The abortion issue by its very nature can logically lead to extremism without much guidance from theology beyond the basic equation of abortion with murder. I should probably make clear my own position here; I'm strongly pro-choice. Yet if one truly believes that embryos and fetuses are fully human beings then it becomes understandable how some might argue that they are entitled to the same rights as, say, three-year-old children. And if one believes that a person or institution is responsible for the murder of, say, ten children per day, then the morality of stopping them is at least arguable. The strongest objection becomes the injustice of a group of citizens taking the law into their own hands. Yet with so many innocent lives at stake, one can certainly hear extremists appealing that "desperate times require desperate measures."

The critical step, therefore, is the first one, and thereafter a certain logic propels the activist without much need of assistance from theology. Operation Rescue's national director, the Reverend Flip Benham, says that Dr. Slepian murdered "countless thousands of innocent children," but that his group still does not condone the murder.[37] Many of his followers probably perceive, I think correctly, that he is being disingenuous for legal and political purposes. But if he were not, I think many might ask how one can fail to support an act that prevents the murder of countless thousands more innocent children. Once one accepts the premises of the antiabortion argument, the physician can very easily be portrayed as a mass murderer of children. And once this idea takes hold in the mind of a man inclined toward violent acts, murder of the provider may come to seem morally defensible and even necessary.

Sociologist Mark Juergensmeyer has probed more deeply into the theology that sustains the antiabortion extremists.[38] In his view, and in that of many other experts, the Reverend Michael Bray wrote the definitive Christian text supporting violent activism.[39] The core conclusion of Bray's work is that Christianity gives believers the right to defend innocent, unborn children with violence, if necessary. He draws a sharp distinction between punishing an abortion provider and stopping one from continuing to perform the procedures. He would not judge the assassination of a retired abortion provider appropriate, because this deed would not prevent any future deaths of the unborn. At least in his published work, Bray also hedges in his support for preventive murders. He says he does not actually advocate such killings, but rather considers them just under some circumstances. He says he is "pro-choice" regarding the killing of abortion providers.

Bray places himself and those who murder abortion doctors in good company. He admires Dietrich Bonhoeffer, the German Lutheran theologian who left his safe academic position in New York to join a secret plot against Hitler and was then executed for his efforts. But Bray's theology and politics differ greatly from Bonhoeffer's. Bray sees America as similar to Nazi Germany and wants to implement a political system based on the Bible. He derives such views from the broader right-wing Protestant movement in the United States to reestablish God's dominion over secular society and politics. We have seen many manifestations of this outlook over the past quarter century, for example, in the Moral Majority and the followers of Pat Robertson.

But Bray and other theorists of militant antiabortion violence draw their views from the most ring-wing regions of this dominion movement, specifically from an approach called Reconstruction Theology. Their theology is complex, but, roughly, the idea is that to bring Christ back to earth, Christians must recapture the nation and, ultimately, the world from a ruinous, satanic secularism. They must bring about the rule of ultra-right-wing Christians like themselves. Bray thinks the path to this new world might be through experiments in the implementation of biblical law on a state-by-state basis. Here, his thinking does indeed parallel that of those who hope, using violence if necessary, to establish the Muslim sharia one country at a time.

Bray has visions that go well beyond the abortion issue. However, he sees abortion as the most pressing issue at present, the one in which Satan most clearly reveals his presence. In his justification of homicide to stop pregnancy terminations, he establishes himself on the extreme end of Reconstruction Theology.[40]

Although Bray's book is the most influential defense of antiabortion violence, it is by no means clear that most perpetrators of such violence found their calling by reading his or any other theological work. Their occasional invocation of Bray may be more in the style of a lawyer who already knows his position and then adduces whatever support he can to buttress his position. Few, I suspect, are converted by reading the work. Moreover, some killers—notably Rudolph—arrived at their militancy down altogether different roads. To the extent that Rudolph had an ideological bent, it came from the Christian Identity movement, more a variant of neo-Nazism than a branch of Christianity. Most antiabortion perpetrators share mainly their militant hostility toward abortion and cannot be described as brothers in agreement on an entire platform of Christian belief.

Though I am hardly an expert in Christian biblical interpretation, the use of biblical references to support antiabortion militancy seems to me somewhat strained. Professor Charles Kimball, a Baptist minister, notes that members of the Army of God derive unambiguous claims to knowledge of absolute truth from biblical passages that "have nothing to do with abortion."[41] Thus, they express certainty that abortion is legalized murder and an abomination to God. They further insist that true Christians must use whatever means necessary to stop the slaughter. But they cite verses like one from the book of Psalms that says: "They sacrificed their sons and daughters to the demons" and one from Galatians that asks: "Am I now seeking human approval, or God's approval? Or am I trying to please people? If I were still pleasing people, I would not be a servant of Christ."[42] In part, they seize on such passages because, as Kimball notes, the Bible does not speak specifically about abortion. One might oppose the practice on the basis of general principles extracted from the text, but this would require a fair amount of interpretation. In contrast, the texts cited by Muslim extremists can very plausibly be read to support the approach they advocate. Considerable humanistic interpretation is required to make such verses compatible with liberal or moderate viewpoints. Christian and Jewish texts dealing with other matters do, as we shall see, create similar problems for modern-minded liberals from these traditions. Yet regarding the source of antiabortion violence, it's hard to put much blame on Christian texts.

The two most telling differences between violent Islam and antiabortion terrorism concern (1) the number of perpetrators and (2) the degree of support from the mainstream. Although lesser forms of antiabortion criminality often have serious consequences and should not be minimized, the total death toll from Christian antiabortion terrorists can be counted on one's fingers. The number of perpetrators of violent acts, even relatively minor ones, is low. I judge protests at the entrance of abortion clinics to be unacceptable, and in some instances, such protests are now illegal. Thousands of people can be summoned to such events. However, such behaviors should be distinguished from violent antiabortion crimes. Nearly all writers on antiabortion violence have profiled the same very small group of people, largely because there aren't many others from which to choose. This situation could change for the worse, but this does not seem to be happening at present.

By far the biggest difference between Muslim extremist terrorism and antiabortion terrorism lies in the degree and nature of support that the extremists receive. Antiabortion terrorists get virtually no support from Christian or other religious organizations in the United States. Most Christian groups are vocal in their denunciations and leave little room for ambiguity on the matter. Even those groups that seek to end legalized abortion in the United States have condemned the terrorists with straightforward language. The Southern Baptists, for example, are one of the most conservative large religious groups in the United States. They strongly oppose legalized abortion and believe unborn life is fully human and deserving of complete protection. However, even they are crystal clear in their opposition to violence against abortion providers. In a 1994 document, they state: "Representatives of a wide range of 'pro-choice,' 'pro-abortion,' and 'pro-life' positions have offered public statements condemning the use of deadly force and the moral justification of such acts. It has been a rare instance of agreement. We join in condemning these killings."[43]

Along similar lines, former attorney general John Ashcroft, probably the most pro-life and religiously conservative attorney general in recent times, made his condemnation of antiabortion terrorism crystal clear. Many analysts credit Ashcroft with improving the law enforcement response to antiabortion violence and—as I write—the violence has lessened. Since the execution of Hill and the capture of Waagner and Kopp, no murderous violence against abortion providers has occurred.[44]

The American public squarely denounces antiabortion violence. There is no undercurrent of public sympathy as there is for Islamic terrorists in some Muslim countries. In 1989, prior to the shootings of antiabortion doctors, pollsters asked a sample of American adults—including those who were pro-life—whether "destroying abortion clinics by arson or bombing" was "an appropriate step for those trying to stop abortions." These bombings were mainly attacks against the physical facilities of the clinics and not directly against people. Ninety-eight percent said no. Only 1 percent said yes.[45] Another poll, back in 1985, found that only one person in twenty would agree regarding the bombings that "[i]f no one is killed or injured, they should be treated as a forceful kind of political protest." Overwhelmingly, Americans said, "There's absolutely no excuse for these bombings, they're the same thing as terrorism."[46]

Such strong opposition to antiabortion violence occurs even though 41 percent of Americans describe themselves as pro-life[47] and only 29 percent believe abortion should be permitted in all cases.[48]

Indeed, only 5 percent of people even support the right of antiabortion protesters to take photographs of people going into abortion clinics and post them on the Internet.[49] Americans are apparently split on many aspects of the abortion issue, but nearly all want the controversies resolved within traditional American rules of political discourse. As one editorialist suggests: "[W]hen some nut does bomb an abortion clinic or shoot someone he finds politically disagreeable, almost all of us recognize right away that he's the one with the problem."[50]

Still, one might fault the Southern Baptists and other strong opponents of abortion for failing to recognize the incendiary impact of their extreme rhetoric on baby killing and the like. Paul Hill has pointed out, not unreasonably, that given the pro-life premises so strongly expressed by the Southern Baptists in their document on the matter, the logic behind their rejection of violence is not entirely convincing.[51] Their rejection of violence may be sincere, but they seem to miss a very likely consequence of their fiery words, one that very much haunted Dr. Slepian himself.

In an eerie letter to the editor of the *Buffalo News* written four years before his death, he warned:

> The members of the local non-violent pro-life community may continue to picket my home wearing large "Slepian Kills Children" buttons. . . . They may also display the six-foot banner with the same quotation at the entrance to my neighborhood. . . . They may continue to scream that I am a murderer and a killer when I enter clinics at which they "peacefully" exercise their First Amendment Right of freedom of speech. . . . But please don't feign surprise, dismay and certainly not innocence when a more volatile and less restrained member of the group decides to react to their inflammatory rhetoric by shooting an abortion provider. They all share the blame.[52]

In my view, to break this link between words and deeds, those in the responsible pro-life movement must evolve a theologically acceptable means for expressing their objection to abortion without asserting that the magnitude of the evil is at the level of killing babies.

A SERMON IGNORED

Disciples rarely realize with precision the plans and purposes of their founder. Thus, Karl Marx might be surprised and dismayed by much of what was carried out in his name. Muhammad, too, would likely object that Muslim clerics have missed key aspects of his message. And were Thomas Jefferson, James Madison, Alexander Hamilton, and other founding fathers to return, they, too, might protest that American leaders often have invoked their names inappropriately. Yet in each of these instances, the founder's beliefs and sentiments appear recognizable as the sources of the resulting movements. No such connection can be readily detected between the teachings of Jesus and the course of Christian history, at least over many centuries.

Perhaps this is not too surprising, because little convincing evidence suggests that Jesus of Nazareth ever intended to found a new faith, much less one following precepts laid down by Paul and centering on the Resurrection. Arguably, one could predict better the course of subsequent Christian history by ignoring Jesus altogether, paying a little attention to Paul, and focusing mainly on the centuries immediately following Christianity's transformation into the state religion of Rome. The requirements of a state religion in late antiquity conflicted so greatly with the teachings of Jesus that these teachings were largely set aside and superseded by a markedly different system of values.

Still, the message set forth by Jesus himself may be where the problem starts. What Jesus actually said, we will, of course, never know, because nothing was recorded in writing until decades after his death and then only by those with strong vested interests. However, Jesus as he appears in the New Testament is the one who matters. And this Jesus offers us a straightforward, crystalline enumeration of his principles in the Sermon on the Mount, as recounted by Matthew. According to Jesus, one should follow his outlined precepts because doing so will lead invariably to heavenly reward and the avoidance of punishment in the world to come. The sermon calls for believers to travel well beyond the dictates of Jewish law at the time; it requires kindly, nonviolent, loving interactions with enemies as well as friends.

In the Sermon on the Mount, Jesus says:

- "Blessed are the merciful, for they will be shown mercy."
- "Blessed are the peacemakers, for they will be called children of God."
- "I say to you, whoever is angry with his brother will be liable to judgment, and whoever says to his brother, 'Raqa [imbecile],' will be answerable to the Sanhedrin, and whoever says, 'You fool,' will be liable to fiery Gehenna."
- "I say to you, offer no resistance to one who is evil. When someone strikes you on your right cheek, turn the other one to him as well."
- "Give to the one who asks of you, and do not turn your back on one who wants to borrow."
- "I say to you, love your enemies, and pray for those who persecute you."[53]

How, one wonders, could a faith built around such core teachings be associated with so much suffering, so many persecutions, doctrinal struggles, and holy wars?

Perhaps by setting the bar too high, Jesus in the Sermon on the Mount established standards that were bound to be ignored. If moral principles exceed human capabilities by too great a margin, they may quickly be deemed irrelevant to day-to-day living. For example, when the sermon claims that "everyone who looks at a woman with lust has already committed adultery," it may in fact weaken the injunction against actual adultery. If one is already a sinner, why, one might plausibly ask, should one stop at mere lusting in the heart? And if anger alone condemns a man, clearly the average fellow has little chance of leading a good life. Giving up altogether on the quest then becomes a reasonable choice. When one is struck in the face and told to turn the other cheek, that person—unless a saint—quickly develops the sense that the scriptural morality is not meant to be taken seriously as a guide for the management of earthly conflict. The net consequences may be, unfortunately, to increase feelings of guilt and to decrease belief in the usefulness of moral precepts.

In any event, while people claiming to act in the name of Jesus and Christianity have been responsible for a substantial amount of good in the world, it is undeniable that they have also perpetrated some of the cruelest deeds in human history. Not all—or even most—evil acts perpetrated by Christians throughout two millennia can be reasonably described as religiously motivated or Christian, much less as instances of religious extremism. Many people who do dastardly deeds of one sort or another may be Christians in name alone, only pretending or perhaps not even pretending to be believers. And even when a sincere, self-defined member of the flock acts badly, say, murdering, raping, or stealing, his or her motivation need not come in any sense from the faith. Here, Christianity could at most be blamed for failing to instill a sufficiently powerful and controlling set of injunctions against misbehavior. And this charge itself would only be sustainable if moral violations by believers were very frequent, as no form of moral indoctrination has ever been flawless. But many, many times in Christian history, believers have felt compelled to commit terrible atrocities precisely because of their faith. Their prime motivating passions have been religious.

Most often, such evil has been associated with a desire to punish or eliminate some form of religious belief or practice that is deemed unacceptable, ungodly, or heretical by Christian authorities, or—much less frequently—by lay Christians acting on their own. The famous antireligious philosopher Bertrand Russell attributes Christian religious intolerance to the monotheism of "the Jews, and more especially the prophets . . . [who] invented emphasis upon personal righteousness and the idea that it is wicked to tolerate any religion except one."[54] Whatever the source of the notion, the English Catholic historian Paul Johnson somewhat similarly places the origins of Christian religious wars in "the assumption that only a unitary society was tolerable, and that those who did not conform to the prevailing norms, and who could not be forced or terrified into doing so, should be treated as second class citizens, expelled or killed."[55] The impulse to root out—often by whatever means necessary—those who believe differently has been an especially prominent, even obsessive, feature of much of Christian history. Inhuman methods have been used in many different eras by many different regimes against pagans, Jews, Muslims, and, no less enthusiastically, other Christians. Indeed, Christians for hundreds of years were willing to put other Christians to death or through merciless tortures over matters that seem incomprehensibly trivial to nonbelievers.

Historians have documented all of this very carefully. But, for our purposes, it is worth taking a closer look at how sincere Christian religious piety readily nourished some of humanity's cruelest deeds. To see Christianity at its true low point, one must go back several hundred years.

Starting in the twelfth century, the Catholic Church launched several Inquisitions in different locales and different eras. All of these Inquisitions were aimed at the conversion, persecution, and/or execution of people alleged to be heretics. Each time, religious motives, to be sure, were accompanied by secular ones, such as a pope's or a king's desire to consolidate power or someone's drive to get his hands on someone else's wealth. But the religious enthusiasm of popes, clerics, and their followers cannot be dismissed because of these other contributing factors.

Of all the Inquisitions, the most infamous started in Spain in 1478, with enthusiastic support from King Ferdinand, Queen Isabella, and many popes. While matters of state may have loomed largest in Ferdinand's thinking—he thought the Inquisition would increase his power and wealth—Isabella's fits the model of a religious extremist. Historian Will Durant describes her faith: "She chose the sternest moralists for her confessors and guides. Wedded to an unfaithful husband, she seems to have sustained full marital fidelity to the end; living in an age as morally fluid as our own, she was a model of sexual modesty. Amid corrupt officials and devious diplomats, she herself remained frank, direct, and incorruptible. Her mother had reared her in strict orthodoxy and piety; Isabella developed this to the edge of asceticism, and was as harsh and cruel in suppressing heresy as she was kind and gracious in everything else."[56] (Incidentally, a strong campaign is currently under way for the canonization of "the Catholic queen," some advocates not knowing, some not caring about her role in the Inquisition and associated events. More than one hundred thousand letters to the Vatican since the mid-1990s have supported her cause.)[57]

This Inquisition was hardly a flash in the pan. It lasted until 1834 and extended to many parts of the New World through Spanish conquests. The final victim was a Spanish schoolmaster, hanged in 1826 for making a slight change in school prayers. He used the phrase "Praise be to God" instead of "Ave Maria."[58]

Although the Spanish Inquisition ultimately targeted Muslim converts (Moriscos), Protestants, and others, the main targets at the start were Jews who had converted to Christianity (Conversos) but who were suspected of maintaining some loyalty to their abandoned religion. The Inquisitors—along with most Christians for hundreds of years—firmly and sincerely believed that God wanted everyone to be Christian. The most enthusiastic believers, including Isabella, perceived other faiths to be "a crass insult to the Deity."[59] The logic of the Inquisitors went a step further and, in a way, made sense once you accepted the premises. Durant explains: "[S]ince any substantial heresy must merit eternal punishment, . . . [the Inquisition's] prosecutors could believe (and many seem to have sincerely believed) that in snuffing out a heretic they were saving his potential converts, and perhaps himself, from everlasting hell."[60]

Jews had been living in Spain for about a thousand years at the time of the Inquisition. They had done relatively well under Muslim rule and, under the Christians, retained much of their economic, social, and political influence. However, as Catholic power gradually extended over much of Spain, massacres, persecution, and barriers to career advancement created significant problems for the Jews. Wishing greater acceptance, or sometimes just to survive frequent pogroms, many Jews converted. Some of these converts were sincere, but many had little love for their new faith. Some continued to practice elements of their abandoned faith in secret. Locating and punishing these Jews became an obsession of the Inquisitors. Jews who remained Jews escaped the Inquisition but—in an early instance of ethnic cleansing—were expelled from Spain in 1492. Any Jew who did not leave was executed with the approval of Ferdinand, Isabella, and the pope.

The tale of the Inquisition is not primarily a tale of numbers. Though the body count was appalling, it was not unprecedented by the standards of that day or our own. What commands our attention is the ease with which religious thinking became a justification for torture and pathological cruelty, and how Inquisitors never paused for a moment to consider the teachings of Jesus or to engage in any genuine ethical reflection.

The crime of the Conversos (also dubbed Maranos, or pigs, by their detractors) was to persist in some trace of Jewish ritual or some shred of Jewish belief after having received baptism. This might mean that they kept a few dietary laws, hoped for the coming of the Messiah, observed the Sabbath, circumcised their children, gave them Hebrew names, or blessed them without making the sign of the cross. "Judaizing," as they called it, might also show up in dozens of other ways, say, changing linens for the Sabbath.

When the Inquisition came to town, authorities issued an edict requiring anyone who knew of such heresy to come forward. Compliance brought secrecy and protection; noncompliance could end in a religious curse and excommunication. If a heretic confessed from the outset, he or she might get off easily, perhaps with a fine and forgiveness. But a full confession required one to name names. Not doing so, or relapsing into Judaizing after forgiveness had been granted, could lead to torture and an "act of faith," or auto-da-fé. This meant, first, a solemn Christian ceremony and then being burned alive at the stake. The burning itself was meant to put the fear of God in potential heretics, but it also had the goal of giving all Christians a foretaste of hellfire.

Once arrested, the presumption was guilt. A person would generally be kept in solitary confinement, chained, and incommunicado. There was no right to confront one's accusers. The person on trial would have to pay for the secret proceedings and swear not to reveal anything about the trial if he or she were acquitted. But getting off was not very likely. As one friar said of an earlier church Inquisition, "[I]f St. Peter and St. Paul were accused of 'adoring' heretics and were prosecuted after the fashion of the Inquisition, there would be no defense open for them."[61] And, of course, even the guilty were never really guilty of much of anything.

Although under such circumstances most people sensed a stacked deck and confessed without torture, a few hearty souls required further encouragement. The Vatican had long since sanctioned torture as acceptable, and the Inquisitors were not shy about using some fairly gruesome methods.[62] With a representative of the local bishop in attendance, they might, for example, tie cords around a person's arms and legs, tightening them until they cut to the bone. Some have pointed out that early Inquisitions were worse, and even this one merely used methods being used by nonreligious authorities. But again, it is the coexistence of such methods with deep religious feeling that requires attention.

When people did not confess, it was often because doing so would require them to implicate their family members, friends, and cobelievers. Sometimes, the Inquisitors would brutalize contradictory witnesses to get at the truth, or they might torture a completely innocent slave just to get the goods on the master.

The mercy of which Jesus spoke in his sermon did occasionally make a cameo appearance. For example, although women, children, and the elderly did not escape torture or burning at the stake, the Inquisitors did prohibit torture of nursing women and those with weak hearts. A majority panel of a tribunal had to vote for the torture, and a physician put a stop to matters if he feared permanent maiming of the victim. Sometimes the Inquisitors showed leniency, letting a person off with a reprimand, a hefty fine, public humiliation, and/or a hundred lashes. The religious authorities did not seem eager to burn someone alive, reserving this penalty mainly for those who reneged on a promise to abandon their Judaizing heresy or those who never confessed and named names. But even at the very end, there might be Christian mercy if a person confessed. They might be granted strangulation prior to burning or even given the last sacraments. Finally, the church never actually killed the heretics; instead, such people were handed over to secular authorities for punishment. But during this dark period in the history of Catholicism, very few churchmen worried much about casting the first stone. And it must be emphasized that the various Inquisitions were not barbaric frenzies but rather deeply religious undertakings in the name of Christ and the holy church.

No one should come away from a recounting of the Inquisitions with the impression that Roman Catholic history was evil, while Protestantism and other forms of Christianity adhered more closely to a reasonable code of ethics based on the teachings of Jesus. The history of Christianity shows that intolerance in the premodern era was well distributed among all the theological approaches. Some sects may have been worse than others in one era or another, but none can point to their history with justified pride.

Thus, millions—perhaps hundreds of millions—of Protestants see in Martin Luther a figure of some moral distinction. Yet Luther wrote that "the pope, his cardinals, and all the rabble of his idolatry and papal holiness . . . [ought] to be taken, and, as blasphemers, have their tongues torn out by the backs of their necks, and nailed in rows on the gallows."[63] He thought that "[e]ven unbelievers should be forced to obey the Ten Commandments, attend church, and outwardly conform."[64] He had no problem endorsing the death penalty for heretics such as "those who teach against a manifest article of the faith . . . for example, if anyone should teach that Christ was not God but a mere man."[65] And although he first reached out to the Jews, when he realized that they were not going to sign on to the Protestant program, he urged: "[L]et whosoever can, throw brimstone and pitch upon them; if one could hurl hellfire at them, so much the better. . . . And this must be done for the honor of our Lord and Christianity, so that God may see that we are indeed Christians. Let their houses also be shattered and destroyed."[66]

John Calvin, the source of inspiration for millions more, set up an unprecedented totalitarian system in Geneva. Elders would visit each house to question occupants on all details of their lives. Card playing, dancing, irreligious songs, extravagant living, immodest dress, theatrical performances, and many other things were strictly prohibited. Blasphemy and adultery could be punished by death. Fornicators would be exiled or drowned. And, as in the Inquisition, torture was used to get confessions.[67]

In the sixteenth and seventeenth centuries, intolerant Catholics and Protestants met each other head-on. The result was one of history's bloodiest eras, where religion was not the only motivation but surely a powerful one.

A PROBLEM MASTERED

Viewed in the light of religious history, the truly amazing thing, then, is not that Christianity once was the source, or accomplice, of so much evil but rather that nowadays things are so much better. This does not mean that Christians have finally implemented the message of Jesus, or even that this entire message merits implementing. But the will and capacity of Christian faith to inspire murder, torture, and intolerance has diminished tremendously. We still see places like Bosnia in the 1990s, where Christian leaders sometimes look the other way in the face of horrible atrocities. But even there, Christian religious belief does not appear to have fueled much hostility. Instead, Christian affiliations have become a marker of ethnicity.[68]

In my view, there is certainly room for greater tolerance in some Christian denominations. But one cannot overlook how mainstream Christian groups have changed dramatically over the past few hundred years. Once, more than a thousand years after the arrival of Christ on earth, his most fervent supporters could—without a touch of moral self-examination—describe a brutal massacre of Muslims and Jews with relish. Consider the words of a chronicler of a Crusader victory: "Wonderful things were to be seen. Numbers of the Saracens were beheaded. . . . Others were shot with arrows, or forced to jump from the towers; others were tortured for several days, then burned with flames. In the streets were seen piles of heads, and hands and feet. . . . It was a just and marvelous judgment of God, that this place [Jerusalem] should be filled with the blood of unbelievers."[69] This Christianity bears no resemblance to most of what passes under that same name today.

The evil that once occurred in the name of Jesus makes our own era with the murderous works of Paul Hill, James Kopp, Eric Robert Rudolph, and the like seem far less threatening than those of past. Even the most outrageous rantings of fundamentalist Christian clergymen somehow seem more temperate when viewed against the backdrop of the churches of old. And, in any case, their power is severely constrained.

But the credit for this improvement does not go entirely, or even mostly, to the Christian religion. Bertrand Russell once suggested that "[i]t is true that the modern Christian is less robust [in persecuting those with different beliefs], but that is not thanks to Christianity; it is thanks to the generations of freethinkers, who, from the Renaissance to the present day, have made Christians ashamed of many of their traditional beliefs. It is amusing to hear the modern Christian telling you how mild and rationalistic Christianity really is and ignoring the fact that all its mildness and rationalism is due to the teaching of men who in their own day were persecuted by all orthodox Christians."[70] Russell's judgment is a bit harsh. The constructive shame of which he speaks is facilitated largely by the core Christian message in sources like the Sermon on the Mount. Even during the worst excesses of the church, that positive message was passed along with the rest. Moreover, many of the reformers whom Russell describes as "freethinkers" would not have considered themselves freethinkers. But Russell does correctly note that the reform of Christianity was not, in essence, an internal development where Christians decided to invoke true Christian precepts. Instead, it came largely in response to external ideas and events.

Harvard professor James Q. Wilson notes that the West has mastered the very difficult task of reconciling religion and freedom. The reason this task is so difficult, he explains, is because people who genuinely believe their own moral rules are superior, God-given, and enforced by fear of eternal punishment will want their country to observe and impose their religious system. "To do otherwise," he writes, "would be to repudiate deeply held convictions, offend a divine being, and corrupt society."[71] Western civilization had to get past this problem in order to establish a society based on religious toleration, freedom of conscience, and—subsequently—the competition of ideas in a realm dominated by reason, science, and open debate.

The history here is well known.[72] Following Luther, new Protestant movements arose, and soon many competing faiths existed in Christian Europe. One attempt to end the period of religious wars rested on the Peace of Augsburg and the principle of *cuius regio, eius religio* (the people follow the religion of their ruler). But this didn't work very well, and murderous religious conflict soon resumed. The Thirty Years' War brought a new level of complexity and bloodshed to struggles of faith. Finally, however, an exhausted Europe began to see the light. At the Peace of Westphalia—which concluded the major religious wars—and in the century that followed, people and their laws gradually began to realize the value of religious toleration. The change did not come all at once, but there was some preliminary recognition of "the essential futility of putting the beliefs of the mind to the judgment of the sword."[73] The 1689 Toleration Act in England applied only to dissident Protestants, and even they could not hold government office. Over time, however, other groups were included—first informally, then formally—and then rights were expanded. The process was also gradual in America, where the Bill of Rights represented a great advance, though not one that immediately conferred complete freedom of conscience and toleration. France and the rest of Europe sooner or later followed paths that increased the rights of religious minorities. The end result of all of this was to permit a wide range of religious beliefs and practices while, importantly, defanging the faith of the majority.

Religious figures could argue against Darwin but they couldn't burn him. The various churches might detest and denounce the likes of Marx, Russell, and Freud, but regardless of religious sentiment, each was free to develop his intellectual program. Thus, in a sense, Christianity did lose some of its freedom in the bargain. Neither the Catholics nor the various Protestant groups could implement their religious visions entirely as they might have wished. What happened, then, by majority agreement and after many struggles, was that the Christian religion and all others in the West became subject to a higher authority. They might continue to believe what they wanted, but they had to act in accordance with constitutional principles. Over time, majorities in every faith in Europe and the Americas came to believe in that reasonable and productive arrangement. Along with John Locke, James Madison, and other advocates of freedom of conscience, a brutal history had taught them that there was no better alternative. As one scholar commented, toleration was "the last policy that remained when it had proved impossible to go on fighting any longer."[74]

It is difficult to overestimate the importance of this development. Bernard Lewis, the renowned historian of the Middle East, makes the point well by drawing a contrast with the prevailing situation in most countries with Muslim majorities. He explains that

> most Muslim countries are still profoundly Muslim, in a way and in a sense that most Christian countries are no longer Christian. Admittedly, in many of these countries, Christian beliefs and the clergy who uphold them are still a powerful force, and although their role is not what it was in past centuries, it is by no means insignificant. But in no Christian country at the present time can religious leaders count on the degree of belief and participation that remains normal in the Muslim lands. In few, if any, Christian countries do Christian sanctities enjoy the immunity from critical comment or discussion

> that is accepted as normal even in ostensibly secular and democratic Muslim countries.[75]

He further argues that, with very few exceptions, "the Christian clergy do not exercise or even claim the kind of public authority that is still normal and accepted in most Muslim countries."[76] What remains unknown, however, is whether these clergy might have a change of heart, were circumstances to change and were they to perceive an opening for increasing clerical power. Thus, while many fundamentalist Christian clerics affirm their commitment to constitutional democracy, it remains an open question how deep this commitment runs.

A VOLCANO WAITING TO ERUPT[77]

On August 4, 2005, Eden Natan Zada—a nineteen-year-old Jewish Israeli—turned his army-issued M-16 rifle on the passengers and driver of a bus he was riding through the Arab-Israeli town of Shfaram. Zada's attack killed four Arab Israelis, two of them Muslim and two Christian; twelve others were wounded. After the shooting, an angry Arab mob killed Zada and injured five policemen who were trying to stabilize the situation.

The date of the shooting is significant. Israel had set August 15 as the deadline when the military would forcibly remove Jewish residents from the Gaza Strip. Although the announcement of the plan did not lead to reciprocal compromises from the Palestinians and did not generate much sympathy for Israel in the international community, most Israelis deemed disengagement to be the best of several bad options available to them. For a large minority of Israelis, however, the thought of Jews tearing other Jews from their homes under such circumstances was unacceptable. Some within this group carried out peaceful protests and organized acts of civil disobedience. A very small number, however, contemplated more radical and possibly violent action to prevent implementation of the government's policy. In the end, there was very little violence of any kind, but in the weeks prior to disengagement in Gaza, no one knew just what to expect.

Eden Natan Zada had deserted his army unit about a month and a half before the bus attack. He had left a note indicating that he would not be a part of an organization that expels Jews. Though Zada's name appeared on some Shin Bet security agency watch lists, the young soldier was not, in any sense, a leader of the antidisengagement movement.

The Israeli government quickly denounced Zada's attack in the strongest terms, and virtually all mainstream groups in Israel followed suit. Prime Minister Ariel Sharon called the shootings "a sinful act by a bloodthirsty terrorist." Gideon Ezra, the public security minister, similarly declared: "This was a terrorist attack in every way. It was an awful terrorist attack." American Jewish leaders issued like-minded condemnations. The Rabbinical Assembly of Conservative Judaism in Boston declared the killings "a desecration of God's Name" and prayed that "never again will a Jew so wantonly spill blood."[78] The Orthodox Union said that "[a]cts of violence in the name of Zionism and/or Judaism must be eradicated from the midst of the Jewish people."[79] Even a spokesman for Kfar Tapuah, Zada's right-wing community, declared: "We totally reject him and everything he did."[80]

No mainstream Israelis had any good words for Zada, though some—principally from among the strong opponents of disengagement—made an effort to classify his behavior as insane. Thus Bentzi Lieberman, chairman of the council that represented settlers in the West Bank and Gaza, said the shooting was the work of a madman.[81] Yet another political leader, Effi Eitam, said: "No one should dare blame the entire right for the crazy act of one crazy man."[82] Zada's parents also attributed the attack to their son's mental instability, noting that they had repeatedly warned the army that he was a danger to himself. It also became clear, later on, that his psychiatric profile probably should have kept him out of the army.[83]

In truth, however, the "lone madman" explanation doesn't suffice here or for most other recent instances of Jewish terrorism in Israel to which it has been applied. Zada's objective was mainly political. He hoped his massacre would provoke an Arab response that would derail the disengagement plan, and—perhaps—in some sense it was also an act of revenge. His plan was poorly conceived and could not work. But it makes little sense to call it insane.

About a year before the attack, Zada had left his home in the mainly secular community of Rishon Letzion to live in the West Bank settlement of Kfar Tapuah. This move accompanied a turn toward political extremism and Orthodox Jewish religiosity. At Kfar Tapuah, he associated with members of the outlawed anti-Arab Kach movement—founded by the extremist rabbi Meir Kahane, who had been assassinated some years earlier in New York by an Islamic extremist. Indeed, Yekutiel Ben-Ya'acov, leader of another extremist group in Tapuah, was one of the few to stick by Zada after the attack. Calling him very pious, soft-spoken, interested in Judaism, and a "very special soul," he said he hoped his death would not be in vain and that it would derail "this sadistic disengagement plan."[84]

During the year prior to his crime, Zada lived in a world where the disengagement plan was viewed as a treacherous act, all the more so because it was championed by a prime minister who had prevailed in an election by opposing precisely such a move. Sharon, after his election, changed and advocated disengagement as means of advancing Israel's security and international status in the absence of a viable Palestinian negotiating partner. Some Israelis rejected disengagement on secular political grounds, stating that since the land involved was Israeli territory, relocating settlers constituted a violation of their human rights. Others objected on security grounds, holding that withdrawal would bring more of Israel within the range of enemy rockets and terrorist attacks. (The rocket attacks by Hamas and Hezbollah before and during the 2006 war showed that these concerns were far from groundless.)

But a deeper, religious motive prevailed for many opponents of disengagement. It was generally believed that Israel would withdraw next from large sections of the West Bank of the Jordan River. These areas, and to a lesser extent Gaza, were viewed as part of Eretz Yisrael (the Land of Israel), which had been given by God to the Jews. According to some Orthodox Jews, no Israeli government had the right to undo an act of God, and Jews had the duty to inhabit the entire land of Israel. When God has established the borders, politicians lose much of their capacity for give-and-take.

This religious foundation for refusing to abandon any territory may seem age-old, but it is fairly new as a practical force in Jewish politics. Israel, of course, did not control the West Bank and Gaza until its victory in the 1967 Six Days' War. In 1948, nearly all Israelis would have been content to occupy peaceably the smaller land of Israel. The acquisition of additional territory in 1967 was, in effect, the accidental result of victory in a war forced upon Israel; it cannot fairly be described as an active attempt by Israel to acquire new territory.

For many Israelis, even those who were not particularly observant, the deliverance into their hands of much of the biblical land of Israel seemed miraculous. Israel's military prevailed decisively over the militaries of much larger nations. The acquisition of the Temple Mount in Jerusalem, Judaism's holiest site, was emblematic of a military result that seemed to call out for a theological interpretation. Just as many Muslims interpreted the 1967 defeat as a message from God that they had been doing something wrong, many Jews saw it as an encouraging message that God had stepped up his interventions on behalf of the Jewish people. Importantly, in conjunction with the Holocaust and the founding of the Jewish state, some messianically inclined Orthodox Jews (like some Christians) saw the victory as a sign of approaching end times.

Novelist David Margolis is one who shares some of the agenda of the Israeli Right, but he does so mainly on political and security grounds. He lives in a West Bank village and worries about some religious thinking he has observed among his neighbors, in particular "the nonsensical tootling about the coming geulah (redemption) that increasingly infects ordinary kitchen conversation on the Orthodox right, with people announcing, as if they just got it in a telegram from God, that the redemption is on its way, to be finalized through the Jewish people's control of a Greater Land of Israel conveniently emptied of Arabs, after which, give or take an apocalyptic war or two, we all live happily ever after, bossed by rabbis."[85] Margolis is especially concerned because the friends who buy into such visions are, in his view, educated, discerning, many Americans and British, people who came to Orthodox Judaism as adults. He asks: "What combination of romanticism, meanness, historical amnesia, and battle fatigue is taking hold of them now?" He further reports that in many circles on the Orthodox Right, "the word 'democracy' is uttered now with distaste."[86]

Thus, the Right in Israel, and the extremist right, draw their motivation from multiple sources—security issues, political issues, and religious issues. It is never easy to determine which is operating in a given individual at a given time. Some may turn to religion to bolster views originally developed on the basis of security concerns. Others may perceive security matters in a particular perspective because it accords with their religious views. Some may simply start with bigotry and use everything else as a cover. Some, like Rabbi Kahane, the founder of the Jewish Defense League in the United States and the Kach movement in Israel, may have commenced with legitimate anger about antisemitism, moved to anger at Arab intransigence, developed racist ideas about Christians and Arabs, and proceeded to use these ideas to justify a host of immoral behaviors. Throughout the process, Kahane and his associates may have mined the long and complex history and theology of Judaism for whatever they could find in support of positions that were social, political, and psychological in origin.

Eden Natan Zada and most other Kach followers cannot meaningfully be described as lunatics. An Israeli journalist, Teddy Preuss, made the point well in his discussion of Baruch Goldstein, an Israeli physician—also associated with the Kach movement—who murdered twenty-nine Muslim worshipers in Hebron in 1994. Preuss wrote:

> Adolf Hitler was no doubt insane. So were the Gazan who stabbed Helena Rapp to death in Bat Yam in 1992, the murderers of the Lapid family, those who butchered the children of Ma-alot and Avivim, and Ami Popper, who shot seven Palestinians to death in Rishon Lezion [*sic*] in 1990. All were as insane as Dr. Baruch Gold-

> stein, who perpetrated . . . [the] massacre at Hebron. But whatever the mutations in the souls of these individuals, they cannot be released from responsibility for the murders they committed. All were sufficiently aware of what they were doing. Their lust for blood was likely the only symptom of insanity they exhibited.[87]

He further notes that "Goldstein didn't grow up in a mental institution, but in the study hall of Rabbi Meir Kahane, who preached expulsion of the Arabs ("dogs") as an act of mercy, or something even worse, if they got what he considered to be their just desserts."[88] The Israeli government agreed and—following the Goldstein massacre—declared Kach and Kahane Chai to be illegal terror organizations. Yitzhak Rabin, the prime minister at the time, said: "We will treat the Kahanists exactly as we treat Hamas." Still, these groups and other similar ones continue to indoctrinate small numbers of supporters beneath the surface of legitimate Israeli politics.

Two weeks after Zada's attack, another Israeli—Asher Weisgan—also shot four Palestinians to death in an attempt to thwart the Gaza disengagement. Weisgan's deeper motivation remains unclear. Though he lived in a predominantly religious settlement, Weisgan himself is not believed to have been particularly observant. He did, however, appear in court wearing a skullcap, typically a symbol of religious identification. There have been a few other acts and attempted acts of terrorism against Palestinians in the decade preceding the deeds of Zada and Weisgan. But not many. One must go back to Goldstein's terrible 1994 massacre in Hebron to find another instance where there were many Palestinian deaths at the hand of a Jewish terrorist. Prior to that, in 1990, an off-duty soldier, Ami Popper, murdered seven Palestinian workers. And in the early eighties, there was an organized campaign of violence against the mayors of Arab towns in the West Bank. Extremist political and religious groups played a role in inspiring most of these acts, but there have been only a few organized plots. Most individuals made the decision to act on their own. There has been a human cost associated with these acts, and also a political one: they undermine the sense of security among Israeli Arabs.

One might, however, wonder why there has not been more Jewish terrorism against Palestinians. After all, Israel has been the victim of countless instances of bloody terror since its founding and, especially, since 2000. Israelis have military experience and familiarity with weaponry. There certainly are many Israelis who feel anger over their losses, and it is human to desire revenge when one's loved ones have been killed. Moreover, there is a large, nationalistic religious establishment, many of whom feel that the Israeli state has been giving away their holy inheritance piece by piece.

There are several answers. First of all, the government and all major political, social, and religious organizations have spoken with one voice regarding the illegitimacy of terrorism. Speaking about one act of Jewish terrorism, *Boston Globe* columnist Jeff Jacoby noted: "Without being prompted, without making excuses, Jewish communities instinctively reacted to Zada's monstrous deed with disgust and outrage, all the more angrily because the perpetrator was a fellow Jew."[89] Several factors contribute to the overwhelming Jewish condemnation of terrorist methods. First, whatever international support Israel retains in the Arab-Israeli conflict depends heavily on Western democracies perceiving a moral difference between the Jewish state and its enemies, most Israelis understand that terrorism is not in Israel's best interests. Second, Jews during the past two thousand years of history, especially prior to the founding of the state of Israel, have been reluctant to use violence as a political approach. This reluctance may derive from religious principles, the Jews' status as a demographic minority, their relative openness to secular principles of human rights, a communal memory of the devastating consequences of violent resistance against Rome in the first and second centuries, or some combination of these and other factors. In any case, when the American public was asked in 2006 which religion is most violent—Christianity, Islam, Judaism, or Hinduism—the smallest percentage chose Judaism, only 2 percent; the majority (64 percent) said Islam, followed by Christianity (9 percent), and Hinduism (4 percent).[90]

The relative infrequency of Jewish terrorism, whether religious or secular, is no basis for complacency about Jewish extremism in Israel. First of all, any level of terrorist violence is unacceptable, and, given the rise in messianic thinking, things could get worse. Secondly, the religious thinking that prevails in much of the Orthodox right may weaken Israel's ability to react pragmatically and intelligently to the political, diplomatic, and military threats it faces, even if this ideology does not lead to terrorism. Thirdly, acts of Jewish terrorism in the Middle East do not have to be frequent or widely supported in order to blow the lid off the region, or even the entire world.

A tiny group of extremists could carry out two threats with devastating consequences: the first a bit less dangerous because it is less likely; the second a nightmare scenario that could happen. The dangers of the first threat become evident when one considers the impact of political violence directed against members of one's own group. When radicals murder or threaten to murder those in their own camp who advocate different policies, the basis for political hypothesis testing and democracy are undermined. This is most apparent today in the Muslim and Arab worlds, where advocacy of certain positions can greatly increase the probability of a premature death. The deadly stances in this world have varied a bit depending on era and locale, but one, defense of Israel and opposition to Islam, is on the list. Another example of the devastating effects of a culture of political assassination was Japan in the interwar period. Thus far, there has been no evidence of this dynamic developing in Israel, and the one significant political assassination of a Jewish leader in post-Independence Israel has had the effect of increasing the nation's commitment to freedom of expression. But there are troubling signs that the Rabin assassination might not have been the last of its kind.

On November 4, 1995, Yigal Amir—an Orthodox extremist—shocked observers throughout Israel and the world by firing two bullets into the back of the Israeli prime minister. Two years earlier, Rabin had signed the Oslo Accords and publicly grasped the hand of PLO leader Yasir Arafat, beginning a process that was supposed to lead ultimately to an independent Palestinian state on the West Bank and Gaza.

The political reaction to this dramatic event included a considerable amount of anger on the part of the Israeli Right, especially among those who believed that God had bequeathed the entire region to the Jews. Rabin himself drew additionally vehement antipathy, in part because he dealt with settler concerns impatiently and dismissively. But Israel was a well-functioning democracy, and few observers there or elsewhere expected the murder of an Israeli prime minister and war hero by a Jewish assassin.[91]

Though, as usual, some on the Right attempted to explain away Amir as a madman, his mental state was at most a contributing factor. According to one expert on the assassination, "He had a desire to prove to himself, his mother, his friends, and others that he could go further than anybody else. Amir noted that he was afraid someone else would kill Rabin before he did, thereby stealing his chance for fame: 'I wanted a thinking person to do it. I was afraid that an Arab might kill him. I wanted Heaven to see that a Jew had done it.'"[92] In addition to this line of thinking, Amir had been depressed for several months since his girlfriend had left him to marry one of his close friends. So psychology provides part of the explanation.

But the murder was far more than the product of individual insanity. Amir had been indoctrinated by the religious Far Right and couldn't let go of the thought that Rabin was evil. Several extremist rabbis had discussed the possibility of putting Rabin and the Israeli government on trial for violation of Jewish laws. Ehud Sprinzak, an Israeli expert on Jewish extremism, explains:

> A *moser* and a *rodef*, according to the Halakha [Jewish law], are among the worst kinds of Jews. They betray the community through acts that could result in the loss of innocent Jewish life. A *moser* is a Jew suspected of providing gentiles with information about Jews or with illegally giving them Jewish property. Since the Halakha refers to Eretz Yisrael [the land of Israel] as the sacred property of the Jewish people, Jews are obliged to kill a *moser*. A rodef is a person about to commit or facilitate the murder of a Jew. The purpose of his immediate execution is to save Jewish life. This rule does

> not apply to a killer caught after the murder, who must go on trial. *Din rodef* [the law of the *rodef*] is the only case in which the Halakha allows the killing of a Jew without trial.[93]

Though their hostile attitude toward Rabin and other pro-Oslo leaders was clear, the rabbis never issued a final judgment about whether the obscure, rarely cited doctrines of *rodef* and *moser* applied to Rabin. According to Sprinzak, "It is almost certain that Yigal Amir had no unequivocal rabbinical sanction to kill Rabin."[94] Amir judged the rabbis "soft" and "political." He "believed he was fully informed of the relevant Halakhic law and had sufficient knowledge of the misery of the Israeli people to act on his own."[95] Amir was apparently also influenced by examples of Jewish zealotry from the biblical past. While never institutionalized in Jewish law, acts might qualify—according to some—as acceptable zealotry if they are conducted in emergency circumstances, guided by awe of God, without a shred of personal gain, and when the zealot is ready to risk his life in the name of God.[96] Thus, Amir killed Israel's leader while believing that his acts were divinely inspired and religiously meritorious. It must, however, be stressed that the principles from which he drew these conclusions were obscure, accepted in the general case by only a small percentage of Orthodox religious authorities and applied by none unambiguously to the situation at hand. I know of no other instances where similar thinking has led to a murder in modern times.

Yet, in 2004, another Israeli prime minister faced similar threats. In the Old Testament, God informs the Jews that whenever they encounter members of the tribe of Amalek, they must kill them. This injunction stems from the memory of terrible atrocities inflicted on the Israelites by this tribe. Whatever the morality of the ruling in the ancient context, nearly all Jews—Reform, Conservative, and Orthodox—nowadays believe it has no relevance and poses no problems simply because there are no Amalekites to be found. Among some extremists, however, the concept has been revived. Jeffrey Goldberg, a left-leaning supporter of Israel and staff writer for the *New*

Yorker, notes that Amalek "in the language of the settler hardcore today, often stands for the Arabs, the existential enemy of the Jews."[97] Goldberg reports a conversation with an Israeli girl in her late teens, wearing religious garb and carrying an M-16. He asked whether the Amalek was alive today. Pointing to an Arab village in the distance, she replied: "Of course. The Amalekite spirit is everywhere. It's not just the Arabs." Then she added a surprise: "Sharon isn't Amalek, but he works for Amalek."[98] However, this young lady stopped short of expressing a desire to kill the prime minister. "Sharon is forfeiting his right to live. . . . It's not for me to do. If the rabbis say it, then someone will do it. He is working against God."[99] Sharon himself reflected: "It pains me that someone who has devoted his entire life to protecting Jews must now be protected from Jews."[100] He spent the remainder of his political life under unprecedented, tight security.

As it happened, no one felt called upon to carry out the deed, though perhaps someone would have had Sharon not experienced a debilitating stroke. The threat did not come from anyone in the organized movement of settlers who opposed the Sharon plan for disengagement. Some discussed breaking the law, but not murder. More stood with Shaul Goldstein, a settler leader who said: "I will not support any act of violence. . . . I do not agree with escalating the struggle although I understand why people would want to. I am in favor of getting people to work together since aggressiveness and forcefulness will in the end fail."[101] Still, according to Israeli security, dozens of people, supported by 150 others, wanted the assassination of Prime Minister Sharon.[102] They did not constitute an organized underground. In July 2004, Tsahi Hanegbi announced his concern about "a lone assassin who sits in a room, takes on himself the responsibility for the redemption of Israel and gets up to carry out the deed."[103] With rabbis still throwing around notions like *din rodef*, albeit more cautiously, it is fortunate that there were no attacks against the prime minister. However, the danger remains that a very small vanguard of extremists might transform themselves into a murderous underground, attempting through assassination to accomplish what they could not through the ballot box or other aspects of the legitimate political process. In view of the powerful internal injunctions against terror within Israeli society, I do not judge this very likely. But it is conceivable. One poll, after all, found that 8 percent of Israeli Jews condoned physical harm to political leaders in order to avert a "looming political disaster."[104] There is considerable distance between what people tell pollsters and what they will do. But the numbers are troubling.

A second threat is more likely and more dangerous. A small group of religiously inspired Jewish activists might succeed in carrying out a major attack against the Dome of the Rock or the al-Aqsa Mosque on the Temple Mount. Such plots have been hatched several times in the past and always failed. Back in 1984, a group of Jewish terrorists brought explosives to the Temple Mount but ran off when they were discovered by a Muslim guard. After they were arrested, it became clear that the plotters belonged to a militantly religious messianic sect. They had hoped to raze the existing mosques in order to prepare for the construction of a new Jewish Temple on its ancient site. This plot was one of the few terrorist attempts by an organized underground; twenty-one people were involved. More recently, in May 2005, three ultra-Orthodox Jewish extremists were questioned in connection with a scheme to fire a missile at the Temple Mount, hoping to disrupt the disengagement from the Gaza Strip, create a new intifada (rebellion), and consequently bring about the expulsion of Arabs from Israel. They were released when it became clear that they had changed their minds about the attack prior to their arrest. Their change of heart came only because they realized they didn't have the money and technical capability to succeed.[105] (Their release does not seem to send a properly robust message to others contemplating similar acts.)

In order to minimize the likelihood of attacks, the Western Wall rabbi Shmuel Rabinovitch issued a religious ruling prohibiting Jews from entering the Temple Mount; though the goal may have been to aid in security, the rationale was religious.[106] Were a plot against the mosques on the Temple Mount to succeed, it is hard to imagine how Israel could repair the situation. As Israeli security chief Avi Dicter has explained: "Jewish terrorism is liable to create a substantial threat, and to turn the conflict between Israel and the Palestinians into a confrontation between thirteen million Jews and one billion Muslims across the world."[107]

The conflict over the Temple Mount involves an unusual clash of two religions, or perhaps three, and the extremists from each might conceivably interact to create a conflagration with worldwide ramifications. Gershom Gorenberg has authored the best study on the topic, noting: "What happens at that one spot more than anywhere else, quickens expectations of the end in three religions. And at that spot, the danger of provoking catastrophe is greatest."[108] Yet Gorenberg concludes that believers need not be governed by their most extreme elements. He notes the history of the Mount and suggests that there are grounds for some hope. Gorenberg explains:

> If we were simply prisoners of a historical pattern, then Israel would not have left the Temple Mount (Al-Aqsa) in Palestinian hands after the Six-Day War in 1967. Even though Israel never officially acknowledged what it had done, its actions were a tremendous, encouraging rebellion against history. The historical pattern in Jerusalem for at least three thousand years is that every conqueror has evicted the previous religion, installed its own, and taken that as a sign that it holds the truth. In 1967, the Israelis came in, conquered the city, and proclaimed, "The Temple Mount is in our hands." That became the official de jure position. But the de facto position is that the Muslims continued to control Al-Aqsa, and the two religions prayed side by side.[109]

Yet one successful terrorist act by Jewish extremists could undo any good that has resulted from Israel's policy. And given the number of religiously inspired messianic thinkers on all sides, there would appear to be many individuals who would perceive such an act as a proof of their devotion to all things divine and holy.

Unfortunately, some who have studied Jewish extremism have attributed the problem irresponsibly and inaccurately to orthodox

Judaism in general, or even to Judaism as a whole. In particular, Israel Shahak and Norton Mezvinsky in their book *Jewish Fundamentalism in Israel*[110] have charged, in effect, that Judaism is an evil religion. In a work that reads more like an angry screed than a work of scholarship, they have nonetheless located numerous inflammatory and incendiary remarks against non-Jews and nonbelieving Jews. For example, they have found ancient texts that they say suggest that it is not murder for Jews to kill non-Jews. Some of the evidence accumulated by Shahak and Mezvinsky can be readily dismissed as inaccurate or misinterpreted. Andrew Mathis has refuted much of Shahak's approach (as manifested in an earlier volume) on a point-by-point basis from a religious perspective.[111] Most of the troubling passages have, for example, been overruled and replaced by more sanguine rulings in definitive rabbinical assessments that are now hundreds or thousands of years old.[112] However, the best assessment of the Shahak and Mezvinsky work comes from an Israeli journalist who understands the dangers posed by Jewish extremism in Israel. Bezalel Stern objects that "[i]nstead of tackling the real issues and problems facing Judaism in Israel today (and many of the various strains of Israeli Judaism do indeed have fundamental problems that deserve to be tackled) Shahak and Mezvinsky succeed only in attacking the imaginary monsters of religious Judaism and Judaism itself, in a way that could easily turn this book into an updated version of *The Protocols of the Elders of Zion* [the notorious anti-Semitic forgery describing a Jewish plot to rule the world]."[113] Stern further notes, correctly, that "Jewish literature, like the literature of all religions, is vast. And, as in all other religions, provocative statements can be found if one seeks them out." The real issue is how the texts are used and interpreted in the contemporary world.

Nonetheless, it remains undeniable that Jewish terrorists have come overwhelmingly from among the religiously observant. Yoram Peri, an expert of the assassination of Yitzhak Rabin, draws a distinction between two camps in Israeli society, the "metros" and the "retros."[114] The metros believe that Israel should be run by humanitarian and universalistic principles; they tend to be urban, liberal, and secular. They see themselves more as Israelis than Jews. Retros see Israel as inherently different from other nations and separate; they see themselves more as Jews than Israelis. No sooner does Peri draw the distinction, however, than he begins to qualify it. He says: "I consider myself metro but my Jewishness is very important to me. There are very few metros who are really as humanistic and universalistic as the ideal type and certainly not all religious people—not even all haredim [ultrareligious Jews]—are completely retro."[115] The question is whether, given these limitations, the ideal types help us to understand what is going on. I'm not sure they do, because so many religiously observant Jews turn out to be politically moderate. What we are really talking about is an extreme retro type.

Journalist Jeffrey Goldberg recently got himself in trouble with some elements of the pro-Israel camp by painting a very unflattering image of some extremist, retro, settlers in the West Bank.[116] If an uninformed person read Goldberg's article in the *New Yorker*, he or she might very well come away with the impression that many Israelis shared the anti-Arab racism, messianic thinking, mindless machismo, and fascistic mindset of the people he describes. However, this was not Goldberg's objective. Instead, his aim was to convey the danger posed to Israel by its extremist fringe. He writes: "The most hard-core settlers are impatient messianists, who profess indifference, even scorn, for the state; a faith in vigilantism; and loathing for the Arabs. They are free of doubt, seeing themselves as taking orders from God, and are an unusually cohesive segment of Israeli society. Hard-core settlers and their supporters make up perhaps two per cent of the Israeli populace, but they nevertheless have driven Israeli policy in the occupied territories for much of the past thirty years."[117]

Although Goldberg probably overstates their impact, these settlers—the extreme retros—are dangerous not only because of their political impact but because it is from their ranks that Jewish terrorists have come and will likely continue to come. Many of these extremists are not people who come from religious families or who have been religious their whole lives. Also, a good percentage come from the United States and the West. Many have adopted the intellectual and theological approach of Rabbi Avraham Kook and his son, Rabbi Zvi Yehuda Kook, though certainly not all followers of Kook are dangerous extremists. Most of the early founders of the Israeli state were secular, but, according to the religious Zionists of the present, God had guided the hands of the nonbelievers and was behind the dramatic successes in the 1967 war. To these believers, the messianic process trumps the peace process. Thus, occupation of the newly conquered territories became an inescapable religious imperative. After Israel's victory, the Arabs declared that they had no interest in granting a lasting peace in exchange for land. Thus, political events necessitated retention of the land and offered the followers of Kook a chance to realize their religious dream. Throughout, Arab intransigence reinforced the religious Zionists' sense that success required a religious program. More generally, religious Jews felt themselves increasingly alienated from the state that had been created by politically, culturally, and socially dominant secular Zionists. Like religious extremists of other faiths and despite their enthusiastic embracing of high technology, they developed a hostility toward many aspects of modern society.[118]

To summarize, it is possible to offer several defensible conclusions about Jewish extremism. First, while many Jews consider themselves traditionally observant and Orthodox, only a tiny percentage have crossed the line into dangerous extremism. Second, the relative unpopularity of extremist violence in Judaism derives from the near-universal condemnation of all forms of terrorism by all elements in the Jewish mainstream—which includes Orthodox, Conservative, Reform, and secular. Third, a still small but somewhat broader segment of the Israeli religious public shares some of the ideas of the extremists, and consequently the situation could get worse in the near future. Fourth, even a tiny group of violent Jewish extremists could through terrorist action, perhaps against the mosques on the Temple Mount, trigger an uncontrollable worldwide conflagration.

Part Two

THE CAUSES OF MILITANT FAITH

CHAPTER 4

Dangerous Books?

Who Really Understands the Bible?

George Went Hensley felt he could no longer tolerate the inconsistencies in his spiritual life, and around 1910 he decided it was high time to implement the will of God. As he told a reporter decades later, he did so by approaching a large rattlesnake in a rocky gap on White Oak Mountain, outside Chattanooga, Tennessee. He knelt down just a few feet away from the reptile, prayed loudly for "the power," shouted, leaped forward, and grasped the serpent in his trembling hands. Descending the mountain, snake in hand, he launched an unusual Christian sect that persists to this day. According to researchers who have studied the group, virtually all members feel the fang sooner or later, and some are bitten repeatedly.[1] Hensley himself died of a fatal rattlesnake bite while preaching at a service in Florida, although it took nearly a half century of serpent handling for this to happen.

The Gospel according to Mark (16:15–18) is the source of the perceived inconsistency that inspired Hensley and that continues to motivate new serpent handlers each year. The crucial lines of scripture concern Jesus's directive to his apostles following the Resurrection. Jesus says: "Go ye into all the world, and preach the gospel to every creature. He that believeth and is baptized shall be saved; but he that believeth not shall be damned. And these signs shall follow them that believe; In my name shall they cast out devils; they shall speak with new tongues; They shall take up serpents; and if they drink any deadly thing, it shall not hurt them; they shall lay hands on the sick, and they shall recover." As a recent convert from debauchery into the Church of God—a Holiness-Pentecostal denomination—Hensley accepted this passage as vitally important and literally true. His problem was that it seemed to require four things, but his cobelievers acted on only three: casting out devils, laying of hands, and speaking in tongues. Why, he agonized, had they omitted the fourth? Why didn't they take up serpents? The passage that dealt with drinking "any deadly thing" said, "if they drink." The passage about taking up serpents contained no "if." Clearly, Hensley reasoned, the snake directive was mandatory.

As one more recent handler put it: "The Bible says, 'They shall take up serpents.' Honey, it means what it says, and says what it means. . . . It won't change for me. It won't change for you. Amen. Thank God. It won't change. . . . I don't care what you try to do, the Word of God is still the same."[2] Another adherent of the sect explained how he could not accept any other explanations of the passage in Mark, ridiculing those who claimed that the line referred to a "spiritual" serpent.[3] Yet another handler offered a description of the experience of holding a rattlesnake that could, one might imagine, resemble to some degree the state of mind of a suicide bomber just prior to the suicide. He explains: "The power of God began to move upon me, and I thought that there was no harm. I began to just look up and let God take my mind, blocked everything out from all around me, and said, 'God, here I am. Just whatever you want me to do, God. Ever how you want to move on me, here I am.' I began to handle that serpent, and like I said, that began to come from another world—something I can't explain."[4] In spite of this willingness to die, however, serpent handlers have not been implicated in any endangerment of anyone except themselves. And one female handler pointed out a possibly positive consequence of the practice: "You really have to have your life in order when you go into that [rattlesnake] box—or you better have—because that could be instant death."[5]

Psychologists and sociologists have offered some theories about why serpent handlers do what they do and why the sect persists into twenty-first-century America. Yet the simplest answer is perhaps best: the believers have been captured by the text. They are prisoners of scripture. This, in any case, is what they themselves contend. Like tens of millions of other Christians, possibly hundreds of millions, they believe that the Bible is literally true, inerrant, and perfectly clear. All they are doing, they insist, is being consistent, while all other so-called believers are being hypocritical or, at least, dead wrong.

There is one small problem. In the earliest manuscripts of Mark's Gospel, Jesus never actually appears before his disciples following the Resurrection and never actually commissions them to go forth into the world preaching the gospel. In other words, the original text not only never enjoins believers to take up rattlesnakes but it never mentions the other signs either. Professor Bart D. Ehrman, a well-known expert on the New Testament, asserts that biblical scholars generally agree on this matter.[6] Interestingly, however, many serpent handlers (who, by the way, are increasingly educated) are aware of this position and persist nonetheless. Some suggest that God, in his infinite wisdom, inspired someone later on to alter the text of the Gospel of Mark in order to bring it in compliance with the divine will. Others have adduced additional biblical verses in support of their position. For example, the book of Job (26:13) says (referring to God): "By his spirit, he hath garnished the heavens; his hand hath formed the crooked serpent." Handlers say this means that Jesus handled snakes too.[7] They insist that he would hardly ask others to do that which he himself would not.

Some theologians have suggested that serpent handlers come closest to a truly literal reading of the scriptures.[8] Yet even they make choices about how to interpret the text. For one thing, they regard the King James Version as definitive, even when this means including text that was probably missing from Mark's original gospel. And their interpretation of the passage from Job springs more from a leap of faith than from any obviously apparent, literal reading. While Christian theologians remain unsure about just what the verse about the "crooked serpent" means, most think it refers to a constellation in the sky. So, when literalists say the Bible says what it means and means what it says, some may wonder whether that is truly the end of the matter—even for them. The overwhelming majority of literalists, after all, do not volunteer to grasp serpents, and not because they question the authenticity of the final portion of Mark's Gospel.

Every year since 1941, the National Bible Association has sponsored National Bible Week around Thanksgiving time, and every year the American president has issued a National Bible Week message. Governors, mayors, and other public officials typically follow suit, adding some holy scripture to the nation's festive menu. Thus, in 2005, Senator Daniel Akaka, a Democrat from Hawaii, told his fellow senators: "The Bible is a resource of profound but fundamental truths that retain relevance throughout the ages. They are the lessons that serve as the building blocks of good citizens, good families, good communities, and good government."[9] President Bush, in his 2005 message, advised that "[t]he Bible is a source of hope for the oppressed, guidance for the faithful and strength for the weary."[10] In 1994, President Clinton's message noted that he includes himself "among those whose lives have been dramatically and personally changed by study of the Bible."[11] About a decade earlier, President Ronald Reagan declared 1983 to be the "Year of the Bible." In his proclamation, President Reagan told us that "[f]or centuries, the Bible's emphasis on compassion and love for our neighbor has inspired institutional and governmental expressions of benevolent outreach such as private charity, the establishment of schools and hospitals, and the abolition of slavery."[12] Consequently, President Reagan had some advice for his fellow Americans, encouraging "all citizens, each in his or her own way, to reexamine and rediscover its priceless and timeless message."[13]

Speeches such as these are, of course, a time-honored American ritual, so we cannot distinguish words that a leader truly believes from those he deems politically advantageous, low-cost, and attractive to potential voters. But what if we were to consider the content of the declarations seriously, as many Americans do? Is there a clear, readily discernible message in the Bible? Presumably, President Reagan did not have serpent handlers in mind when he urged each citizen to search the text "in his or her own way." And he wasn't thinking of the centuries of the Spanish Inquisition when he alluded to the governmental consequences of the Bible's emphasis on compassion and love. Similarly, Senator Akaka probably was not thinking about John Calvin's totalitarian Geneva when he spoke of scripture as the basis for "good families, good communities, and good government." What would be the net effect of, say, one hundred million Americans taking the message of National Bible Week to heart? Would there be a change in morals, political views, family relations, or other behaviors? Would the change, if any, be for the better? And, if one acknowledges that some readings of scripture might lead to detrimental consequences, which methods of study might help readers to avoid these undesirable outcomes?

The National Bible Association Web site tells us that many celebrities read the Bible, including former heavyweight champions Evander Holyfield and George Foreman, country music legend Dolly Parton, sales guru Zig Ziglar, poet Maya Angelou, music legend Elvis Presley, movie star Mel Gibson, comedian Dick Van Dyke, pop musician Bono, and former *New York Times* columnist William Safire. Among historical Bible readers, the list includes Ulysses S. Grant and Robert E. Lee, Christopher Columbus, Martin Luther and Martin Luther King Jr., Oscar Wilde, Mother Teresa, Theodore Roosevelt, and William Shakespeare.[14] The list, of course, could go on and on. But we are not told *how* these people read the Bible. One wonders what we would find if we were to study the Bible-reading experiences of these luminaries, past and present. Would there be any common ground? And suppose we were to add in some of the more poorly regarded readers of scripture? Would there then be any shared lessons? If so, what would these lessons be?

Certainly none of the American political leaders and celebrities—and few of the historical figures—cited by the National Bible Association had in mind the ideas of Rousas John Rushdoony, author of *The Institutes of Biblical Law*.[15] Rushdoony's plan was for establishing biblical theocratic republics, where every aspect of life would be subjected to Christian religious law. He regarded all other systems of law as fundamentally anti-Christian. Yet Rushdoony and his supporters believed that all knowledge stemmed from the Bible and only from the Bible. How did they—and so many others whom the mainstream devout consider misguided—go astray?

Many believers within and outside Christianity see their faith as grounded exclusively, or almost exclusively, in scripture. But most religions inherit a larger religious tradition than scripture alone, sometimes a much larger one. In faiths where the original scripture dominates heavily—some Protestant denominations, for example—each generation or even each person may, at least in theory, feel free to interpret verses and passages anew, without agonizing too much about how these passages were used and interpreted in the past. They may take guidance from a particular pastor, group of pastors, or denomination. But they do not—again, in theory—consider themselves bound by officially recognized, ancient readings of the text. Where the religious tradition includes additional sacred works and perhaps centuries of recorded commentaries and opinions—as in much of Islam and Judaism—there is a tougher path for individuals or theologians who wish to reinterpret scriptural text freely, without reference to past theology.

In Judaism, for instance, the Torah (i.e., the first five books of the Jewish Bible), stands at the pinnacle of holiness. But there are also the remaining books of the Jewish Bible (i.e., the writings and the prophets in the Old Testament), the oral law as passed down through the generations, the Mishneh and Gemara (which record and discuss this law), the various compendia of Jewish law in later eras (such as Maimonides' *Mishneh Torah* and Joseph Caro's *Schulchan Aruch*), and the responsa (opinions) of rabbis from the medieval era through the present day.[16] All of these sources may provide ideas, inspirations, sources, and rulings. If one seeks to return to the Torah to offer an altogether novel interpretation, one typically finds that one's idea has already been considered, and the rabbis probably have rendered an opinion on the acceptability of the interpretation. Newer interpretive works generally (but not always) supersede older ones. Many passages of the Jewish Bible have essentially been declared inoperative or inapplicable, perhaps even two thousand years ago. When a new question arises, the real question doesn't concern the validity of various doctrines but rather which doctrines apply to the situation at hand.[17] Each religion has its own mechanisms of interpretation and change, but Catholicism and Islam bear at least some resemblance to Judaism in assigning great value to the opinions of sages from the distant past.

Yet many Jews, like many in all faiths, reject what their religious leaders say. When enough people disagree along similar lines, a new sect, branch, denomination, or style of worship may be born. Hence, in Judaism, Reform, Conservative, and, most recently, Reconstructionist movements have developed among many who have disagreed with rulings of the Orthodox rabbis. People within the Conservative, Reform, and Reconstructionist movements may feel the most liberty to offer their own interpretations of the sacred texts, picking and choosing, often without even bothering to consult scripture, rabbis, or classic commentaries. They may do so even when they act in direct conflict with the official positions of their movement.

As we have already seen, the question of how individuals and religious groups interpret their sacred scriptures—the Jewish Bible, the Catholic Bible, the Protestant Bible, and the Koran—is critical. No matter what believers may say, none is truly a literalist. Everyone picks and chooses, at least a little. Everyone interprets. When there are additional religious traditions and additional sacred books, the importance of interpretation extends beyond scripture to these sources as well. The same texts in each faith can be used to support diametrically opposed political, social, psychological, and theological stances. Hence, understanding how religionists make decisions concerning the interpretation of their religious texts and traditions is the key to deciphering when and how religion becomes a force for evil in the world. (This is the topic we consider in the next two chapters, focusing here on the dynamics of interpretation within Christianity, Islam, and Judaism and targeting in the next chapter the psychology of religious belief.)

But first, we must address a preliminary concern. It has been suggested that people do not in the first place really make any religious choices at all.

The Accident of Birth

Many sociologists have argued that a person's religious identity is largely determined by factors of time and place. In other words, nothing determines our religious beliefs more than where we are born and among whom we live. Sociologist Phil Zuckerman makes the point well.

> The likelihood that a child born this morning in Sakakah, Saudi Arabia, will be Muslim is far, far greater than the likelihood that she or he will be Episcopalian, or a worshiper of the Aztec mother-goddess Tonantzin. The truth is, the overwhelming majority of people who are Muslim or some other religion today aren't Muslim or some other religion because of brain chemistry or even some individual/personal choice or life event. . . . Rather, they were born at a specific time in human history and in a particular place (i.e., city, state, or region) that made such a religious identity possible, or, rather, inevitable—if not downright imperative.[18]

Zuckerman does not deny the occasional exception, but he believes that by focusing on exceptions we may miss the broader truth. To understand, for example, why most African Americans, more than 80 percent, are Protestant Christians, we should attend less to their individual psychologies and more to the facts of history, specifically, that most of their ancestors were enslaved by Protestant Christians.

Quite a lot of evidence can be marshaled in support of the sociological argument. For one thing, if people are raised in a religion, they tend to stay in that religion. In the United States, 80 percent of people who are born Catholic stay Catholic (in the sense that they never convert or renounce their religion). Ninety percent of people who are born Protestant stay Protestant. Fewer than one American in a hundred convert to an entirely new religion.[19] And when people do convert, Zuckerman argues, it may have more to do with their social relationships than with theology or psychology. He writes that "while religion may have to do with a connection or attachment to God or some other Supreme Reality Out There, more significantly (and observably) it has to do with a connection or attachment to mom or dad or husband or wife or sibling or friend right here on planet Earth."[20]

The sociologists have established a simple yet important truth, one that is often acknowledged in principle, then overlooked in the heat of religious debate and conflict. It hardly seems sporting to criticize a person for arriving at the wrong religious (or nonreligious) position when that position has not been adequately presented as an option. A similar problem arises for religious traditions that, as a condition of salvation, require people to follow all the details of a faith, even though they hail from an entirely different part of the world.

Still, geography is not necessarily destiny. Setting aside deeper philosophical questions about whether people ever exercise free will, they do seem to make selections from among the range of religious options available in their environments. In some places—for example, the United States—people are exposed to a large array of religious theologies and lifestyles. Most often, however, they make choices *within* the religious tradition of their birth. Christians are unlikely to become Muslims. Muslims are unlikely to become Christians. Members of both faiths are unlikely to become Jews. However, the room for choice within each tradition remains so great that a liberal Christian's experience of faith may resemble that of a Reform Jew more than that of a fundamentalist Christian.

In my own case, I slipped from slight observance of Conservative Judaism during childhood to substantially more observance and belief during my teenage years to nonbelief but slight practice as a Reconstructionist Jew during early adulthood. Throughout, no one much cared in my family or the surrounding Conservative Jewish community.[21] The changes—though personally significant, theologically large, and psychologically stressful—fell well within the parameters of social acceptability in American Reform and Conservative synagogues. Choices can easily be made, but within limits. Had I moved to the Reform movement, the change would have raised similarly few eyebrows. Had I become strictly Orthodox, it would have necessitated some lifestyle changes and posed some practical problems for family and friends, primarily because of the dietary laws. However, there would have been no strong social, communal, or familial consequences. Had I dropped my Jewish religious connection altogether but not assumed a new religious affiliation, I suspect there would have been about the same amount of social disruption. Had I moved to Israel, but maintained any of the above styles of belief, there would have been many changes in my life, but most Jews would have viewed the choice as a defensible one.

But had I joined a right-wing Orthodox community of West Bank settlers, many Jews I know would have thought that I had lost my mind. Had I married a non-Jewish woman who converted to Judaism, there would have been at most a mild disruption. On the other hand, had I actually converted to a Christian denomination, even a liberal one, the decision probably would have necessitated very major changes in familial and social relationships. In spite of the possibility of some social sanctions, however, all of the above decisions would have been understandable in the sense that they were on the radar. In view of the popularity of new age movements, some Western forms of Zen Buddhism might also have been in the realm of possibility. I know some Jews who have followed each of the paths mentioned here. Still, some options are more or less off the radar, in my case, for example, Islam, Hinduism, Shinto, Zoroastrianism, Mormonism. The odds would be overwhelming against any of those changes, for me or for most American Jews.

Yet had I been born in India, the odds—as noted above—are overwhelming that I would have been a Hindu or a Muslim with an entirely different set of religious options. But I would not have been confined to the exact same religious spot where I had been born. People very frequently modify their approach to the religion of their birth, sometimes because they have been won over by preachers, sometimes because they imported neighboring traditions, and sometimes because they made a choice to support some other decision, say, concerning marriage or a career. Thus, the real choices people make about religion are constrained by their era and geographical circumstances. But people do make choices.

No one is born with the unchangeable destiny of becoming an extremist. If we examine Osama bin Laden's very large family, we find among his relatives many observant Muslims, though not all equally observant. Many are Wahhabis, as one might expect in Saudi Arabia. But only a very small number are supporters of an aggressive anti-Western jihad. More than a few are apparently pro-Western.[22]

All people who are affiliated with a religion must assume an attitude toward that religion's inherited traditions. Texts, history, clergy, and traditional practices can provide guidelines and constraints on what constitutes acceptable interpretation. Unfortunately, the holy scriptures of all the Abrahamic faiths provide quite a bit of textual material that can seem, at least on initial inspection, to be pushing people in the wrong direction, at least when judged against the standards of Western liberal civilization.

TROUBLING TEXTS

A series of incidents in the book of Judges shows how poorly the Bible sometimes fares as a guide to moral behavior in the contemporary world. Consider the following story. A certain traveler from the tribe of Levi had deliberately chosen not to stop in Jerusalem for the night because the place, still known as Jebus, was not yet an Israelite town and he judged an overnight stay there unadvisable. The Levite's decision proved disastrous. He and his traveling companions, including his concubine, lodged instead in the house of an old man in the town of Gibeah, the only one who would take them in, and soon some members of the tribe of Benjamin came by and pounded on the door. We are led to believe that the Benjaminites constituted something of a problem tribe. They demanded that the Levite be sent outside so they could "know" him, something everyone understood to mean sodomy, a great abomination in the eyes of the Lord.

The master of the house, a hospitable man, was appalled. "Nay, my brethren," he said, "Nay, I pray you, do not so wickedly, seeing that this man is come into mine house, do not this folly." He proposed an alternative. The Benjaminites could take his own daughter, who was a virgin, and the Levite's concubine. They could do as they pleased, the man said, but he enjoined them to leave his male houseguest alone. Their plans for this Levite guest, he said, would be a very evil thing.

The Benjaminites still wanted him, but when the Levite sent out his concubine, the hostile crew seemed to accept her. She was abused through the night and then released. On closer examination, it became clear that she had not survived the ordeal. The Levite, who had recently reconciled with his concubine (and may have loved her), was horrified. In his grief, he cut her into twelve pieces. These he sent throughout the Israelite realms, probably with an account of what happened. The gory packages had their desired impact. When the Israelites received them, they said: "There was no such deed done nor seen from the day that the children of Israel came up out of the Land of Egypt until this day."

They then gathered an army, went to the Benjaminites, and demanded the perpetrators of the crime so that they could be put to death. The tribe of Benjamin refused. War followed, and with God's assistance, Benjamin suffered a terrible defeat. The tribe's towns were devastated—as retribution for their evil ways—and when it was all over, the other Israelite tribes realized with remorse that Benjamin, one of the tribes of their people, might soon disappear.

The biggest problem blocking repopulation of the tribe was a shortage of women. But, unfortunately, the members of the other tribes had previously sworn not to give any of their daughters to the Benjaminites, on pain of death. To solve the problem, they came up with a scheme. The tribal leaders realized that no one from the town of Jabesh-Gilead had come to aid the war effort against the Benjaminites. So, with God's blessing, they killed all the male residents of Jabesh-Gilead and all the women who had slept with them. But they found four hundred virgins, and these they gave to the Benjaminite males for wives.

Still, they needed more women and so came up with a new plan. At the time of the annual festival of the Lord in Shiloh, some women from the town would each year come out to dance in the vineyards. They advised the wifeless Benjaminites to hide there, waiting for the dancers to arrive. Then they were to capture their wives. When the fathers and brothers of these women came to protest, the other Israelites would explain the difficult situation and urge them to be understanding.

This, apparently, is what happened. Then the Benjaminites rebuilt their towns, and without God or anyone else uttering so much as a peep, lived—more or less—happily ever after. The book of Judges concludes the story by saying: "In those days there was no king in Israel; every man did that which was right in his own eyes." In other words, the book—written during the monarchical period—lays the pragmatic and, perhaps, moral groundwork for appointing a king. But there is no clear, or even implied, condemnation of the sordid behaviors toward women, or the killings, or the other offenses we observe in this tale. God makes several appearances, but nearly always addressing matters that modern people would deem morally peripheral. He offers battle advice and mainly sanctions decisions made by the Israelite leadership.

Commenting on the above story, one atheistic critic observes that "[o]bviously these women were repeatedly raped. These sick bastards killed and raped an entire town and then wanted more virgins, so they hid beside the road to kidnap and rape some more. How can anyone see this as anything but evil?"[23] The author of these remarks doesn't think much of the Bible. His Web site, EvilBible.com, offers viewers a specific, hard-to-defend, seemingly immoral "evil Bible" quote for each day of the year. He announces that the "web site is designed to spread the vicious truth about the Bible." For far too long, he insists, "priests and preachers have completely ignored the vicious criminal acts that the Bible promotes. The so-called 'God' of the Bible makes Osama Bin Laden look like a Boy Scout. This God, according to the Bible, is directly responsible for mass-murders, rapes, pillage, plunder, slavery, child abuse and killing, not to mention the killing of unborn children."[24]

EvilBible.com and some similar antireligious compendia make a strong point, but they are also unbalanced for three reasons. First, they neglect to mention that many religious denominations have long ago evolved methods that render the most problematic passages inoperative. Second, they fail to include counterbalancing positive messages that are also abundant in the texts. And, most important, they rarely concede that—understood historically—the Bible was a step forward even if one would be ill-advised to take it literally as a guide to moral behavior in the present. In essence, however, the very moral standards used by most nonbelievers to criticize the Bible are, at least partly, the consequence of a historical process that started (but did not end) with the Bible itself.

Nonetheless, it is hard to escape the conclusion that those who have scoured the Bible, the Koran, the Book of Mormon, and other classic religious sources have been very productive in their searches, finding many, many troubling passages with which all believers must contend—one way or another. And that such passages remain in books that are deemed sacred means that some religious extremists may always be able to return to them for support. Well-intentioned and benign reinterpretations of such passages sometimes fare poorly because they are inherently more complex than a straightforward reading of the words as written.

The scriptures of the Abrahamic faiths contain many different varieties of "hard passages," ones that most modern members of Western societies find difficult to accept at face value.[25] Sometimes the text demands behaviors that believers are unwilling or unable to follow. Sometimes, a modern problem calls out for an ethical ruling, yet the scriptural text is mute on the matter. Biblical requirements, laws, injunctions, and statements of fact can also be unclear, illogical, or too hard to swallow in light of the findings of scientists. In my view, the most dangerous scripturally based problems arise from two sources: (1) the founding narrative of the faith, and (2) rules, stories, and examples concerning the treatment of those outside the faith. Both require more attention.

TALES FROM THE FOUNDING: JUDAISM AND CHRISTIANITY

Historians could host a lengthy and heated debate concerning just when the events of the Jewish Bible took place, when they were recorded, and when Judaism as a religion began. No one really knows whether any of the events described in Exodus occurred. Nearly everything prior to the sojourn in Egypt is unsubstantiated. Even if the early stories derive from a kernel of truth passed down orally, this kernel is coated in so many layers of myth that it might as well be made up. As late as the period of Saul, David, and Solomon, we may be dealing with legends that do not have a substantial factual basis. The earliest books of the Jewish Bible were committed to parchment, perhaps some time around the split of the Jewish kingdom into two parts: Israel and Judah. The latest parts were completed about two centuries before Christ. Thus, if we wish to develop a serious understanding of the moral lessons of these scriptural texts, we should place them in the context of social, moral, and political life in the ancient Middle East over a period of many centuries. Unfortunately, although there are other sources, most of what we know about this place and time comes from the Bible itself. We can construct a reasonably good guess about what was going on outside of the Israelite community, however. And in this context, many unpalatable events—and there are many—may actually reflect behavior that was more moral than that of surrounding tribes. Still, most religious people are not interested in defending their scripture merely as a remarkable historical advance. They see it as a guide, perhaps an inerrant guide, for present-day living.

One doesn't need to be a biblical expert to note some of the problems that arise from this approach. Why, for starters, did God feel justified in wiping out the whole human race, except for Noah and his family? How bad could the people have been? And if no one outside of Noah's clan met the requisite moral standards for survival, might not those standards have been a bit stringent for their era? And couldn't God have spared the firstborn children of Egypt, especially because he himself had apparently hardened Pharaoh's heart? Was there no other way for a being of such power to accomplish his goals? And why, when Joshua learned that Achan has done some looting of Jericho, did God apparently sanction the execution not only of this villain but also of his sons, daughters, and animals? And wasn't God showing illiberal tendencies when he sanctioned the mass murder of those misguided souls who put their faith in a golden calf? And what about poor Onan, slain for spilling his seed on the ground when he should have used it to impregnate his late brother's wife? Of course, one always wonders about the judgment of Abraham, who on the basis of his perceived communication with God was willing to murder his child. What lesson might that send to extremists who sense that God is telling them to act against their better judgment and to violate conventional moral standards?

Even the most observant Orthodox religious Jews are not fundamentalist in the sense of taking the Bible literally; what matters most to observant Jews is Jewish law, something that has filtered scripture through an oral tradition and rabbinical interpretation. Still, the lessons of the Bible—and especially the Torah—are given a prominent position of honor, read regularly in Jewish prayer services, and treated by all Jews, at the very least, as a valued source of inspiration.

Let us examine some of the most troubling passages in the Old Testament, those that seem to encourage the mass murder of entire tribes or ethnic groups. It is hard to imagine a moral standard more basic to the definition of a civilized society than "Thou shalt not commit genocide." Yet, in several places, the Old Testament seems to encourage precisely this.

We don't know much about how the "conquest" of Canaan really happened. But the biblical account is the one that matters and it calls for a brutal style of holy war. In the book of Deuteronomy, God explains that, on the way to the Promised Land, the Israelites will have to do battle with seven nations. Each of these nations—Hittites, Girgashites, Amorites, Canaanites, Perizzites, Hivites, and Jebusites—would, under ordinary circumstances, overpower the Israelites, but God promises that he will deliver victory. And when the Israelites prevail, God insists that they "shalt smite them, and utterly destroy them; thou shalt make no covenant with them, nor show mercy unto them" (Deut. 7:2). The plan did not call for vengeance for its own sake. The concern was that leniency would lead to cultural intermixing and that the conquered peoples would teach Israelites to mimic their abominations and sinful ways (Deut. 20:18). God later offers refinements on the rules of holy war, noting, for example, that battles must be preceded by an offer of peace at the price of forced labor. When victory comes in battle, only men—not women and children—are to be killed. But women may be taken as "wives," whether or not they approve, provided they are given a month to mourn for their slain husbands (Deut. 20 and 21). The books of Deuteronomy (2:26–35) and Joshua (10:26–38) provide several examples of how the Israelites purportedly conducted their holy war. And it was not a pretty picture.

The treatment of the people of Amalek was uniquely severe. The Amalekites were the first enemy to attack the Israelites on their way out of Egypt, when the Israelites were still tired and weak. Instead of meeting God's people squarely in battle, they apparently launched sneak attacks at the rear, killing primarily women, children, and the elderly. The Israelites finally confronted them directly. According to the tale, whenever Moses held his hand up, Israel prevailed; when he let it down, Amalek started to win the battle. So Aaron and Hur assisted him in holding up his hands, and Israel won the day (17:12). God, however, remained very angry with the Amalekites, and though the Bible doesn't specify precise crimes, they are widely understood to represent evil incarnate. What the Bible does say is that the fear of God wasn't in Amalek (Deut. 25:18). In the book of Exodus, God says that he will blot out the remembrance of Amalek from under heaven (17:14). Then Moses adds: "The Lord has taken his oath that there will be war with Amalek from generation to generation." In the book of Deuteronomy (25:19), a few word changes put the burden on the Israelites themselves (rather than on God) to see to it that the memory of Amalek is cut off from the earth. And the command was to be taken seriously. One of King Saul's great sins was that, after he defeated the Amalekites in battle, he spared the life of the Amalekite king, Agag, after being specifically told by God to kill them all (1 Sam. 15:3).

From the very beginning of the Rabbinic period, sages perceived the moral problems with the biblical passages concerning Amalek and over the centuries have evolved a variety of mechanisms for rendering them inoperative. For two millennia at least, Jewish law has attempted and largely succeeded in undoing the damage of these dangerous biblical passages, though not always achieving the moral clarity one might desire.[26] The rabbis start from the position that Jewish law cannot be found in a literal reading of the Bible; the scripture must be interpreted, largely based on the Oral Law, something that observant Jews believe comes from God and has been carried down by learned people through the ages. Some of the rabbis' arguments include the following:

- The (ancient) Talmud notes that punishing children for the crimes of their parents is wrong.
- Even though another part of the Talmud says that Jews *are* obligated to kill Amalekites, most statements in the Talmud are not binding law.
- Haman, the villain in the book of Esther, is a descendant of

Amalek. Yet the Talmud also states that descendants of Haman, including Rabbi Samuel ben Shilath, studied Torah in Bnei Brak. So, clearly, it is acceptable to ignore the rule about killing Amalekites and to judge each on an individual basis.

- For thousands of years, it has been essentially impossible to identify Amalekites or their descendants because, as the Bible says, the lineage of many nations has been confused.
- Amalek is not really an ethnic group but rather a symbol of evil, armed might. A permanent war exists between the sword and the book, and the war against these Amalekites of the spirit must be waged "with the book," not physical destruction.
- The obligation is only to wipe out the memory of the glory of Amalek, not Amalek itself.
- The original directive to kill Amalekites stemmed from horrible but unmentioned behavior by the Amalekites, including the cutting off of circumcised penises from live Israelites and throwing them into the air to challenge God.

Rabbi Joseph Telushkin, in his best-selling book *Jewish Literacy*, states that "[t]he eternal animosity that the Torah mandates against Amalek is highly unusual, even inexplicable."[27] The nonbeliever may well express disbelief at the acrobatic efforts used by Jewish scholars over the centuries to escape the implications of an age-old sacred ruling that they know is wrong. However, it is worth noting that they have—in this case, at least—evolved a method that effectively handles a potentially dangerous text. Less observant Reform and Conservative Jews have been able to reject the teachings concerning Amalek with much greater ease and complete clarity.

Some very observant Jews have even managed to extract a moral message from the seemingly hateful text that resonates fairly well in the modern world. Thus, one rabbi writes:

> No longer a foreign nation, today's Amalek is unholy cynicism. That little voice inside each of us that derides, belittles and attacks truth

> and goodness; our irrational tendency to mock people who act morally, to be cynical when we see altruism, to doubt our own or other's sincerity—these are the modern day Amalekites. They wage a lethal war with our soul. . . . There is only one effective response to Amalek's attacks: Annihilation. . . . The most inspiring, uplifting and profound moment of spiritual awakening can be dismissed in an instant by Amalek's sarcastic taunts. . . . You can't fight cynicism with reason. Just wipe it out. . . . Next time your cynical Amalekite raises his ugly head, stomp on it.[28]

It's not at all clear how this author gets from the verses in the Bible to this inspiring piece of cognitive therapy. But he has, in effect, gutted a potentially dangerous part of the scriptures. Yet, as we have seen, the mere existence of the Amalek verses may provide an inspirational tool for at least a few Orthodox Jewish extremists on the West Bank. They could use the verses not as binding law but rather as a motivational metaphor.

Probably by the time of Christ, and certainly during the years following the destruction of the Second Temple by the Romans in 70 CE, the religious lives of most Jews did not resemble very much the ones ordained and described in the books of the Jewish Bible. It is a mistake to picture the Jewish ethical tradition springing instantly into existence in adult form. Instead, Jewish ethics evolved slowly, and perhaps initially in response to the Babylonian exile, and then, the dispersion by the Romans. Absent a homeland central to most religious rites, Jewish identity depended on forging a new and sustainable relationship to God. This, in turn, required much reflection, including some analysis of misbehaviors that might have produced the misfortunes suffered by God's "chosen" people.

By the time Jesus arrived, a good many of his ethical notions were already being discussed and considered by Jewish rabbis.[29] His views—even as presented in the New Testament—did not constitute a revolutionary break with the past but rather a refinement of various traditions within Jewish thought. In all likelihood, the ideas and beliefs of the historical Jesus were even more a part of the existing panorama of religious, ethical, and political thought.[30] The later contributions of Paul and Jesus's other followers introduced far greater changes in the religion, though perhaps not so much to its core ethical vision. As in the case of the Old Testament, the New Testament evolved over centuries and cannot be regarded as an objective history of events. Some Christians see the New Testament as a fulfillment and replacement of the old; this, in effect, frees them of the need to deal with the host of moral ambiguities in the older books. Other Christians adopt different attitudes toward scripture, some of which require them to wrestle with many of the problems faced by Jewish believers. Yet the foundational narrative of Christianity in the New Testament itself presents problems.

Unlike Judaism and Islam, Christianity did not guide any state policies until after the writing of scripture was complete. Jesus's rise to prominence did not have any military component, and neither did the spread of Christianity in its earliest centuries. The dangerous Christian extremists throughout history were not often people who had a fanatic desire to follow the example of the life of Jesus. They were, more often, people who developed and followed a theology that fenced off and ignored the life and teachings of Jesus. Little, if anything, in the accounts of the behavior of Jesus might have led even the most perspicacious first-century observers to predict the mess of doctrinal wars and murderous activity that would come to dominate European and world affairs in the name of Christ.

Thus, to the extent that misguided policies of church-dominated states had religious origins, they typically came from later manifestations of doctrine and religion. For example, Saint Augustine reasoned that men fought and had always fought; therefore, Christians should fight too, provided they had been commanded by God (never an insurmountable restraint). When war was designed to convert the heathen or destroy the heretic, it was especially meritorious. Later, several popes added the idea that anyone who died in a war conducted on behalf of the church would get a heavenly reward or rank as a martyr.[31] But none of this was in the New Testament. There, for the most part, Jesus led a peaceful ministry and so did his followers. Later theologians had to look hard for support for their brutal policies. But, as the record shows, they were up to the task.

Many arguably difficult passages found in the New Testament deal with nonbelievers and misbehavers in ways that do not seem to square with contemporary values. In addition, we find sections that seem, in the opinion of some, to be inconsistent with the psychological well-being of the believer. The antireligious philosopher Bertrand Russell writes, "There is one very serious defect to my mind in Christ's moral character, and that is that He believed in hell. I do not myself feel that any person who is really profoundly humane can believe in everlasting punishment . . . one does find repeatedly a vindictive fury against those people who would not listen to His preaching."[32] This spirit, for example, comes across when Jesus tells his disciples that when they encounter those who do not welcome them and their message, they should "shake the dust off your feet when you leave that home or town. I tell you the truth, it will be more bearable for Sodom and Gomorrah on the day of judgment than for that town" (Matt. 10:15–16).

As a consequence of this and many similar verses, Russell and others have argued that millions have lived their lives tormented by thoughts of a future in hellfire where a worm that does not die will gnaw at them and where they will burn in a fire that is not to be quenched. Russell writes that the whole system depends on fear, and that fear in turn is the "parent of cruelty."[33] This position, of course, can be debated. It is, however, a matter of fact that the New Testament, for better or worse, does feature fear of hell prominently.

Many authors have suggested that the virtues taught in the New Testament are also psychologically damaging. Thus, another atheist writer, George H. Smith, has suggested that "the ruthless consistency of Christian virtues—such as humility, self-sacrifice, and a sense of sin . . . without exception, are geared to the destruction of man's inner sense of dignity, efficacy and personal worth."[34] According to Smith, it is no accident that pride is deemed a major sin. He suggests: "A man lacking in self-esteem . . . a man ridden with guilt and self-doubt, will frequently prefer the apparent security of Christianity over independence and find comfort in the thought that, for the price of total submissiveness, God will love and protect him."[35] Critics of the New Testament have also argued often that the text creates psychological troubles by arguing against the normality of sexual feelings, as, for example, when it warns to "abstain from fleshly lusts which war against the soul" (1 Pet. 2:11). If the charges of Russell, Smith, and like-minded critics are valid, the primary victim—though perhaps not the only victim—is the believer himself.

The New Testament also contains numerous passages that clash with prevailing Western views on some social issues. For example, Alexander Stephens, the vice president of the Confederacy during the Civil War, used passages from the Old and New Testament to argue in favor of slavery. The Holy Book says: "Slaves, submit yourselves to your masters with all respect, not only to those who are good and considerate, but also to those who are harsh" (1 Pet. 2:18). On the basis of this and other verses, Stephens was able to argue with some plausibility that "[t]o maintain that slavery is in itself sinful, in the face of all that is said and written in the Bible upon the subject, with so many sanctions of the relation by the Deity himself, does not seem to be little short of blasphemous! It is a direct imputation upon the wisdom and justice, as well as the declared ordinances of God."[36]

The New Testament also contains many statements that clash very clearly with even the mildest forms of modern feminism. The book of Timothy contains a passage that is especially jarring to modern ears: "A woman should learn in quietness and full submission. I do not permit a woman to teach or to have authority over a man; she must be silent. For Adam was formed first, then Eve. And Adam was not the one deceived; it was the woman who was deceived and became a sinner. But women will be saved through child-bearing—if they continue in faith, love and holiness with propriety" (1 Tim. 2:11–15).

Although many conservative Christian groups favor corporal punishment of children, it is worth noting that most biblical sources of the practice come from the Old Testament (especially in the book of Proverbs) and none from Jesus himself.[37] However, the New Testament does seem to include some support for vigorous punishment in child-rearing. In particular, we are told: "For the Lord disciplines him whom he loves, and chastises every son whom he receives. It is for discipline that you have to endure. God is treating you as sons; for what son is there whom his father does not discipline? If you are left without discipline, in which all have participated, then you are illegitimate children and not sons" (Heb. 12:5–8). Those who support corporal punishment say this verse endorses, and perhaps requires, the practice, though the words are open to other interpretations as well.

Some questions raised about the New Testament, in truth, apply to all Abrahamic religions. The text requires believers to accept things that fly in the face of reason, experience, and science. We have already encountered, for example, the directive to drive out demons, speak in tongues, and heal the sick through the laying of hands. It may be possible for some modern Christians to accept such magic-laden thinking, while many others will balk at a literal reading of such passages.

Ultimately, some have objected that the Christian Bible and perhaps all sacred scriptures are excessively flexible documents, resembling Rorschach inkblots. George Smith has complained about a tendency found in many of the theologians he considers most reasonable. He writes, "To avoid disclaiming the teachings of Jesus, theologians continue to do what they have done for centuries: they *interpret*. Passages unfavorable to Jesus are reinterpreted in a more favorable light, or they are dismissed as unauthentic interpolations. Anything will do as long as it permits the theologian to profess agreement with the ethics of Jesus; the minute he ceases to conform in this respect, he is no longer a theologian, nor can he continue to pass himself off as a Christian."[38] The problem as he sees it is that "Christian theologians have a strong tendency to read their own moral convictions into the ethics of Jesus. Jesus is made to say what theologians think he should have said."[39]

However, it is also possible to see this theological tendency not as the problem but as part of the solution. When the text doesn't seem to advance a reasonable position, find a way to knead it and shape it until it does. This strategy, unfortunately, is capable of creating the opposite problem. For example, when the text does not speak with sufficient clarity against abortion, find a verse that seems somewhat related and then interpret and reinterpret until it ends up saying what you wanted it to say from the outset.

We will return to this problem and to the matter of what the Christian Bible says about the treatment of nonbelievers. But first we look at some aspects of the foundational narrative of Islam.

TALES FROM THE FOUNDING: ISLAM

For devout Jews, Christians, and Muslims, the detailed accounts of ancient living in the sacred books are anything but the dry, irrelevant minutiae of history. Believers can come to regard these happenings in distant lands of long ago as far more applicable to their daily lives than the present goings-on of their own nations and communities. More precisely, the holy literature can provide a lens—from their perspective, the only useful lens—through which a believing person may come to understand the here and now.

On July 28, 2006, several weeks into the Israeli-Hezbollah conflict, Hassan Nasrallah's Muslim militants began firing a new and more powerful rocket, the Khaibar-1, deep into Israeli territory.[40] These Khaibar rockets, like the more frequently used Katyushas, had no specific target. Their objective was to kill as many Israeli civilians as possible. The name of the rocket meant nothing to most citizens of the West. However, it was rich with meaning for Muslim believers. Hezbollah had apparently renamed an Iranian-supplied Fajr-5 rocket in the hope of inspiring its fighters.[41]

The new name brought several desired mental associations, the most important being with the prophet Muhammad's victory over some Arabian Jews at the Battle of Khaibar. Just why this particular battle took place is something we will never know for sure. Prior to the religious, political, and military rise of Muhammad and his followers, there were several Jewish tribes in Arabia and these tribes were relatively wealthy.

Muhammad, at first, had considerable respect for the Jews and their traditions and (like the Protestant Martin Luther in a later era) expected them to convert in droves. This, however, did not happen, and during Muhammad's time in Medina, tensions grew between Muslims and the various Jewish tribes there. According to Muslim sources, one tribe, the Banu Nadir, was expelled from Medina because it broke a treaty with Muhammad. (We have no Jewish or third-party sources for any of this.) Another tribe, the Banu Qaynuda, was also expelled, in this case possibly because of an incident involving a Muslim woman's honor. (According to one story, a Jew apparently did something to reveal a Muslim woman's undergarments. Her male companion, in defense of her honor, killed the Jew. The other Jews then killed him, and, as a result of the escalating conflict, the Banu Qaynuda were forced to accept exile.)[42]

The most troubling incident, however, occurred in 627. It should be noted up front that while this event is part of the Muslim tradition and well known, the details come from sources considered to be of questionable reliability by some Muslim and Western scholars. It is not recounted in the Koran. According to the story, a Jewish tribe—the Banu Qurayza and other Jews associated with them—had made an alliance with Muhammad's pagan enemies from Mecca. The Jews in this story and others are sometimes portrayed as instigators of the pagans.[43] That they made common cause against the Muslims was perceived as especially egregious because it was in violation of their treaty obligations with the Muslims.

Soon after the battle (called the Battle of the Trench) started, the pagan Meccans under the command of Abu Sufyan were easily defeated by the Muslim armies. The Meccans retreated to avoid further losses, and, consequently, the Jews of Banu Qurayza—who never actually fought in the battle—were abandoned and demoralized. They, too, retreated.

Then the angel Jibril told Muhammad to wage battle against the

Banu Qurayza, which he did. Even without the help of Jibril, Muhammad perhaps realized that his military situation had improved greatly after the defeat of the Meccans. After a short siege, the Jewish tribe surrendered unconditionally. The question remained what to do with those who surrendered. Muhammad, apparently at the request of some allies of the Jews, agreed to accept the judgment of Sa'd ibn Mu'adh. Previously a friend of the Banu Qurayza, he had recently converted to Islam and had been seriously wounded in battle. For whatever reason, Sa'd ibn Mu'adh ruled that all the males of the Jewish tribe should be killed.[44] The women and children should be taken as prisoners.

According to one hadith (a saying attributed to Muhammad), the prophet then said: "O Sad! You have judged amongst them with (or similar to) the judgment of the King Allah."[45] According to the early Muslim historian Ibn Ishaq, the Muslims and Muhammad "struck off their heads in those trenches as they were brought out to him in batches. Among them was the enemy of Allah Huyayy b. Akhtab and Ka'b b. Asad their chief. There were 600 or 700 in all, though some put the figure as high as 800 or 900."[46] After the killings, the spoils were divided, and, in a manner not uncommon at the time (and, as we have seen, also approved in the Old Testament), the men took wives from among the women. Muhammad himself selected a woman, Rayhana, from among the widows of the slaughtered Jews.

The Battle of Khaibar took place soon afterward. Muhammad's motivation remains unclear, although the defeat of a potential enemy and the acquisition of spoils to fund his later victorious battle against the Meccans seems to have played a role. In any event, the Jews of Khaibar knew about the fate of the Banu Qurayza Jews and, therefore, fought hard. But they, too, were defeated. At a critical point in the battle, Ali—a great hero of the Shiite Muslims and, later, the person around whom the Shia sect started—killed a Jewish leader with so powerful a stroke of the sword that he split the helmet, the head, and the body of his opponent. He also lifted a door of the fortress to use as a shield; it was so heavy that it later took eight men to return it to its original location.

Thus, Khaibar acquires a special importance for Shiites fighting Jews. The defeated Jews of Khaibar fared much better than those of Banu Qurayza, however. They were allowed to continue to work the land of their oasis home, although this became the property of Islam. They simply had to turn over half of what they produced to the Muslims.

Muhammad again took a wife, this time Safiyya bint Huyayy, the young and beautiful wife of a slain Jewish leader and the daughter of another tortured, beheaded Jew. She soon converted to Islam (though another Jewish woman from her tribe tried to poison Muhammad in revenge). A few years later, the caliph Umar expelled the Jews from Khaibar and all Arabia, relying on a provision of the surrender that said that the terms could be revoked, if the Muslims so desired.

When Hezbollah named their missile Khaibar-1, therefore, it portrayed its battle against Jews and Israel as a continuation of one started in Muhammad's day. This position is not supported by Muhammad's own statements regarding the Jews or by hundreds of years of more subtle and accommodating Muslim thinking. But images from the prophet's day can be powerful ones. Hezbollah also wanted to remind militants that there was a time when Muslims easily won one battle after another against the Jews and Jews were forced to assume their rightful, subordinate place in the social order. For the Shiites in Hezbollah, Khaibar recalls one of the glorious and powerful exploits of their hero, Ali. And they may see little reason to question the morality of their own deeds in the present, since they have found, or think they have found, precedents in the days of the Holy Prophet. The single word *Khaibar* conveys so much to Muslim ears, all missed by the West. The Palestinian Sunni militant organization Hamas, similarly, has employed the Khaibar name in its slogan: "Khaibar, Khaibar, O Jews, [Muhammad's] Army will return."[47]

Koranic and early Islamic images are salient in the lives of many devout Muslims, including Muslim extremists. But the moderate devout may differ from the extremist devout by emphasizing different stories and drawing different lessons from them. Thus, when Osama bin Laden became a father of a girl shortly after the September 11 attacks, he named her Safia. Hamid Mir, his Pakistani biographer, asked why. According to Mir, bin Laden replied: "I gave her the name of Safia who killed a Jewish spy in the days of Holy Prophet [Muhammad], so that is why." The writer inquired about the little girl's age. Bin Laden answered: "Just one month. She will kill enemies of Islam like Safia of the Prophet's time."[48]

From the "Children's Corner" of an Islamic Web site, we learn the story of Safia bint Abdul Muttalib, presumably the namesake of bin Laden's infant daughter.[49] Of noble lineage, Safia was one of the first to join Muhammad's faith and, later, his army, serving mainly as a nurse and in other supporting capacities. At the age of sixty during the Battle of Uhud, when things weren't going so well for the Muslims, Safia dropped the water bag she was carrying, picked up a spear, and challenged the unbelievers.

Her greatest fame, however, comes from her deeds a bit later in the Battle of the Trench, the one that ended with the massacre of the Banu Qurayza Jews. Muhammad had secured the women and children of his group in a fort and, sensing that they would be safe, did not follow his usual practice of providing male guards. Safia noticed a Jewish man trying to gather information about the Muslim families at the fort and she understood this activity to be in violation of the Jews' pact not to harass the Muslims or ally with their enemies. She decided that the man was trying to determine whether there were any Muslim men at the fort. If he learned that the women were unprotected, he might use this information to the advantage of Muhammad's enemies. Possibly the opposing army, or their Jewish allies, might take the women as prisoners and, thereby, interfere with the Muslims' ability to focus on the battle. So Safia tied a bandana over her head and another cloth around her waist in the style of a warrior. She waited behind a door with a *lathi*, a type of club, and, when the suspicious man entered, she struck him on the head repeatedly. Then, she cut off his head and tossed it to the man's colleagues who were waiting for him to return. Thinking that there were indeed numerous male guards on duty, the Jewish men fled, and the women and children were then safe.

The historical accuracy of this tale is irrelevant. But it bears some similarity to other tales of heroic women, for example, the Old Testament story of Ya'el, who used a tent peg to slay an enemy general. Understood as a tale of female valor and taken in its historical context, the Safia story is perhaps a tad gory but poses no major moral problems. The difficulty is when the tale is used to indoctrinate children from birth with a mission to kill Jews and other infidels in the modern world.

It should be noted that the early Muslim treatment of the Jews was not so very different from the way winners treated losers in many parts of the world. Groups often went to war with no justification at all, or for the flimsiest of excuses. W. Montgomery Watt, a Western biographer of Muhammad, writes, regarding the Qurayza massacre, "It has to be remembered . . . that in the Arabia of that day when tribes were at war with one another or simply had no agreement, they had no obligations towards one another, not even of what we would call common decency. The enemy and the complete stranger had no rights whatsoever. When men refrained from killing and being cruel, it was not from any sense of duty towards a fellow-man but out of fear of possible retaliation by the next of kin."[50]

When Christian writers suggest that similar behaviors would not have followed from the teachings of Jesus, they are probably correct. But such teachings were essentially irrelevant. All evidence points to actual Christian armies behaving no better. Ancient imagery, even when it is used by Osama bin Laden, must be adapted to the modern world. He adapts the story of Safia in an inflammatory way. Others might use the same story to build respect for strong women who act decisively and on principle. Similarly, one might focus on Jews as the eternal enemies of Muslims or, benignly, on the need to confront those who behave unjustly. One might emphasize the appropriateness of brutal methods in warfare or, more positively, the need to protect children from harm.

WHAT TO DO WITH INFIDELS

Ask believers of any faith to identify their most important belief and you will generally be led to a point of theology. Jews might tell you the contents of the *Shema* prayer, "Hear O Israel, the Lord our God is one," or possibly list the Ten Commandments. Christians of various stripes will recount different points of dogma, sometimes about the Resurrection, the Trinitarian nature of God, or the importance of faith as the path to salvation. Muslims may explain the *Shahada*: "There is no god but God, and [Muhammad] is his Prophet," or they may tell you about the "Five Pillars of Islam," adding to the *Shahada* the five daily prayers, fasting during Ramadan, giving alms, and taking the pilgrimage to Mecca at least once in a lifetime.

Probably somewhat fewer believers would identify as the central tenet of their religion an ethical directive like the Golden Rule in one of its various forms, or some other ethical precept. But almost no believers will point to the one area that matters most critically with regard to the propagation and development of religious extremism and evil, namely, how a faith and its sacred texts treat those who do *not* believe.

The tendency to berate, reject, stigmatize, or even dehumanize nonbelievers or incorrect believers (or some of them) can be extremely dangerous. Scripturally based religions often lead believers to conclude that their own way comes from God, directly or by divine inspiration, and that other ways do not. Some believers even conclude that different faiths have satanic roots. The Abrahamic faiths, and most others, include teachings about the value of charity, hospitality, goodwill, respect, and other virtues. But it must be determined to whom such principles of behavior apply.

On the face of it, the Golden Rule, as generally formulated, runs counter to human nature. In fact, religions that preach universal application, in practice, may use the virtues sparingly and principally for in-groups. Others limit the application of the virtues in theory but use them more widely. There is, as far as I can tell, no powerful correlation between what the text and faith preach and how the believers conduct their lives, though this is not something I can readily prove. When one thinks about all the evil that has occurred in the name of religion, one might conclude that the most workable ethical formulations would not call for loving one's enemy or spreading love throughout the world. Similarly, they would not require having absolutely equal emotional reactions to the suffering of all groups, or absolutely equal desires to bestow charity on everyone around the world. Emotions don't seem to work that way. In any event, "Do unto others as you would have them do unto you" or even "Live and let live" would seem a more reachable goals than "Love thy neighbor (and everyone else) as thyself."

In assessing the way various religions approach nonbelievers, we might ask several key questions. Is there a sanctioned method for those outside the faith to lead a righteous life? Is failure to convert and see the light viewed as inherently sinful? Are all, or most, nonbelievers destined for eternal damnation? How should nonbelievers be treated when they are in the minority?

Special concerns arise when one or more groups of nonbelievers are portrayed negatively by the founding narrative of the faith. When this is the case, it becomes necessary to determine whether subsequent interpretation extends the tarnish to all (or some) members of the offending group in subsequent generations. Big problems also arise when a faith requires nonbelievers to follow some of its customs, rituals, and prohibitions. The Danish cartoon controversy is one dramatic example.

In itself, the missionary impulse is natural not only to some religious faiths but also to many secular belief systems. There is, after all, nothing inherently nefarious in trying to spread what one believes to be the truth. One might, to the contrary, worry about those who are not willing to share the way. But when this missionary impulse becomes very powerful, it can cross the line into harassment of nonbelievers, diminishing tolerance, and reducing any tendency to "live and let live." Moreover, an intense focus on acquiring new believers can create a sense that nonbelievers are to be valued and tolerated only until they make it crystal clear that they are not interested in conversion.

Judaism, Christianity, and Islam encompass huge traditions, and it is impossible to identify any one approach to nonbelievers that has been applied across time and place. Individuals within each tradition have run the gamut from complete tolerance to utter cruelty. However, it is possible to examine what some of the religious traditions say about the treatment of infidels.

Although conversion to Judaism is possible, Jews do not actively seek to convert nonbelievers and never have sought to do so. Instead, traditional Jews offer a clear pathway for non-Jews to follow if they wish to be righteous and procure a place in the world to come. Non-Jews must adhere to the biblical Noahide laws.[51] They must not murder, steal, or eat a limb torn from a living animal. They must refrain from certain sexual activities, including incest, adultery, homosexuality, and bestiality. They must not deny God through idolatry or commit blasphemy, though idolatry, for example. (There does not appear to be a specific prohibition against atheism, perhaps because it was not a common stance.) Another requirement is for nonbelievers to set up fair courts of justice. But if non-Jews adhere to the Noahide rules, they are—at least in principle—deemed just as righteous as religiously observant Jews. The main theoretical difference between Jews and non-Jews is that Jews must follow many more requirements in order to be deemed righteous. For this reason, and no doubt others, many rabbis have felt a duty to dissuade potential converts.

The real debate in traditional Judaism concerns just which individuals and non-Jewish faiths fit the bill. A strict adherent of Islam would probably fit well. There is more disagreement about whether the belief of some Christians in a Trinitarian conception of God is consistent with the Noahide rules. It is if it means three senses of one God but not if it is a challenge to monotheism. Some debate also arises with regard to Hinduism.[52]

In general, biblical Judaism called for harsh treatment of idolaters. The book of Deuteronomy (17:2–8) conveys the general approach. If any Israelite is found to have broken the covenant by doing evil and worshiped and served other Gods—for example, the sun and the moon—"thou shalt stone them with stones, that they die." To be sure, there must be at least a couple of witnesses, but death is the consequence of an Israelite going over to the service of idols. However, there is a progressive take on this seemingly barbaric provision. The Bible, apparently, is concerned with abolishing the rituals of child sacrifice and bestiality that typically accompanied much idolatry in those days. Though the words do not so specify, some modern interpreters have suggested that there was far less emphasis on the persistence of polytheism as an intellectual choice.[53] In this sense, the harshness toward idolaters might be seen, in part, as a historical step toward improved human rights. In effect, it was a method of ending some ancient human rights abuses.

Most Jews think of themselves as God's chosen people, a belief that has perhaps aggravated hostility toward them over the millennia. For example, in 1973, following the Yom Kippur War, the Soviet Union's ambassador to the United Nations charged that "[t]he Zionists have come forward with the theory of the Chosen People, an absurd ideology. That is religious racism."[54] There isn't a theological basis for this accusation. Jews think of themselves as chosen in the sense that God has revealed his word to them first and they have been selected to make God known to the world, not by proselytization but by example. The doctrine does not include any component of greater rights for Jews and, in fact, imposes a large number of additional requirements. Still, Mordecai Kaplan—the founder of Reconstructionist Judaism—has dropped the concept altogether. He judged it too likely to lend itself to misinterpretation and also too ethnocentric for the contemporary world, in that it implied God might play favorites.

For many centuries, until the founding of Israel, Jews were always the minority wherever they lived, and usually the persecuted minority. Thus, there were few opportunities for taking hostile action against nonbelievers, and virtually none was contemplated. In Israel, despite years of conflict, the Jewish state has made major efforts to respect the religious privileges of Christians and Muslims as, for example, in the preservation of Muslim control over the Temple Mount, Judaism's holiest spot.[55] Though Israel's record with regard to the rights of other faiths is imperfect, it is far better than that of other states in the region.

In modern times, and even before, Jews have not often taken violent actions against "idolaters" and "blasphemers" within the faith; I don't know of any recent examples.

Yet traditional Judaism, in part as defensive measures in dangerous times and in part out of ethnocentrism, developed a system of laws that treated non-Jews differently than Jews. The Schulchan Aruch is a compilation of Jewish laws and customs that dates back hundreds of years but is considered current by many very observant Jews. The book includes thousands of details telling the believer how to live the religiously observant life; some of these rulings are ethical but most concern the proper implementation of rituals. Few Jews, if any, observe all the rules, but observant Orthodox Jews aspire to do as much as they can. Among the rulings, one finds many that distinguish between Jews and non-Jews. For example,

- "If a Jew is in possession of evidence in favor of a non-Jew who has a lawsuit with another Jew in a non-Jewish court, then if by his testimony, he will cause his fellow Jew to become liable to a larger sum than he would be in a Jewish court, he is not allowed to testify. Otherwise, he may testify. If the non-Jew had arranged with the Jew that he would testify in his behalf, and if he should not do so, the name of God will be desecrated (by the Jew's breach of faith), he must give his evidence under all circumstances."[56]
- "If one is accompanied by his wife, he may . . . be alone with another woman, because his wife watches him. However, a Jewess, must not be alone with a non-Jew, even if his wife is present; even if there are many non-Jews with their wives, she must not be alone with them."[57]

While these rulings provide evidence that Jewish religious law dealt very differently with Jews and non-Jews, in historical context they likely were efforts to arrive at fair solutions in communities that themselves were frequently unjust by modern standards and often inhumanely hostile to the Jewish community.

The Schulchan Aruch, however, dealt harshly with those who left the faith. It states: "All those who deviate from the community by casting off the yoke of precepts, severing their bonds with the people of Israel as regards the observance of the Divine Commands, and are in a class by themselves; also apostates, informers, and heretics—for all these the rules . . . of mourners shall not be observed. Their brothers and other next of kin should dress in white, eat, drink, and rejoice that the enemies of the Almighty have perished."[58] In effect, if you quit the club, the club throws you out—unceremoniously. You are ostracized when alive and not mourned upon death. But beyond that, there were seldom any violent punishments that ensued.

To the extent that the above rules and views are invoked nowadays, it is almost always by the Orthodox. Still, within that approach to Judaism, there have been countless attempts to improve interreligious relations. For the vast majority of Reform, Conservative, and Reconstructionist Jews, the sacred religious texts are merely inspirational and respected guidelines, perhaps divinely inspired but viewed mainly as products of a vastly different historical context and consciousness. For these Jews, the pursuit of social justice, respect for fair-minded people in all religions, and the contemporary tenets of equality have become, in effect, a substitute for (or, as they might say, a fulfillment of) the traditional approach. An important group of Reform rabbis have agreed, for example, on the following as part of the guiding principles of Reform Judaism: "In Judaism religion and morality blend into an indissoluble unity. Seeking God means to strive after holiness, righteousness and goodness. The love of God is incomplete without the love of one's fellowmen. Judaism emphasizes kinship of the human race, the sanctity and worth of human life and personality and the right of the individual to freedom and to the pursuit of his chosen vocation. Justice to all, irrespective of race, sect or class is the inalienable right and the inescapable obligation of all. The state and organized government exist to further these ends."[59] How exactly this perspective emerged from the Bible and classical Jewish texts is a complex tale but arguably not a fabricated one. The existence of revised religious ethics in Judaism and other faiths should give pause to those who argue that all religion is essentially part of the problem.

Christian scripture has a very different way of thinking about the nonbeliever. In the Gospel according to John (14:6), Jesus announces: "I am the way and the truth and the life. No one comes to the Father except through me." Earlier in that Gospel (3:3), he explains the consequences of unbelief to Nicodemus, a member of the Jewish ruling council at the time: "No one can see the kingdom of God unless he is born again." A few verses later, Jesus adds a bit more detail, saying: "For God so loved the world that he gave his one and only Son, that whoever believes in him shall not perish but have eternal life. For God did not send his Son into the world to condemn the world, but to save the world through him. Whoever believes in him is not condemned, but whoever does not believe stands condemned already because he has not believed in the name of God's one and only Son." This passage, taken literally, seems to suggest that the only way to avoid hellfire is to accept Christ and his path, a message confirmed in Acts (4:12). Here, Peter says: "Salvation is found in no one else, for there is no other name under heaven given to men by which we must be saved."

If God did in fact inspire these lines, the divine message would seem clear. Only Christians go to heaven, and everyone else is damned eternally. This is the favored reading of most Christian fundamentalists, and—understandably—an unequaled tool in the hands of the evangelist. Yet there are many lines of text in the New Testament that could be used to mitigate this verdict, or perhaps to construct an altogether different message.

However, Ajith Fernando, a Christian who lives and works among many non-Christians in Sri Lanka, attempts to justify in modern terms a strict reading of the texts on non-Christians. He explains the perspective of the biblical Christian as he sees it: "The biblical Christian says, 'We are not headed in the same direction. Some of our practices may be similar. We may learn from each other, but there is a sense in which we cannot live harmoniously with each other. We seek to bring all who are outside of a relationship with Christ into such a relationship, and that necessitates the forsaking of their former religions.'"[60] He suggests that the good features in other religions are partly bad, because these features may lead potential Christians to resist efforts at their conversion.

Roman Catholics started with a similar doctrine: *Extra Ecclesiam Nulla Salus*, meaning "there is no salvation outside the Church." When first formulated, the doctrine was probably directed mainly at Christian heretics and schismatics, not at unbelievers. After Christianity became the state religion of the Roman Empire, however, St. Augustine "stressed that those who had heard the message of the Gospel but had not become Christians were guilty because of their rejection of the Gospel message, and their salvation could be found only in the Church. . . . Thus, the axiom *Extra Ecclesiam Nulla Salus* began to apply to anyone who was outside the Church such as pagans and Jews. Much later Muslims, referred to as Turks, were added to the list."[61] In 1302, in the papal bull *Unam Sanctam*, Pope Boniface VIII made it tougher still to gain salvation, adding the requirement that one must acknowledge papal authority. When, in the era of exploration, Europeans encountered huge masses who had never even heard of Jesus, Catholics added the proviso that those who are ignorant of the true religion would not be held strictly accountable by God on that account.

Things changed dramatically in the 1960s as a consequence of the Second Vatican Council. The document *Nostra Aetate* announced: "The Catholic Church rejects nothing of what is true and holy in . . . [other] religions. She looks with sincere respect upon those ways of conduct and of life, those rules and teachings which, though differing in many particulars from what she holds and sets forth, nevertheless often reflects a ray of that truth which enlightens all men."[62] The church continues to maintain that its way is *the* way. But the spirit of the encounter with non-Christians has been modified substantially, to the point where the following advice is offered to "sons of the Church" to "prudently and lovingly, through dialogue and collaboration with the followers of other religions, and in witness of Christian faith and life, acknowledge, preserve and promote the spiritual and moral goods found among these men, as well as the values in their society and culture."[63] This liberalization of church attitudes toward those outside the faith has been interpreted differently by various theologians, but there can be no denying that its impact has been real.

Many non-Catholic Christian churches have made similar changes in their approach to nonbelievers. They have, in effect, adopted the position of the influential Catholic theologian Karl Rahner, who maintained that non-Christians may find Christ through their own faiths without even knowing it. Such people might, according to this view, be seen as "anonymous Christians."[64] Some Christians go even further than Rahner, holding that all religions are equally valid ways of getting to the truth, or that different religions take believers to equally important but different truths.[65] Even Billy Graham, a firebrand fundamentalist for decades, has found a way to include nonbelievers. Asked by *Newsweek* magazine whether good Jews, Muslims, Hindus, Buddhists, or secular people would be excluded from heaven, he said: "Those are decisions only the Lord will make. It would be foolish for me to speculate who will be there and who won't . . . I don't want to speculate about that. I believe the love of God is absolute. He said he gave his son for the whole world, and I think he loves everybody regardless of what label they have." But then his spokesman adds a bit of qualification, noting that, for more than six decades, "Mr. Graham has faithfully proclaimed the Bible's Gospel message that Jesus is the only way to Heaven." And then, the spokesman seems to change direction, adding that salvation is God's work and "only he knows what is in each human heart."[66]

Nearly all students of antisemitism have spoken of its roots in Christianity. In fact, documentation of Christian theological hostility to the Jews could fill many volumes.[67] For example, St. Thomas Aquinas, one of the most thoughtful Christian theologians of all time, wrote: "It is true, as the laws declare, that in consequence of their sin [of rejecting and crucifying Jesus] the Jews were destined to perpetual servitude, so that sovereigns of states may treat Jewish goods as their own property."[68] In fact, Christian antisemitism was so extreme and so widespread that Adolf Hitler could tell a Catholic bishop in 1933: "As for the Jews, I am just carrying on with the same policy which the Catholic Church had adopted for 1500 years." Two recent historians conclude with some justification that "[n]o other religious tradition has condemned a people as the murderers of its god, a unique accusation that has resulted in a unique history of hatred, fear, and persecution. When it came to the Jews, the central doctrine of Christianity, that Jesus was providentially sent into the world to atone by his death for mankind's sins, was obscured."[69]

Yet even among those who recognize the horrific consequences of Christian anti-Judaism, there is considerable debate about how much the New Testament itself is responsible. Also, some hostility toward the Jews in the Jesus story may have been written into the scripture. This may have been an effort to differentiate Christians from Jews in the eyes of the Roman government. After the destruction of the Second Jewish Temple in 70 CE, and the suppression of the Bar Kochba revolt decades later, the Romans had come to think of Jews as traitors, radicals, and enemies of the state. Christians wanted to ensure that they could spread their faith without being regarded as just another sect of this despised group. According to anthropologist Marvin Harris and others, the focus on Jesus as a pacifist who wanted to render unto Caesar the things that were Caesar's may have had a similar origin.[70] The point was to avoid arousing too much Roman anger, something that might impede the growth of the new religious sect.

For whatever reasons, the version of the Jesus story enshrined in the New Testament portrays Jews as godless and heartless, knowing the right thing but not doing it. They are hypocrites and picayune. In the Gospel according to Matthew (27:25), the Roman Pontius Pilate says: "I am innocent of this man's blood. . . . It is your responsibility." And, as if on cue, the Jewish crowd responds: "Let his blood be on us and on our children." Still, many fair-minded critics, including Professor Bart Ehrman, conclude that Matthew and the other gospels fall short of antisemitism in that they direct negativity toward specific Jewish leaders viewed as corrupt.[71] Ehrman is somewhat more critical of the treatment of the Jews in the book of Hebrews. This book argues in no uncertain terms that Judaism is in many ways inferior to Christianity and, in so doing, treats many aspects of the parent faith disparagingly. Ehrman opines that Hebrews stands "only at the beginning of a trajectory of thought that leads to [antisemitism]."[72] The book does not urge taking action against the Jews, and most of the hatred came later.

But historians Perry and Schweitzer offer a more scathing assessment of Christian scripture, noting that

> [n]umerous . . . examples could be cited of how New Testament images of the Jew—the Jew as deicide, the Jew as satanic agent, the Jew as antichrist, the Jew as liar and deceiver, the Wandering Jew—persist down the centuries and resonate in contemporary antisemitism. It is all a reprise of the cycle of criminal guilt against the divine and of inevitable revenge and punishment for the perpetrators. The New Testament teaches a high morality and contains a message of salvation that continues to inspire. But judging from the role it has played in Jewish history, it needs to be said . . . that the New Testament is the most dangerous antisemitic tract in human history.[73]

It is very hard to get clear, unbiased information on how believers of any of the religions think, feel, and act toward unbelievers, as this is the most sensitive of topics. But in the current political environment, it is most difficult to get an objective reading on Islamic views and behaviors toward those outside the faith.

Certainly the Koran contains many passages about unbelievers and violence that seem to conflict rather sharply with modern norms of tolerance:

- "Allah is the enemy to those who reject Faith. We have sent down to thee Manifest Signs; And none reject them But those who are perverse" (2:98–99).[74]
- "Those who reject the Faith, And die rejecting—On them is Allah's curse, And the curse of angels, And of all mankind" (2:161).

- "And believe no one Unless he follows Your religion" (3:73).
- "Fighting is prescribed Upon you, and ye dislike it. But it is possible That ye dislike a thing Which is good for you, And that ye love a thing Which is bad for you. But Allah knoweth, and ye know not" (2:216).
- "Those who reject Faith—Neither their possessions Nor their (numerous) progeny Will avail them aught Against Allah; they are themselves But fuel for the Fire" (3:10).
- "O ye who believe! What Is the matter with you, That when ye are asked To go forth in the Cause of Allah, Ye cling heavily to the earth? Do ye prefer the life Of this world to the Hereafter? But little is the comfort Of this life, as compared With the Hereafter. Unless ye go forth, he will punish you With a grievous penalty, And put others in your place" (9:38–39).

After listing some of these (in a different translation), and dozens more similar verses, Sam Harris, author of *The End of Faith*, concludes: "On almost every page, [the Koran] . . . instructs observant Muslims to despise nonbelievers. On almost every page, it prepares the ground for religious conflict. Anyone who can read passages like those quoted above and still not see a link between Muslim faith and Muslim violence should probably consult a neurologist."[75] Often the hadiths are even less consistent with current norms of human rights; one, for example, says: "Whoever changes his religion [from Islam], kill him." Another hadith announces: "Jihad is your duty under any ruler, be he godly or wicked." Yet another states: "He who dies without having taken part in a campaign dies in a kind of unbelief."[76] When the lines are examined together, a clear picture does indeed emerge. Still, I think Harris overstates his case.[77]

As always in matters of scripture, such verses might, in theory, be interpreted in ways that square better with prevailing social norms in the West. Harris uses the following translation of sura 5, verse 57: "Believers, do not seek the friendship of the infidels, and those who were given the Book before you, who have made of your religion a jest and a pastime."[78] Another translation says: "O ye who believe! Take not for friends and protectors those Who take your religion For a mockery or sport—Whether among those Who received the Scripture Before you, or among those who reject Faith."[79] I don't know which translation is more accurate, but the second suggests a somewhat more progressive interpretation. Don't take as a friend or protector someone who makes fun of your religion. That may be reasonable advice. More generally, it is worth remembering that the content of the Koran did not prevent Muslim political philosophers from penning works of political and moral philosophy that are still well regarded. Inflammatory or not, the words themselves were transformed into a fairly reasonable foundation for a civilization for quite some time, at least when viewed against the backdrop of what was occurring elsewhere during the same eras. During the many years when Islam ruled a large portion of the world, scripture was reconciled with progressive as well as regressive outlooks.

There are many passages in the Koran that might (or might not) provide a foundation for the promotion for moderate religious worldviews. Consider the following:

- "O ye who believe! Stand out firmly For justice, as witnesses to Allah, even as against yourselves, or your parents, Or your kin, and whether It be (against) rich or poor: For Allah can best protect both. Follow not the lusts (Of your hearts), lest ye Swerve, and if ye Distort (justice) or decline to do justice, verily Allah is well-acquainted With all that ye do" (4:135).
- "Let there be no compulsion in religion: Truth stands out Clear from Error: whoever Rejects Evil and believes in Allah hath grasped The most trustworthy Handhold, that never breaks" (2:256).
- "Nor would thy Lord be The One to destroy Communities for a single wrongdoing If its members were likely to mend. If the Lord had so willed, He could have made mankind One people: but they Will not cease to dispute" (11:117–18).

- "Would that you knew what the Height is! It is the freeing of a bondsman; the feeding, in the day of famine, of an orphaned relation or a needy man in distress" (90:12–16).[80]
- "Fight in the cause of Allah Those who fight you, But do not transgress limits; For Allah loveth not transgressors" (2:190).
- "That was why We laid it down for the Israelites that whoever killed a human being, except as a punishment for murder or other wicked crimes, should be looked upon as though he had killed all mankind; and whoever saved a human life should be regarded as though he had saved all mankind" (5:32).[81]

Such verses may create problems for intellectually honest extremists who must determine how to reconcile them with their outlook.

The Koran—like the Old and New Testaments—places women in a subordinate position. For example, it says: "Men have authority over women because Allah has made the one superior to the others, and because they spend their wealth to maintain them. Good women are obedient" (4:34).[82] It also condones slavery and is out of step with some other modern Western perspectives on social relationships, but no more so than the Old and New Testaments. Similarly, there has been much discussion in recent years about whether Islam is fundamentally incompatible with modern, constitutional, democratic institutions. However, it is worth pointing out that Judaism and Christianity, as manifested in their scriptures and much later theology, also provide, at most, only the flimsiest of bases for that which we observe in Western political systems. These were largely secular developments.

There is a major difference between scriptural Christianity and Islam that requires attention. As historian Bernard Lewis has pointed out, Muhammad was his own Constantine,[83] whereas Abraham never led any large polity and Moses never made it to the promised land. The religion of Jesus and his followers developed, for several centuries, as a faith of the downtrodden. Only when Constantine started to move Rome in the direction of Christianity did it become necessary to develop a political theory of leadership. Jesus himself played a much smaller role in the development of Christian civilization than did Muhammad in the development of the Islam world. This is why one author's ranking of the most influential people in history put Muhammad first, ahead of Jesus (who was third).[84]

Muhammad achieved great political and military success in his lifetime. As a result, he had to reconcile his ethical teachings with the demands of war and governance. This tension is reflected often in the Koran and the hadiths.

Muhammad was put on a pedestal by believers. As Professor Menahem Milson explains, "Modern-day Islamists regard the days of the Prophet [Muhammad] and of his immediate successors—the era of Islam's far-reaching conquests—to be the exemplary era in Islam and the source of their inspiration. Indeed, even in mainstream Islam all Muslims are required to follow the tradition of the Prophet and to seek guidance in the conduct of his companions and successors."[85] But along with Muhammad the religious teacher, we have Muhammad the seventh-century military and political leader who had to face situations never encountered by Jesus, Abraham, and Moses. Christians in power later addressed the tension between religious beliefs on the one hand and political and military requirements on the other. They often made decisions that look inhumane in retrospect. But such decisions are not recorded in the New Testament because Jesus and his early followers had long since died. It is often said that Islam had to encourage militaristic values in order to spread as far as it did. Christianity spread equally far—also not entirely because of the appeal of the values expressed in the Sermon on the Mount. Meek religions tend to become forgotten religions.

Bernard Lewis explains a core difference between Christianity and Islam that resulted from circumstances surrounding the founding of the two faiths:

> In classical Islam, there was no distinction between Church and state. In Christendom the existence of two authorities goes back to the founder, who enjoined followers to render unto Caesar the things

> which are Caesar's and to God the things which are God's. Throughout the history of Christendom there have been two powers: God and Caesar, represented in this world by *sacerdotium* and *regnum*, or, in modern terms, church and state. They may be associated, they may be separated; they may be in harmony, they may be in conflict; one may dominate, the other may dominate; one may interfere, the other may protest. . . . But always there are two, the spiritual and the temporal powers, each with its own laws and jurisdictions, its own structure and hierarchy. In pre-Westernized Islam, there were not two powers but one, and the question of separation, therefore, could not arise.[86]

Those who wish to build constitutional democracies in the modern world have had to address this issue. Some have found in Islam sufficient flexibility to permit progress in the direction of constitutional democracy; others have not.[87]

As we have already seen, many present-day adherents of Islam are deeply antisemitic. As I have argued elsewhere, the anti-Jewish imagery that prevails in many parts of the Muslim, especially Arab Muslim, world, compares in rancor and extremity to the rantings of *Der Sturmer* and other Nazi periodicals. We are talking about a hatred that—given the means—in all likelihood would not pause before taking a genocidal turn. Clearly, this antisemitism has been aggravated by the Arab-Israeli conflict, but it cannot be attributed entirely to that conflict. There was first the fertile ground of religious belief in which it could thrive.

Islam's historical contribution to contemporary antisemitism is more complex than is generally recognized.[88] Two things can be said with confidence about the centuries in which Jews lived under Muslim domination in many lands. First, Jews generally fared better under Islam than under Christianity. Second, this is not saying much, as Muslim anti-Jewish prejudice and discrimination was often very unpleasant. It is a myth to say that Jews were treated well under Islam.

Bernard Lewis explains that "[i]t was not until comparatively modern times that the idea was imported from Europe that the Jews are a separate race, with evil and enduring racial characteristics"[89] and that "[w]ith rare exceptions, where hostile stereotypes of the Jew existed in the Islamic tradition, they tended to be contemptuous and dismissive, rather than suspicious and obsessive."[90] The situation of the Jews "was never as bad as in Christendom at its worst, nor as good as in Christendom at its best."[91]

Indeed, the Islamic religious tradition provides the present-day antisemite with abundant source material, starting with Muhammad's earliest interactions with the Jews in Arabia. The Koran picks up a theme from Christian antisemitism; addressing the Jews, it states: "We gave Jesus the son of Mary veritable signs and strengthened him with the Holy Spirit. Will you then scorn each apostle whose message does not suit your fancies, charging some with imposture and slaying others? They say: 'Our hearts are sealed.' But Allah has cursed them for their unbelief. They have but little faith. And now that a Book confirming their own has come to them from Allah, they deny it, although they know it to be the truth. . . . Evil is that for which they have bartered away their souls" (2:87–89).[92] The passage then poses a pointed query to the Jews: "Why did you kill the prophets of Allah, if you are true believers?" (2:91). The text then provides "proof" that the Jews know they are wrong, suggesting that if their claim were true, they would long for death and the rewards it brings. Yet the Jews "will never long for death, because of what they did; for Allah knows the evil-doers. Indeed, you will find that they love this life more than other men; more than the pagans do. Each of them would willingly live a thousand years" (2:94–96). To modern Western ears, this is an odd insult. Yet it sent a very clear message to early believers and, no doubt, continues to resonate in the thoughts and feelings of many of those who provide a more current rationale for their animosity toward Jews and Israel.

The Koran is filled with statements that might be interpreted as anti-Jewish, even though such statements coexist with more positive assessments. More generally, Islamic law assigned a protected, but clearly subordinate, *dhimmi* status to Jews and Christians—protected because they were "peoples of the Book" and subordinate because they failed to accept the true faith.[93]

These protections did not in theory apply to members of other faiths, though, at some times, Hindus and others were treated as "peoples of the Book."

One goal of Islamic law was to convey clearly that Jews and Christians were inferior, thereby pressuring the *dhimmis* to convert and warding off any thoughts believers might have of leaving the faith. Humiliation and belittlement were considered suitable means of achieving this goal much, though not all, of the time. Sometimes distinctive dress was required. Nearly always, the Jew or Christian was expected to acknowledge the superiority of the Muslim in personal interactions. Synagogues and churches generally were not to be destroyed, but there were limitations of construction and repairs. Any criticisms of Islam or Muhammad were punishable by death. So were efforts to convert Muslims. Many laws did not apply if Muslims were the perpetrators and Jews or Christians were the victims. Despite the laws of *dhimma*, neither Jews nor Christians were allowed to live in Arabia, and to this day, the laws apply. Over the hundreds of years, there were good times and there were bad times. But there was never equality or anything approaching it.

Thus, the roots of contemporary Muslim Jew-hatred (and hostility to Christianity) are deep, and, as in the case of Christian antisemitism, part of the blame belongs to the religious tradition, including the sacred books. For example, to energize their soldiers prior to the 1973 Yom Kippur War, Egyptian leaders distributed brochures citing Koranic passages such as the following: "Cursed were the children of Israel. Surely ye will find that of all men the most hostile to the believers were the Jews and the Polytheists."[94] Similarly, the mufti of Lebanon told a primed and understanding audience in 1968 that Jews "were the most atrocious enemies of Islam and the Moslems in the age of our prophet" and that their leaders were conceited, stubborn, wicked, and megalomaniacal.[95]

Still, on the whole, the Christian religious tradition provided a stronger foundation than the Islamic one for antisemitic beliefs. Partly, this is because Muslims quickly achieved a monumental victory over the Jews as well as many other tribes in and around Arabia. Thus, the Jews emerge from the Koranic tale as wrongheaded losers and unworthy rivals. As such, they were generally incapable of arousing the same level of anger that flowed from the Christian charge of deicide. Muslims also tell of Jews conspiring to kill Jesus, whom they honor as a prophet. But in the Muslim version, the Jews are unsuccessful in their efforts. Other aspects of early Christian history and theology were also more favorable to the development of an obsessive, anti-Jewish hostility.[96]

Thus, it is important to avoid the "ancient animosities" explanation that so often has clouded understanding of contemporary conflicts (e.g., Bosnia and Rwanda).[97] Such explanations tell little about how distant events and traditions become psychologically relevant and meaningful for individuals and cultures. The thirteen-hundred-year-old doctrine of jihad; the division of the world into the House of Islam and the House of War; the emphasis on military force in spreading the faith; the harsh punishments for apostasy; the required subjugation of Jews and Christians; and Koranic anti-Jewish imagery have all, at times, pushed believers toward extremism and hatred. However, on other occasions, such concepts have been interpreted and reinterpreted in ways that have permitted and advanced moderation and tolerance.[98] The culprit therefore is not Islam but rather the interpretations of Islam offered by militants, especially as they have developed in recent years.[99]

INTERPRETATION AND ITS DISCONTENTS

What happens to babies who die without baptism? Until recently, this was the sort of easy question generations of Catholic schoolchildren dreamed about seeing on a test. The church position, clear for centuries, had been articulated many times. For example, Pope Pius X in 1905 said: "Children who die without baptism go into limbo, where they do not enjoy God, but they do not suffer either."[100] The theory was that as a consequence of original sin, infants could not get through the doors of heaven, but neither would a merciful God send them to hell; hence, a compromise solution. Limbo was better than hell.

But now limbo may be abandoned by the church. No one suggests that reality has changed or that new evidence can be brought to bear on the matter. But in response to a request by the late Pope John Paul II, a group of thirty top theologians were convened at the Vatican in 2005 to reconsider the existence of limbo (officially called the Limbo of the Babies). Apparently, the notion was never official church doctrine and in recent years has grown unpopular due to its harshness and weak theological base. Though it did not seem to disturb generations of priests in earlier centuries, no sacred scripture refers to limbo; it was, in essence, a product of gradual philosophical deduction by the likes of St. Augustine, St. Thomas Aquinas, and others. And nowadays, it gets in the way of winning converts, especially in places where infant mortality is high. It is harder to sell a religion that tells bereaved mothers that their babies definitely will not be going to heaven. Better to leave some possibility of a good outcome or, at least, to say that their fate is unknown.

If limbo does disappear, and many expect it will, the new theology will bear witness to the Catholic Church's ability to change important components of its theology. But, as many have pointed out, the church often lumbers like a giant, changing over centuries, rather than months or even years. However, the current pope, Benedict XVI, two decades ago when he was a cardinal, said, "Limbo has never been a definitive truth of the faith. . . . Personally, I would let it drop, since it has always been only a theological hypothesis."[101] So it looks like even the world's most stable religious institution is about to change its views on how humans relate to eternity, at least partly in response to market pressures and changing public sensibilities. As James J. O'Donnell, the provost of Georgetown University, explains, the church is essentially saying: "Let's progress back to ignorance rather than remain mired in assertion that brings with it perhaps more complication and more trouble than it is worth."[102]

The signs in front of churches may proclaim: "Under the same management for 2,000 years." But, at least in the earthly domain, this statement is patently untrue. And with new managers come new policies. Rituals, core theologies, scriptural interpretations, and ethical rules change in every faith, sometimes dramatically. It is even fair to say that the believers from one era might feel very uncomfortable were they able to visit members of their own religion in another era. While those from the most liberal and modern sects would perhaps notice differences, even the conservative adherents would often be shocked. Imagine, for example, a conversation on how to be a good Jew among six strictly observant Jews, one from the early days of the prophets, one from the Rabbinic period around the time of Jesus, one from Spain in the twelfth century, one from Poland in the seventeenth century, one from Morocco in the early twentieth century, and one from New York today. While they certainly could find a few points of agreement, I suspect the discussion would rapidly degenerate into a series of disputes. The real question is not whether religions change but rather how they change and by which procedures and mechanisms.

These procedures and mechanisms depend on the attitude one adopts toward scripture, religious laws, and sacred traditions. Those who believe in the literal truth of scripture and the notion that sacred texts come word for word from God would seem to have the toughest time adapting their faith to current circumstances and values. It has been suggested that "[t]he doors leading out of scriptural literalism do not open from the inside." Still, some psychologists of religion have written that it is a "stereotype to think that fundamentalism has a closed system of thought, consensually held and forever fixed. . . . [N]othing is more variable than the perception of absolute truth! . . . Fundamentalists easily separate when they disagree on what their sacred text says, indicating that, like all who seek to understand, they are open to change and interpretation."[103] Such believers justify modifications as emanating from the scripture, but they are, despite their protestations to the contrary, influenced by outside forces.

Sam Harris may be missing the point, partly, when he writes:

"[C]oncessions to modernity do not in the least suggest that faith is compatible with reason, or that our religious traditions are in principle open to new learning: it is just that the utility of ignoring (or 'reinterpreting') certain articles of faith is now overwhelming."[104] By responding to the need for "utility," however, believers are demonstrating a bit of rationality and capacity for new learning. There may be a basis for some hope in the capacity of the faithful to reinterpret scriptures in the interest of utility and other nonscriptural arguments.

Religious people may also view their texts as inspired by God but written in a manner appropriate for an earlier historical epoch. They may even see scripture primarily as a source of religious stories that ought not to be judged by whether or not they are objectively true. A good story should ring true and make a good point, effectively and accessibly. A scriptural story might aim to instruct a person on how to live a good life or it might provide them with some psychological comfort. And if a story does not achieve its goals, it may be abandoned or ignored.[105] Scripture and the religious tradition for these believers still serve as authorities, but not as the only authorities. The messages they contain are viewed as "tentative, contingent, and continually susceptible to change."[106] In the eyes of the fundamentalist, such tremendous flexibility indicates that religion has surrendered its greatest strength, purpose, and usefulness. But they, too, will sometimes change when the need becomes sufficiently pressing.

Religions have adopted a great variety of procedures for interpretation and modification. There is sometimes a tendency among nonbelievers to view the most flexible traditions as best. This view, however, misses the point that many recent instances of religious extremism have been precisely the consequence of the modification and abandonment of traditional religious principles. Talk of a return to old-time religion notwithstanding, Christian fundamentalist hostility to some developments in evolutionary biology and other areas of science is fairly recent. Lawrence Principe, a prominent historian of science, has argued convincingly that for much of the past, Christianity has a far more complex and often supportive relationship with science.[107] And extremist Islam has acquired its most dangerous ideological infusions from very novel readings championed by such figures as Sayyid Qutb, though such interpretations are presented as if they are the only authentic way of reading the Koran.

Many writers have likened religious interpretation to constitutional interpretation.[108] The framers intended constitutional change to be difficult, yet possible. In a similar vein, there is nearly always a strong norm against abandonment or abrogation of existing religious ways, though perhaps a bit more openness to the addition of new ideas and practices. Sometimes, change occurs because of unacknowledged, unsanctioned, possibly clandestine, or even subconscious influences.

Religions differ greatly in terms of who is empowered to reinterpret and change the faith. Most often, such power resides in the hands of an individual or an elect few defined by superior scholarly achievement, religious ordination, acknowledged holiness, or position in a religious hierarchy. By limiting interpretation to such individuals or groups, the faith is able to ensure that no one messes with tradition without first undergoing an arduous process of socialization and indoctrination. Thus, attorney Alan Dershowitz recalls the reactions from his Orthodox Jewish teachers when he decided to challenge some religious rules. He explains that he was told he did not understand the true reasons for the prohibitions in question: "I spent years hearing this kind of one-upmanship from my Hebrew teachers. 'You must learn a lifetime,' they admonished, 'before you have the right to challenge.' The editor of an Orthodox newspaper put it this way: 'Unless you have completed the study of the entire Talmud (over 60 volumes) and its many commentaries, you are not capable of discussing our religion.' Pretty clever! They get you to learn for years, and by the time you're prepared to challenge, you've committed yourself to the system."[109] Religions may slow down the process of change even more by requiring that the sanctioned few who are authorized to reinterpret and make substantial modifications are spread out over generations.

Over the years, religions have also approved certain ways of achieving a successful reinterpretation. When faiths acknowledge that

God communicates through fallible human beings, it becomes possible to modify messages through source analysis and historical understanding. In some instances, even fundamentalists use these methods. Texts may, on the basis of archaeological discoveries, now appear to be forgeries or later additions. Difficult verses may take on new meaning when viewed in the light of ancient politics, psychology, and social life. Nearly always, the most questioned lines of scripture are those that conflict, or arguably conflict, with other scriptural sources; hence, one verse can be used to criticize a second. Another way religions change is through revelation, usually to a leader, although nowadays this most often happens in cults (or new religious movements, as sociologists prefer to call them).

All of the above ways of changing a faith can be religiously sanctioned, but they are not necessarily religiously inspired. Believers sometimes develop a need for change based on observation of norms outside the religion. Social psychologists would speak of a cognitive dissonance that results when the faith one professes is in conflict with the values one possesses, especially when the perceived conflict reflects poorly on one's self-esteem. When this unpleasant cognitive dissonance surfaces, people feel pressure to change either their religion or their values.[110] Sometimes the need for some modification of faith originates in science, in logic, in cultural values, or in the observation of other religions. Sometimes people decide they want change because the existing religious culture doesn't seem to fit their personalities or lifestyles; it is psychologically unfulfilling or discordant. It may clash with intuitions about what is right, conducive to happiness, or otherwise suitable for the world in which people live. When this happens, many people will fall away from the faith or pick and choose among its elements. At such times, the chaperones of the official religion often will—sooner or later—respond to the need for change and find a suitable mechanism to accomplish it.

Not all of these changes concern the development of religious extremism. From this vantage point, changes may be constructive, destructive, or irrelevant. In general, it is not difficult to identify the sorts of beliefs that lead to extremism and ought to be discouraged. All of these beliefs conflict with the presently prevailing ethos of most liberal democracies They assert explicitly or implicitly:

- All nonbelievers are destined for eternal damnation.
- Some nonbelievers (such as polytheists, atheists, members of particular religions) are hated by God.
- The government ought to treat believers differently from nonbelievers.
- The faith should be spread by military means.
- People cannot freely convert out of the religion.
- Nonbelievers must also follow some religious rules or prohibitions, even if they have no secular foundation.
- Nonbelievers must not blaspheme against God.
- Those who violate religious rules deserve harsh earthly punishments.
- Certain geographical locations must be controlled by members of the religion and nonbelievers may not live there.
- Any method is justified if it is used to implement God's will.
- God prefers men to women, or prefers to see women in a subjugated role.
- God prefers some races or ethnic groups to others.

These beliefs can and have shown up in all the Abrahamic religions and in others as well. Some of them continue to form a central part of the mindset of extremists in Judaism, Christianity, and Islam—and not because the extremist believers have miscomprehended their faith. Arguably, the truer reading may be the more extreme one, but that, I suppose, is a matter for the faithful to debate.

Why Islam Currently Has the Biggest Problem with Extremists

Three extremist beliefs are most dangerous because they, in effect, obstruct a religion's ability to repair itself. These beliefs—ones that conflict directly with democratic political theory—are the prohibition against blasphemy, the enshrinement of religion in the fundamental rules of the state, and the willingness to implement violent sanctions against those who leave the fold. Above the other troubling beliefs, these three render debate, discussion, and market pressures useless in changing or repairing a religion. In effect, they very powerfully stack the deck against reform.

This is why Islam currently has the biggest problem with restraining extremists. The Islamic world has not experienced the unique confluence of historical events that ultimately produced in the West a tradition of tolerance and a check on religiously inspired hatred. There was no Renaissance, no Reformation, no Peace of Westphalia, no Enlightenment, no theory of the separation of church and state, and no Vatican Council II. In the West, religious messages nowadays enter public debate primarily through the tempering prism of modern culture and constitutionally based values. In the world of Islam, the dictates of the faith can have a more direct and deleterious impact on social and political affairs.

In view of the dangers that accompany any confrontation of extremists, it is noteworthy that numerous reformers have publicized competing progressive visions of Islam.[111] Such reformers sometimes offer major moral revisions, sometimes relatively minor quibbles. And to a large extent, they represent much of the hope for the future. But even they must conduct their criticism within tightly constrained rules. It is against the law in Pakistan to engage in "willful defiling, damaging or desecration of the Holy [Koran], and directly or indirectly, by words either spoken or written or by visible representation, or by an imputation, innuendo or insinuation defiling, the name of the Holy Prophet." The mandated punishment is imprisonment or death, and the law is not merely an ancient obscurity that remains on the books. It has been used.[112]

Even in the West, when an author like Ibn Warraq wants to write a critical analysis of Islam from a secular humanist perspective, he must do so under a pseudonym.[113] Speaking in February 2005, Iranian leader Ali Khamenei had the following to say about the death sentence imposed sixteen years earlier by his predecessor, Ayatollah Khomeini, against author Salman Rushdie for writing a work deemed insulting to Islam: "The day will finally come when the apostate Salman Rushdie will receive his due punishment for his disgraceful and slanderous move against the [Koran] and the Prophet."[114] He added that the death sentence was irrevocable. The message is not lost on non-Muslim writers in the West, much less on Muslims in the heart of the Middle East.

Warnings abound. In 2004, the influential Sunni cleric Sheikh Yousef al-Qaradhawi declared: "For Muslim society to preserve its existence, it must struggle against *ridda* [apostasy] from every source and in all forms, and it must not let it spread like wildfire in a field of thorns. . . . There is no escape from struggling against and restricting the individual *ridda* so that it will not worsen and its sparks scatter, becoming group *ridda*. . . . Thus, the Muslim sages agreed that the punishment for the *murtadd* (one who commits *ridda*) . . . is execution."[115] Responding to this and other statements of Qaradhawi's position on apostasy, the progressive Egyptian writer Sayyed al-Qimni explains:

> According to Qaradhawi, punishment [for *ridda*] does not apply only to someone who decides freely to leave Islam for what satisfies his heart and his conscience—whether this be another religion or nothing at all. It applies in principle [also] to the Muslim who clings to the laws of his religion . . . but disagrees with those who have appointed themselves the priests of Islam and who call themselves religious sages . . . because . . . [the priests] have determined that their understanding of the holy scriptures is the only [permitted] understanding and the absolute truth, and anything else is absolute falsehood. . . . Any attempt at new thinking in reading the scriptures is thrust away [on the pretext] of [accusations of] abandoning the

> religion . . . and the punishment for new thought or expressing a different opinion is death.[116]

Another progressive Muslim writer, Shaker al-Nabulsi, attempted to draw a distinction between the Koranic chapters on belief, mainly revealed in Muhammad's early years in Mecca, and the chapters on legislation, the life of the Prophet, his relationships with his wives, and other matters. He said: "Frankly, there are many verses that we call political and military verses, that is, 'verses of the sword,' that are connected to circumstances that existed in the past but exist no longer. . . . Politics are fluid, not static; therefore, the laws built on a political foundation are also subject to movement, and are not static."[117] What al-Nabulsi was doing with the Koran was what many progressive Christians and Jews have done to bring their own scriptures more in line with current conditions. But lecturer Ibrahim al-Khuli from the renowned Al-Azhar University left no doubt about how this and similar strategies would play in the mainstream Muslim world. Al-Khuli said:

> Al-Nabulsi and Nasr [Hamid] Abu Zayd and their gangs speak of the historic aspect of Koranic scripture . . . Nasr Abu Zayd went so far as to say that the Koran is a human text that developed and crystallized, and is a cultural product. This is a lie, [and therefore] the Egyptian court's sentence regarding him was the sentence of *ridda*—and had he not left Egypt he would have been executed . . . Al-Nabulsi is not worth holding a discussion with, or of me mentioning him. He lied when he said that there are Koranic verses that contradict one another. When you say that in the Koran there are verses contradicting one another, you commit apostasy, and you leave the fold of the [Muslim] community through its widest gate. I take responsibility for these words.[118]

These are not the words of a terrorist but of a mainstream lecturer at Sunni Islam's most revered institution of higher learning. The situation faced by liberal theologians in the West is hardly comparable. So when people in the West encourage Muslims to defend a truly moderate interpretation of Islam, they should realize that they are asking a lot. The task is intellectually similar to that religious criticism in the other Abrahamic faiths, but it is socially, politically, and physically dangerous.

A few years ago, Lina Joy, a Malaysian who had been born a Muslim, started proceedings in civil court to obtain the right to marry her Christian fiancé and have children. She maintained that she had converted from Islam to Christianity and, consequently, did not need the permission of the Islamic sharia courts that typically governed such matters for Muslims in Malaysia. The lower civil courts ruled against her, and ultimately she brought the case to the nation's highest court, which—in May 2007—rejected her appeal. Thus, her official identity card still designates her religion as Muslim. The high court ruled that one cannot, at one's whim and fancy, renounce a religion. Lina Joy continues to endure many death threats from Muslims who consider her an apostate and she lives in hiding. Malik Imtiaz Sarwar, a Muslim human rights lawyer who helped with her case, has received one death threat that was widely circulated by e-mail. This e-mail featured his picture, with the heading "Wanted Dead" and the text "This is the face of the traitorous lawyer to Islam who supports the Lina Joy apostasy case. If you find him dead by the side of the road, do not help."[119] Without the freedom for intellectuals to critique a faith or dissatisfied members to leave in search of greener pastures, it is hard to imagine how reformists will prevail.

WHY NOT DO AWAY WITH SCRIPTURE ALTOGETHER?

Canadian social psychologists Bob Altemeyer and Bruce Hunsberger think of fundamentalism as "[t]he belief that there is one set of religious teachings that clearly contains the fundamental, basic, intrinsic, essential, inerrant truth about humanity and deity; that this essential truth is fundamentally opposed by forces of evil which must be vigorously fought; that this truth must be followed today according to the fundamental, unchangeable practices of the past; and that those who believe and follow these fundamental teachings have a special relationship with the deity."[120] One might point out that without scripture, the belief in god, or religious traditions, the potentially dangerous syndrome they have identified could not exist.

For this reason, some atheists and skeptics ask a very controversial question about holy books, faith traditions, and religious law. Why not jettison the whole necrotic mess and start from scratch? They argue that too much killing, hatred, and distress has resulted from books purporting to speak the word of God. Perhaps a better way of life might be grounded in science, humanism, or something else. Religion, they argue, serves no useful purpose, or least none worth the price that has been paid. Repair and reform are too difficult, maybe impossible. There is, they suggest, no reliable way to separate peaceful fundamentalists from potentially deadly extremists, and no method to ensure that more liberal believers will not fall prey to dangerous impulses sooner or later.

This critique is impractical. Religion speaks poignantly to the needs and desires of billions of people. A more attainable goal, in my opinion, is to focus our efforts on identifying and understanding the appeal of extremist religious visions and the circumstances under which they are most likely to thrive. To do so, we must start by considering why people turn to religion in the first place, and why, sometimes, their needs are not met by less perilous forms of faith.

CHAPTER 5

Vulnerable Minds and Sick Societies

An Affair of the Heart

Sometimes the religious lives of extremists cry out for psychological analysis. Malika El Aroud is a Belgian Muslim whose husband, Abdessatar Dahmane, traveled halfway around the world to swear an oath of loyalty to Osama bin Laden. Dahmane was a thirty-nine-year-old Tunisian man who had settled in Belgium. Two days prior to the September 11 attack on the United States, he and an associate carried out a suicide bombing against Ahmed Shah Massoud, the military mastermind of the Afghan Northern Alliance. Massoud had been dubbed the Lion of Panjshir for his successful guerrilla exploits against the Soviets. He was a Muslim who had served in a Muslim government in Afghanistan prior to the rise of the Taliban. His assassins acted under direct orders from bin Laden, who intended the murder as a gift to Taliban leader Mullah Omar. The al Qaeda head probably ordered the assassination to solidify Omar's support in the coming struggle against the Americans.

After Dahmane's death, his widow penned a memoir in which she recalled the precise moment at which her husband first decided to go to Afghanistan to offer his services to al Qaeda. Bin Laden had appeared briefly on the television news, and her husband was deeply impressed. "Look at that face, don't you think that it is beautiful?" he remarked. Dahmane's wife dutifully replied that he, Dahmane, was also handsome. But he persisted. "I love him." And she responded, "Me too, I love him." In her book, she later explained that her husband "was alluding to the light of faith illuminating his face." Bin Laden, she explains, called for "combat against the aggressors of the poor and the unarmed, the Muslim community." At that moment, "[s]omething had just put a shadow over the happiness of Abdessatar: he was scared of dying without having made the supreme effort on the path of God: Jihad. And he had the impression that it was to himself in particular that Osama was delivering a message."[1]

Malika El Aroud does not see herself and her husband as extremists; they were, simply, a "religious Muslim couple to which history threw up an unexpected act."[2] They were, by her account, very loving toward each other. She reports that her husband's last words to her were that he would love her to the end of her days.[3]

Malika reflected on why, in Jalalabad, Afghanistan, "[i]n every family the first born was called Osama." Bin Laden, she suggests, "was loved because he was combating injustice. He wanted to liberate the Islamic lands. That was the opinion of everyone. He was rich, he had money and he put his money at the service of his community and to spend it on others. That is worthy of being respected and loved. It is not everybody who does this. It's normal that we love him and he is a hero for us, a big brother."[4] Surprisingly, in view of her husband's acknowledged role in one of bin Laden's terrorist deeds, Malika insists: "I don't believe for a minute that he ordered the 9/11 attacks."[5]

Extremists, in every faith, arrive at their fanaticism through a combination of personal peculiarities and religious ideology. W. W. Meissner, a psychoanalyst and Catholic priest, notes that "[o]ne can distinguish between the belief system, as an aspect of consensual group ideology and identity, and the personalized belief system of the individual believer. These are not synonymous. Belief systems, as they come to be individually internalized, always bear the stamp of the individual's personality."[6] To understand the origins of destructive faith, it is not enough to scrutinize the religious ideologies themselves, but one must understand the role played by faith in an individual's psychological makeup.

Malika El Aroud offers reasons for supporting bin Laden that seem, on the surface, quite reasonable. Would not many good people want to help a man with the traits and beliefs she attributes to bin Laden? Yet, at least to most of us in the West, she is providing at best a skewed image of the al Qaeda leader. Is she simply misinformed? Or is she being influenced by deeper psychological forces?

In their still relevant 1956 book, *Opinions and Personality*, psychologists M. Brewster Smith, Jerome S. Bruner, and Robert W. White explored the way people's opinions, including their religious opinions, helped them "to meet and master" their world. In technical terms, they looked at "the adjustive functions of personality . . . served by the formation and maintenance of an opinion." Thus, they asked how holding and keeping a particular opinion was socially and psychologically useful.[7] The authors identified three functions, which they called object appraisal, social adjustment, and externalization. When an opinion helps with object appraisal, it provides "a ready aid in 'sizing up' objects and events in the environment from the point of view of one's major interests and going concerns."[8] Thus, for Malika, her husband, or—probably—both, extremist Islam may have "provided a creative solution to the problems posed by the existence of disparate internal demands and external or environmental demands." Unfortunately, we will, very likely, never know enough about this family to understand for certain just what these demands might have been. In Malika's case, she had not always been a convinced Muslim. She had received a Western education and, in her teen years, rebelled against many Islamic rules. One consequence of this rebellion was her involvement in several unhappy conjugal experiences. More generally, she grew dissatisfied with modern life in Belgium. She also felt guilty about disappointing her father. Thus, by intensifying her commitment to Islam, she was able to make some sense of her failure to thrive as a modernized, francophone Muslim. To her mind, perhaps, the standard Western narratives did not explain her predicament very well, but the radical Islamic worldview seemed consistent with her life experience.

When a person's attitudes perform the second psychological function—social adjustment—they facilitate, disrupt, or maintain an individual's relations with other people and groups. By holding specific opinions, "one identifies with or, indeed, differentiates oneself from various 'reference groups' within the population."[9] Of course, we would still need to explain why it mattered so much for Malika and her husband to identify with some groups and separate themselves from others. But a desire to attain the celestial status of martyr in the Islamic extremist community may have been significant. For Malika, very much a product of Europe, signing on with the most extreme wing of Islam was one way to establish quickly the genuineness of her Muslim credentials. Moreover, had she rejected Islamic extremism after her husband's act of terror, she would have been an outcast in every community. By celebrating his deed, she became a heroine in the world of the extremists.

The final personality function—externalization—occurs when a person uses opinions to manage, often unconsciously, some unresolved inner problems or psychological difficulties he or she may be experiencing. For example, extremists may adopt a view of the nonextremist world as a corrupt and perverted place by unconsciously projecting outward their own feelings of guilt, corruption, and perverse sexuality, feelings that are too provocative of anxiety for them to face within themselves. When a psychoanalyst reads that "something had just put a shadow over the happiness of Abdessatar," she might typically wonder whether that "something" had to do with Abdessatar's hidden, unconscious life. She might also wonder whether Malika's self-described descent into gloom and darkness during her prereligious years was the consequence of inner psychological conflicts involving guilt and sexuality. If so, extremist Islam may have helped her to handle the threatening fires that burned within her unconscious.

But how, in particular, did the specific personalities of Abdessatar Dahmane and Malika El Aroud lead them to extremism when many Muslims in Belgium (who also had their share of problems) ended up elsewhere? Certainly Malika paints a portrait of bin Laden as the classic charismatic leader, an image confirmed by statements from other supporters. But why did she and, even more, her husband respond so powerfully to the man and his message? Many times, in discussions of Hitler's popular appeal in prewar Germany, people have spoken of his "hypnotic" ability to get people to suspend their better judgment. But this ability to hypnotize was largely an ability to pronounce energetically a message that people wanted to hear.[10] In Hitler's case, the message was partly political and partly psychological. One might presume that bin Laden and his ideology meet some political needs and some psychological needs that are common to a subset of the radical Muslim population. And for some individuals, signing on to bin Laden's program, even to the point of death, might seem preferable to persisting without him. In short, a few may be drawn to extremism by the idiosyncrasies of their psychic makeup, but there could be an extremism-prone personality, or perhaps several such personalities, common among many fanatics.

Yet Malika's account of her husband's road to al Qaeda does not point clearly to the elements of any well-defined syndrome of religious militancy. Was one of them—or were both of them—seeking to repent from some real or perceived sin? Were they reacting to a sense of alienation from their lives in Europe? Did they have personal connections to someone who was perceived to be a victim of Western policies in the Mideast? Was extremism a method they developed to bolster self-esteem in the face of a family economic crisis or a seemingly irresolvable marital problem? There is no end to this sort of speculation. In the case of Malika El Aroud and Abdessatar Dahmane, we have an entire book of data and we are still left without an adequate understanding of their motivation. If the psychoanalysts are correct, the true pull of extremism in every faith would hardly be apparent to the extremists themselves; more likely, fanatics would be inclined to deny psychological sources of their beliefs and, in their place, offer up all manner of rationalization.

One place to begin probing how destructive and militant religion functions is by understanding the needs met by nonmilitant religion. William James once suggested that the abnormal provides a superb window on the normal. The reverse is also true. Psychiatrist Eli Chesen no doubt oversimplifies when he says, "With very few exceptions, most religions become harmful only when taken incorrectly or in overdosage."[11] But we shouldn't underestimate the importance of understanding why and how people "take" their religion.

Why People Turn to Religion in the First Place

The story of Jean Barois is one place to explore the appeal of religious faith. Barois is a fictional character created by Roger Martin du Gard, the brilliant but largely forgotten 1937 French Nobel Prize winner in literature. A young man in late nineteenth-century France, Barois abandons and rejects the Roman Catholicism of his upbringing. He soon becomes a leading atheist writer and editor, strongly opposing the Catholic religious establishment of his day. His work overflows with well-developed arguments against religion and faith. None would have reason to question his sincerity or resolve.

Then, without warning and at the height of his intellectual power, Barois finds himself stuck in a horse-drawn carriage headed for a serious crash. "Pale with terror," the author writes, "Barois huddles back against the cushions. A sense of utter helplessness . . . and the certainty of disaster flash like lightning through the chaos of his thoughts. He utters a low cry. 'Hail, Mary, full of grace."[12]

Awakening in bed after the accident, Barois at first smiles as the "joy of life regained" sweeps through him. He reflects on death through his long-established atheistic framework. Life, he notes, is "no more than a series of transformations, so why be frightened of *that* one? It's not the first and, presumably, not the last incident in the . . . [process]

of becoming."[13] But then he grows very disturbed, recalling his utterance at the critical moment before the crash. He becomes obsessed with the fear that he might one day return to religion and thereby negate his life's work. This fear is particularly intense and plausible because he lives with the knowledge that his own nonpracticing father had himself returned to the religious fold on his deathbed.

Barois decides he must record his current views for posterity. Propped up in bed and still recovering, he writes: "This is my Last Will and Testament. What I write today, in my early forties, in the full mental vigour of my prime, should obviously outweigh anything I may say or think or write at the close of my existence, when my intellect and judgment may well be impaired by the infirmities of old age."[14] He proceeds to explain his philosophy in detail, pausing to note: "I deserve to die, combatant and defiant, as I have lived, without capitulating, without whoring after idle hopes, without fearing my return to the primal matter that nourishes the slow processes of evolution."[15] He enumerates his many views on life, saying that he knows his "personality is but an agglomeration of particles of matter, whose disintegration will end it absolutely."[16] He also records his belief that man "is incapable of forming conceptions of the Absolute and the Infinite. He has invented names for what transcends himself, but these have not got him any further; he is a victim of his terminology, for those words and names do not, so far as human understanding is concerned, correspond to any cognizable reality."[17]

Despite all this, years later, ailing and awaiting death, Jean Barois does, in fact, return to the Catholicism of his upbringing. When visited by a still unrepentant friend from his intellectual days, Barois declares: "I'm sorry for you, old chap. You're still at the resisting stage. You're putting up a fight. . . . But what's the good of struggling? You know quite well that in the end you too will come to this." Barois holds a crucifix and says: "Only see for yourself how calmly I can face death, now I know I shall live again beside him."[18]

And what becomes of his last will and testament? His loving and very pious wife—a woman to whom he returned after many years of abandonment—tosses the document into the fireplace, telling only her priest. And in his view, this final "sacrifice" of Barois is perhaps due to the church for all it has done to ease the man's passing.

Martin du Gard is a fine storyteller, and the tale of Jean Barois's return to faith cannot be explained at one level alone. His life was very much tied to his country, class, and era. France changed greatly during the adulthood of Jean Barois, in part because of the passage of the 1905 law for the separation of church and state. Barois's family life and upbringing were unusual. So his story was not the story of everyman.

Yet the fear of physical decline, death, and what follows proved decisive for Barois, a man of unparalleled intellectual capacity and integrity. His adult theories ultimately, after many detours, proved no match for the lessons he had imbibed at his mother's knee. How much the more so, then, would religion's capacity to comfort carry the day for many others? Barois may be a fictional character, but his story is instructive. Religion for Barois, in his declining years at least, and for others, perhaps throughout their lives, makes claims to meet needs to which the intellect alone cannot minister.

The case of Irene Smith is more recent and real. Smith's son, Leon, was a firefighter who died in the September 11 attacks. Five years later, she told reporters: "If I didn't believe in God I wouldn't be here, I'd be in a mental home someplace."[19] With this judgment, Smith joins countless millions throughout the ages who have seen religion as an essential component of mental health, especially under conditions of adversity.

For many, Irene Smith and the fictional Jean Barois included, religion addresses specific needs for comfort in the face of death. But, as the well-known psychologist of religion Kenneth I. Pargament has noted, "[p]art of the unique power of religion may lie in its capability to respond to so many needs in so many different ways."[20] Psychologists who study such matters identify at least five dimensions of an individual's religion: (1) religious belief and ideology; (2) religious rituals and practice; (3) religious experiences and feelings; (4) religious knowledge; and (5) the consequences of religion for other aspects of a person's life.[21] The appeal of religion may lie in any of these dimensions, or in some combination of them.

Thus, people may turn to religion because they find the ideology appealing, but they may also pay very little attention to ideology or beliefs. It may be far more important for some to engage in a life of highly structured ritual and practice. Still others may ignore both ritual and ideology, drawn instead by the emotions and/or alterations in consciousness that, for them, accompany prayer and the quest for mystic experiences. Yet others may care little for any of the above, adhering to a religious life because they see it as a way of combating loneliness, maintaining an alcohol-free existence, coping with difficult-to-manage sexual urges, or overcoming anxiety or depression. Finally, there are undoubtedly those who stay with a faith in response to social pressures or simply because they know no other way.

Numerous writers, generally religious ones, have suggested that the abandonment of existing religions will create a vulnerability to new methods of coping, not all of them constructive. Back in 1972, when rapid cultural change was in the air, Catholic priest and sociologist Andrew Greeley suggested that "[i]f there is one thing clear in all the deviant streams running through youthful American culture—drugs, rock, protest, communes, superstition—it is that the younger generation quite explicitly wants something to believe in and norms which follow from that belief according to which they can live."[22] He further suggested that "the conventional wisdom," which he read as hostile to religion, was "in no position to cope with the renewed interest in bizarre and esoteric forms of the sacred . . . [and that] if industrialized society attempts to ignore the sacred in substantial segments of men's lives, and if the churches listen to those divinity school professors who believe that contemporary man no longer needs or wants the sacred, then it is going to spring up in all sorts of odd and unexpected places."[23]

More recently, Sarah Taggart, a therapist and minister, arrived at a similar conclusion: "The trouble with not believing in something is that one will then believe in anything. And anything in this context can mean all sorts of odd and destructive cults and gangs and sects."[24] Greeley and Taggart may or may not be right in their assessment that finding replacements for religion must be a step in the wrong direction. However, arguments such as theirs point to the importance of understanding just which needs are most important and addressed by religion in its many manifestations.

Through the years, psychologists have offered many different answers to the question of why people seek religion. Sigmund Freud, once described as "the last great representative of the Enlightenment, the first to demonstrate its limitations," saw reason as embattled and opposed by all sorts of irrational forces but still as humanity's guiding light.[25] He had little patience for theology or faith and thought it an illusion "to suppose that what science cannot give us we can get elsewhere."[26] He rejected the pragmatism of William James and others with the judgment that "[i]gnorance is ignorance; no right to believe in anything can be derived from it."[27]

For Freud, all humans feel helpless in the face of death, disease, disasters, and other challenges of life. He suggests that "once before has one found oneself in a similar state of helplessness: as a small child, in relation to one's parents. One had reason to fear them, and especially one's father; and yet one was sure of his protection against the dangers one knew."[28] Thus, using the model of the father, people create an illusory figure called God and a method of relating to him called religion. Both times, in childhood and adulthood, there is someone of superior wisdom and power whose love and protection can be won by obeying commands and avoiding transgression of prohibitions. Religion, in short, is infantile wish fulfillment, something essentially neurotic that stands in the way of humanity's maturation and reliance on reason.

Freud conceded that various religious doctrines had "historical worth." They had aided in the development of civilization by contributing to the necessary repression of aggressive and sexual instincts. He writes: "When civilization laid down the commandment that a man shall not kill the neighbor whom he hates or who is in his way or whose property he covets, this was clearly done in the interest of man's communal existence, which would not otherwise be practicable."[29] And the addition of God, heaven, hell, and the like greatly increased the potency of such rules. Yet Freud argues that religion has, on balance, not done enough to make people happy or civilized and that it is time for a change. He expects religion to wither away in time and this he would view as a welcome development.

From the outset, Freud's views on religion generated controversy, even among those who accepted most tenets of psychoanalysis. Some objected that he had little to say about religious experiences, that he limited his analysis to certain Western religions, and that he himself did not even claim to prove that religious beliefs were untrue—only that they served the function of wish fulfillment. Among his religious critics, some rejected his conclusions but agreed he had unearthed an underlying psychological mechanism of some "immature" religious belief.

Unfortunately, Freud's one-size-fits-all analysis does not get us far in distinguishing among the psychological characteristics of moderate and extremist faith. Moreover, his confidence in reason's ultimate ascendancy over religion seems harder to justify in the current era of revitalized religious militancy. Freud formulates one argument that he then dismisses too quickly, that "[i]f you want to expel religion from our European civilization, you can only do it by means of another system of doctrines; and such a system would from the outset take over all the psychological characteristics of religion—the same sanctity, rigidity and intolerance, the same prohibition of thought—for its own [defense]."[30] This rejected argument probably deserves reconsideration when the decline of traditional religion has at times been accompanied in turn by the rise of Nazism, communism, and religious extremism.[31]

Since Freud, the most influential psychological writers generally have offered more sympathetic assessments of religion—though, often, they endorsed religious experiences and quests rather than adherence to traditional dogmas and practices.[32] Numerous humanistic and existential psychologists—including Gordon W. Allport, Erich Fromm, Abraham Maslow, Viktor Frankl, and Ernest Becker—saw in religion a way to somehow provide one's life with meaning, or, at least, a perception of meaning. According to Allport, people have a need for a "unifying master sentiment," and religion contributes to mental health by providing ultimate meaning and a source of long-range guidance and goals. Fromm did not believe in God, but he saw the concept of God as a potentially useful source of growth, freedom, and autonomy. In his vision, the right kind of religion could potentially meet two human needs: first, provide a way of understanding the world, and second, provide a set of ideals in which people could place faith.[33] Viktor Frankl—author of an influential memoir on life in a Nazi concentration camp and the founder of a school of therapy called logotherapy—highlighted a human need to search for and discover meaning in one's life. According to Frankl, obedience to one's conscience made sense only if one understood that conscience to transcend one's self. Religious people were those who gave the name God to the entity to which they were ultimately responsible.[34]

Maslow, one of the originators of the humanistic approach in American psychology, focused on religion as a way of attaining two desirable and related goals: peak experiences and self-actualization.[35] For Maslow, once people meet their basic lower-level needs, they strive to become what they are capable of becoming, in other words, to achieve their inner potential. As they move toward this state of self-actualization, they begin to show signs of "better" values in many areas of life. For example, they increasingly accept themselves and nature, they get along better with others, they are more creative, they are better at problem solving, and they are less bored. They also tend to have more peak experiences, which Maslow describes as "transient experiences of bliss, ecstasy, or joy which tend to evoke emotions of awe, reverence, and wonder and have a transforming effect on the subject of the experience."[36] Such experiences might come from many sources, including art, athletics, love, or even LSD. Yet Maslow thought that he had discovered the general scientific category through which one could explain religious experiences and even endorse their desirability. While he generally was no friend of traditional faiths, he did believe that religion could be a contributor to growth and self-actualization.

Ernest Becker was trained as a cultural anthropologist, but in his 1973 Pulitzer Prize–winning book, *The Denial of Death*, he developed an approach that is increasingly influential among psychologists. According to Becker, "Man is literally split in two: he has an awareness of his own splendid uniqueness in that he sticks out of nature with a towering majesty, and yet he goes back into the ground a few feet in order blindly and dumbly to rot and disappear forever. It is a terrifying dilemma to be in and to have to live with."[37] In Becker's view, people may say that they can handle this problem and that other things concern them more. But the truth, he says, is that the fear of death has merely been repressed—and perhaps not very effectively. What would it mean, Becker asks, to be wholly unrepressed? He answers, "It can only mean to be reborn into madness."[38] Thus, many of the things about which people seem to care are, in actuality, "vital lies."

Becker's theory of human nature speaks directly about the appeal of religion. He suggests that, psychologically speaking, religion can solve

> the problem of death, which no living individuals can solve. . . . The two ontological motives of the human condition are both met: the need to surrender oneself in full to the rest of nature, to become a part of it by laying down one's whole existence to some higher meaning; and the need to expand oneself as an individual heroic personality. Finally, religion alone gives hope, because it holds open the dimension of the unknown and the unknowable, the fantastic mystery of creation that the human mind cannot even begin to approach, the possibility of a multidimensionality of spheres of existence, of heavens and possible embodiments that make a mockery of earthly logic—and in doing so, it relieves the absurdity of earthly life, all the impossible limitations and frustrations of living matter.[39]

Unlike Freud but like the fictional Jean Barois, Becker does not believe that reason alone will stand up well to the existential challenges of life. To the extent that he also views nonreligious means of fulfilling these challenges as "vital lies," he is understandably more tolerant than many of religious solutions. As one of the proponents of his theory explains, "[B]ecause all personal and cultural immortality projects, strategies, and ideologies function to allay the terror of mortality, finitude, insignificance, and nothingness, in a very real sense all of these are 'religious to the core.'"[40] However, Becker's own religious views never emerge clearly, and since he died shortly after completing *The Denial of Death*, scholars have been left guessing.

Nowadays most psychologists of religion—drawing heavily on the humanistic and existential theorists—would locate the need for religion in "the desire for *self-transcendence*."[41] Although this term, perhaps understandably, is never defined in a way that meets strict scientific standards, it is possible to elaborate on it a bit. People seek to expand their consciousness so they can experience a "wider and deeper" version of themselves, one that goes "beyond the limits of our everyday consciousness." People also turn to religion to overcome undesired feelings of aloneness by forging "bonds of love and solidarity with others." Perhaps the main appeal of religion lies in its efforts to "put life into some kind of ultimate context, to discover its ultimate meaning and destiny."[42]

If religion meets important psychological needs, and if it does so in a manner superior to nonreligious approaches, one might expect to witness a higher level of psychological well-being among the faithful. But some psychologists—such as the influential founder of Rational-Emotive Behavioral Therapy, Albert Ellis—would expect precisely the opposite. Drawing on clinical research, theory, and his personal experience, Ellis maintains that emotionally healthy people should be, among other things, self-directed, tolerant, flexible, scientific, and self-accepting. They should also have a considerable supply of concern for their own self-interest. Ellis concludes that, far from advancing these traits, religion "doesn't help at all; and in most respects it seriously sabotages mental health."[43]

Hundreds of psychological studies have tried to assess whether the effects of religion are good or bad. In short, they have not produced sufficiently powerful findings to change many minds in either direction. With so many types of religious belief, so many modes of expressing such belief, and so many ways to measure well-being, the studies often seem to be comparing apples and oranges or to be hopelessly mired in confusion. Happiness, after all, is not even the main goal of most religions. And how does one quantify the immense satisfaction that may, indeed, flood the feelings of an extremist who has carried out a socially destructive act?

Yet another problem is that most studies have been done with American Christian subjects, and it would be unreasonable to speak of their findings as if they applied to other religions and places.[44] One prominent textbook author, Raymond Paloutzian, concludes his review of research on religion and well-being by saying: "Religious persons, as far as personality and psychological adequacy are concerned, appear to be neither better off nor worse off than other persons. They are only different—slightly better off and worse off, each in specialized ways."[45] In short, the quantitative studies do not teach us all that much because, shall we say, the devil is in the details.

Whatever one's views about the merits of the religious enterprise as a whole, the central question remains of why so many people in the contemporary world have sought to meet their religious needs in ways that have proved so destructive. While no large, well-developed body of psychological or sociological research addresses this matter directly, we are able to extract some important clues from what has been written.

GOOD FAITH, BAD FAITH

Rollo May, one of the most influential proponents of the existential approach in American psychology, rightly notes that "[i]n any discussion of religion and personality integration, the question is not whether religion itself makes for health or neurosis, but what kind of religion and how is it used?"[46] He then offers a list of questions that might provide insight into the psychological value of an individual's faith. For example,

- Does it serve to break one's will, to keep one stuck at an infantile level of development, or to shelter one from humanity's necessary encounter with freedom?
- Does it keep one from a mature assumption of personal responsibility?
- On the other hand, does it give a person an experience of meaning in life that affirms personal dignity and worth?
- Does it encourage courageous acceptance of life's limitations?
- Does it help a person to cope with anxiety?
- Does it help develop personal capabilities including the capacity to love fellow human beings?[47]

Others psychologists have offered their own methods for separating good faith from bad faith.[48] Gordon Allport distinguishes between mature and immature faith. Among other things, he thinks mature religion can provide a person with a sense of meaning and harmony, as well as a comprehensive philosophy of life. Mature faith also brings with it an insightful capacity for self-criticism. It is typically accepted as a heuristic map to living one's life, a map that will certainly need corrections from time to time. Allport also thinks mature faith is capable of enlisting the total energy of an individual, something that one might reasonably associate with fanaticism. However, given the other aspects of mature religious belief, Allport deems this sort of believer unlikely to become an extremist.[49]

Erich Fromm's well-known approach holds that good religion is humanistic while bad religion is authoritarian. In authoritarian faith, a person exchanges self-worth, independence, and integrity for a sense of belonging and being protected. The worst sin in authoritarian faith is disobedience, not because God represents high virtues but because God has the most power. For the believer of this sort, all of humankind's best traits are projected onto God. What's left is a greatly diminished self. Thus, people feel empty and sinful. And understandably, because of this state, they are unable to bring much love into their worlds. Religious moral principles exist, but mainly as a justification for the faith. They remain distant and detached from believers' lives.

Humanistic religion, on the other hand, prefers adherents to use their minds and emotions to achieve meaningful religious experiences. God becomes a symbol of what humans can attain, and not a tyrannical boss over them. The aim of religion here is for people to overcome egotistical issues and to become capable of more love, joy, and social concern.[50]

The "good" faiths endorsed by Fromm, Allport, and May seem psychologically constructive and consistent with humanistic moral values. Thus one might conclude that they fulfill William James's pragmatic standard, that religions should be judged by their fruits. However, as the philosopher A. J. Ayer has argued, this claim is "in line with the view of some contemporary theists that the doctrine associated with the religious practices in which they engage is acceptable as a useful myth . . . it does appear open to the practical objection that the satisfaction which most believers derive from their acceptance of religious doctrine depends upon their not judging it as mythical. A myth which is generally seen to be a myth must be in some danger of losing its utility."[51]

Putting aside questions about how we might define and measure the somewhat nebulous criteria suggested by Fromm, Allport, May, and others, we are left uncertain about how well the "good" faiths will satisfy the needs that led people to seek out religion in the first place. These include fear of death, desire for immortality, and the need for clear answers to large questions. Nowadays, in the face of centuries of scientific success, many mainstream believers have accepted what one student of extremism has called a "controlled secularity," where religion reigns only in the private sphere of the family, personal beliefs, and leisure. As for politics, economics, and science, these have been ceded to secular approaches.[52] This type of solution—probably satisfactory in the main for many humanistic psychologists—does not work as well for a sizable segment of believers. And herein may lie part of the explanation of why the "bad" faiths have often thrived even in modern times.

If our objective is to distinguish between the psychologies of extremist and moderate religions, there remains an additional problem. One would not expect to find many humanistic, mature believers among extremists as we have defined them. But it seems likely that the overwhelming majority of immature, even authoritarian, believers will never turn dangerous, and some may be found among those who show commitment to political moderation.

Why Moderate Religion Fails I: A Matter of Psychology

Erik Erikson, the noted psychoanalyst and social theorist, was no foe of religious belief.[53] Born Jewish and later a professing Christian, he engaged in a lifelong religious and spiritual quest. Yet Erikson was keenly aware of the possibility that many central parts of religion could be readily corrupted. Believers could develop illusory and narcissistic images of perfection, and they could then organize their lives around the pursuit of these false "Gods." They could be tricked into mistaking the forms of religion for its substance. They could become self-righteous or unreasonably legalistic. And, perhaps most dangerously, their religious ideology could be corrupted into fanaticism.[54]

Erikson did not provide much detail about how or why such corruption takes place. Drawing on historical analysis and subsequent work in the social sciences, we are now able to shed much more light on the core psychology of religious extremism. The worst manifestations of militancy in recent times seem to involve all or most of the following elements:

- Idealization of some past era combined with the belief that the world has gone awry
- Declared certainty of the correctness of one's religious vision
- Unwillingness to compromise with those who disagree
- Powerful denunciation of people with different lifestyles, especially when they involve forms of sexual liberality

- Devaluation of events in this world and intense focus on life after death
- Willingness to assume the role of God's "hit man," defending the deity and his representatives against all perceived insults
- Veneration of some religious leader or leaders
- Lack of concern for earthly evidence, except of the sort sanctioned by the religious system
- Frequent acceptance of the desired ends as justification for unsavory means
- Adoption of numerous defensive methods for avoiding serious encounters with conflicting systems of belief and their adherents
- Preference for keeping women in traditional, subordinate roles

These elements of fanaticism seem to cut across religions, applying to extremists in Christianity, Islam, Judaism, and other faiths. This may be because most religions, by their very nature, require to some degree that one let go of one's intellectual inhibitions and give oneself over entirely to an idealized other, called God. In addition, religions often involve idealization (or sanctification) of a whole array of objects, for example, crucifixes, holy books, churches, remains of saints, and much more. The process of abandonment of the rules of everyday thinking is part of what gives religion its tremendous power to influence the lives of believers, sometimes for the better, as in the case of Alcoholics Anonymous. But the same process also feeds the tendency toward fanaticism.

As psychologist James V. Jones argues: "If a religious institution insists that it is pure and without error; if expositors insist that a text is infallible; if a teacher or master insists that he or she is perfect, then the devotees will be kept in a state of developmental arrest, no matter how deeply they love that institution, or that text, or that teacher, or how powerful the emotions are that are evoked."[55] Most dangerously, the insistence that the faith is perfect leads to a splitting of the world into camps of good and evil, the first step down the path of extremism. If the nonbeliever is demonic and impure, he or she should be dealt with accordingly.

A central part of the mindset of the religious militant involves close-mindedness.[56] In a work on moral behavior that does not deal specifically with religious fanatics, psychologist Derek Wright makes apparent why and how various elements of religious extremism might fit together in the close-minded individual:

> Whatever the nature of the ulterior motives at work in the closed mind, their presence is betrayed by a variety of signs. Since the degree of certainty felt usually goes well beyond what is justifiable in terms of evidence and reasoning alone, it has to be defended in other ways. The most simple and characteristic of these is the appeal to authority. If the moral rule can be derived from an authority which is regarded as absolute and infallible then at one stroke the problem is solved. Not only is the subjective certainty justified but there is the additional security generated by the knowledge that other problems can be solved in a similar way.[57]

Wright further maintains that "[s]ince beliefs function as a kind of defensive carapace holding the personality together, the existence of other people who think differently is threatening to personal stability."[58] As a result, the close-minded person adopts a wide range of strategies with a common purpose, to "divert the individual from actually listening sympathetically to what his opponent has to say, considering it on its own merits, and learning from it."[59] As Milton Rokeach, the first student of the psychology of close-mindedness, puts it: "If doubt is cast on any portion of the belief system, doubt can be cast on any other portion, and this threatens the cohesiveness and solidarity of the group as well as the inner psychic stability of the individual believer. This threat can reach psychotic proportions, in which it is equivalently the threat of inner disintegration, loss of self, and psychic death."[60]

Thus, militant believers, past and present, have dealt with nonbelievers by avoidance, ostracism, derision, shouting down, claims of eternal damnation, proselytization, and explaining away through the attribution of disreputable motives. After these tactics fail, and sometimes even before that, fanatics progress to threats, physical violence, and murder. Nonbelievers come to be seen as obstacles that must be overcome, manipulated, or eliminated. And, for extremists, all means—no matter how inhuman and no matter how much in seeming conflict with the tenets of the faith—can be justified.[61] By far the most dangerous omen is when believers decide that, to protect their psychological balance, they must personally sign on as hit men or assassins for God, enjoined by the deity to accomplish what he (or she) alone apparently cannot do.

The whole syndrome probably "begins with the perception that the public world has gone awry, and the suspicion that behind this social confusion lies a great spiritual and moral conflict, a cosmic battle between the forces of order and chaos, good and evil. Such a conflict is understandably violent, and this violence is often felt by the victimized activist as powerlessness, either individually or in association with others of his gender, race, or ethnicity."[62]

Close-mindedness can characterize an individual or an ideology. When it affects both, the danger is multiplied. Under such circumstances, the possibility for compromise becomes very slight. Absent is the type of bargaining that typically makes up the lifeblood of ordinary diplomacy and world affairs. Add God to the equation, along with the prospect of sincerely anticipated recompense in the world to come, and few will make deals even in the face of very likely defeat. In an eternal stakes game with such terms, believers may be willing to wait eons for fulfillment of their objectives. Compromise may be seen as out of the question because "[y]ou can't sell half your soul to the devil."[63]

The most important benefit that the believer gets from extremist faith may be the simpler solution it provides to existential problems. This may be what initially draws most people to religion in its various forms. For some, militant faith may work better (or seem to work better) than moderate faith in helping people to

- manage anxiety about death,
- believe life has meaning,

- overcome feelings of ultimate aloneness and bolster a sense of identity,
- escape from the overwhelming challenges brought about by too much freedom,
- address needs for strong self-esteem, and
- cleanse a sense of sinfulness.

As Ernest Becker and others have argued, people will go to tremendous lengths and expose themselves to all sorts of risks and dangers solely to "prove" that the myths they live by are true. The extremist sometimes gets to a place where he can only confirm the truth of the faith by exhibiting and testing a willingness to die for it. One historian of philosophy discusses a recurring theme in existential thought, that "[t]hough terrifying, the taking of death into ourselves is also liberating: It frees us from servitude to the petty cares that threaten to engulf our daily life and thereby opens us to the essential *projects* by which we can make our lives personally and significantly our own."[64] Becker would call these projects immortality projects, where people devote most of their psychic energy to creating symbols of immortality that serve to tame the terror that arises when they focus on their own mortality. In short, some people will do almost anything to prove to themselves that their stories about the world to come are completely true. The seeming paradox is that to ward off the fear of mortality they may in fact hasten it.

Policy analyst Michael J. Mazarr sees this psychology as central to the motivation of the suicide bomber. He writes: "The ultimate manifestation of an authentic life, according to at least some of the existentialists, is to regain control over the manner and purpose of one's death."[65] With this in mind, he suggests, "one is hard-pressed not to think of the stolid, brutal authors of September 11, going about their placid lives and smoothly traversing their petty cares sustained by the conviction that they had taken their death inside, bought and owned it, and thereby achieved wholeness, achieved greatness, achieved authenticity."[66]

Another problem that feeds extremism is that the experience of freedom to choose is not universally experienced as a positive one. Too much freedom can be psychologically threatening to some.[67] Thus, large numbers of people have shown a preference for totalitarian solutions to the many forms of uncertainty in life. We have seen this force at work in the appeal of communism and fascism, and no doubt it assists those who sell visions based on claims to an absolute knowledge of God's will. Charles Kimball explains that "[t]he need for fixed stars, for certainty in the midst of our tenuous lives on a dangerously unpredictable planet, is real and understandable. Religious leaders who can package and deliver absolute truths find receptive audiences."[68]

However, the surrender to religious authorities of a good chunk of one's essential humanity comes at a high cost. People who do this believe that they are engaging in a deal whereby they acquire the right to depend entirely on God or faith to meet their needs. When, as often happens, the deal does not work, the individual feels cheated and resentful.[69] Thus, submissive and dominating tendencies may go hand in hand. As Goethe has noted: "[E]ach, incompetent to rule His own internal self, is all too fain to sway His neighbor's will, even as his haughty mind inclines."[70] The angrier and more confused people become, the deeper their commitment to fighting off alternative perspectives and the people who hold them.

The human condition can also involve feelings of intense and ultimate aloneness, and these feelings can lead some to extremism. As the singer says, "Sooner or later you die in your own bed." To counter such feelings, people strive to achieve high self-esteem and identity, a sense of who they are. Very often, such self-esteem and identity become tightly linked to one's membership in an ethnic, religious, racial, or national group.

If members of a group feel slighted, they may react by becoming increasingly hostile toward people in other ethnic and religious groups. What matters is the perception of a threat from outside the group, not the reality. People will, when they experience threats to their identity, tend to reassert the core, or formative, values of their group (as they see them).

When groups feel powerless, or even insufficiently powerful, members may turn to militancy in an attempt to overcompensate. Psychoanalyst W. W. Meissner comments that "[c]losed belief systems reflect underlying needs to compensate for feelings of inadequacy and self-hate by excessive concerns over power status."[71] Thus, people from groups that have been experiencing severe identity threats will tend to get very defensive, especially when the symbols of their group are treated disrespectfully. The problem, however, is that militant believers have developed finely honed antennae that detect all real insults and some imagined ones, judging none sufficiently small enough to ignore.

Sometimes people seem drawn to extremist faith as the best means to alleviate guilt they've experienced because of certain misdeeds—major, minor, or purely imagined. By asserting their boundless commitment to their religion, they may be able to escape their consciences and achieve expiation in a way they could not with moderate faith. It would seem that religion, in some form, had to be there initially to implant the seeds of guilt. But those who have been tempted by some aspect of nonbelief may come back to the fold with a fury.[72]

Several psychoanalysts have detected a connection between religious extremism and feelings about sex. The hostility of most militants toward homosexuals, the exaggerated concern about the sexual goings-on of other people, the angry reaction to permissive mainstream media broadcasts, the preference for women in nonrevealing garb, and the insistence upon a male-dominated power structure can all be seen as suggestive of difficulties in the management of sexual impulses. Perhaps militants fear their own sexual impulses or the conflict of these impulses with their declared ideological commitment. One need not be a card-carrying psychoanalyst to agree that such people therefore construct a system of controls that makes the task of impulse control easier, but at the cost of intense frustration, anger, and resentment, directed especially toward those with a freer lifestyle.

It would, however, seem more a caricature than description to maintain, as one analyst does, that "[Christian] Fundamentalists live in a world obsessed with sexuality. . . . [Morality] is about avoiding certain sexual sins and fixating on that dimension of life to the virtual exclusion of everything else."[73] Psychoanalyst Walter Davis argues that, for the Christian fundamentalist, "[s]exuality has been transformed into the festering wound out of which *resentment* is born, because every time desire rises up one experiences again one's powerlessness to break the stranglehold the superego [or moral component of the personality] has over one's sexuality. A jaundiced eye then casts its gaze on all who have succeeded where one has failed. Malevolent envy rises up, offering one the only exit from inner conflict—hatred of the sexual and unending war upon it."[74] What are we to make of this argument? Perhaps that it remains highly speculative and, in any case, probably constitutes no more than a portion of the motivation for some extremists in Christianity and other faiths.

Even within cultures where extremism thrives, many individuals resist the pull. Psychologists do not possess conclusive evidence about which individuals are most apt to develop into enthusiastic proponents of religious militancy, but we should perhaps be most concerned about those who

- are in late adolescence and early adulthood,
- come from families lacking in normal love and support,[75]
- are frustrated and consumed by thoughts that their lives have been spoiled or wasted,
- are preoccupied with issues of pride,
- feel personally humiliated,
- feel their group has been humiliated,
- experience with intensity real or imagined threats to their identity or self-esteem, or
- have bound together tightly their religious, ethnic, and personal identities.[76]

Some of the points from Eric Hoffer's old classic *The True Believer* are still relevant. People, he suggests, are brought to radical movements by "the consciousness of an irremediably blemished self. Their chief desire is to escape that self—and it is this desire which manifests itself as a propensity for united action and self-sacrifice."[77] And, as Hoffer notes, "To lose one's life is but to lose the present and, clearly, to lose a defiled, worthless present is not to lose much."[78] When one expects to gain eternal salvation in exchange for loss of life, the loss may be barely noticeable.

Why Moderate Religion Fails II: Society and Politics

Psychology speaks of individuals, yet militant religious movements arise in groups, social classes, countries, cultures, and civilizations. It would be a mistake to think we have explained the origins of extremism once we have uncovered the psychology of the phenomenon. Various brands of religious fanaticism have emerged across the globe in the past half century, but they have assumed very different forms. And the most dangerous strains of extremism have not taken root in all places where demagogues have sought to implant them. Certain countries, cultures, and groups have been much more vulnerable than others.

Here it is worth recalling a famous psychological study concerning a very different situation. Hadley Cantril investigated those who believed Orson Welles's fictitious 1938 Halloween news broadcast about an invasion from Mars. Thousands of Americans became panic stricken amid what they thought was a real alien attack. They never bothered to change the station or seek confirmation of any kind. One thing Cantril learned was that many of these people

> had preexisting mental sets that made the . . . [invasion broadcast] so understandable to them that they immediately accepted it as true. Highly religious people who believed that God willed and controlled the destinies of man were already furnished with a particular standard of judgment that would make an invasion of our planet and a destruction of its members merely an "act of God." This was particularly true if the religious frame of reference was of the eschatolog-

> ical variety providing the individual with definite attitudes or beliefs regarding the end of the world. . . . [Also, some] persons had built up such fanciful notions of the possibilities of science that they could easily believe the powers of strange superscientists were being turned against them, perhaps merely for experimental purposes.[79]

Cantril also determined that many people possessed no existing standards of judgment sufficient to engender disbelief. Moreover, the circumstances described by Welles were so far beyond people's capacity for understanding that many were desperate in their need for interpretation and, consequently, likely to accept the first interpretation offered to them.

The parallels between the credulous radio listeners of 1938 and the religious extremists of the present day are far from perfect. However, those who become religious fanatics may be similarly motivated by a desire to come to terms with a world situation that they perceive as dangerous and incomprehensible. In the face of such anxiety-provoking confusion, they may be tempted to believe in great conspiracies and to interpret and frame events through the prism of a previously established religious worldview.

Cantril believed that the roots of credulity in 1938 lay importantly in the broader social, economic, and political instability of the years immediately preceding World War II. He wrote:

> The prolonged economic unrest and the consequent insecurity felt by many of the listeners was another cause for bewilderment. The depression had already lasted nearly ten years. People were still out of work. Why didn't somebody do something about it? Why didn't the experts find a solution? What was the cause of it anyway? . . . [W]hat would happen, no one could tell. . . . [A] mysterious invasion fitted the pattern of the mysterious events of the decade. The lack of a sophisticated, relatively stable economic or political frame of reference created in many persons a psychological disequilibrium. . . . [The invasion] was another phenomenon in the outside world beyond their control and comprehension.[80]

When events in the world and people's personal lives are unexpected, confusing, threatening to self-esteem, and potentially dangerous, many will become amenable to simplistic explanations. This may be part of the reason for the rise of extremist and near-extremist worldviews in many places.

Nearly everyone agrees that one must seek the sources of contemporary religious fanaticism in the global upheavals unleashed by modernization.[81] Historian Bruce Lawrence sees the origins of the fundamentalist challenge as "inseparable from the specter of its declared enemy: the Enlightenment."[82] He explains that "[t]he Enlightenment undergirds the modern world. It also launches the modern study of religion. It looks at everything human, yet considers its own viewpoint as observer and interpreter to be superior. It is that implicit assumption of superiority that offends."[83] He sees a "core contest between two incommensurate ways of viewing the world, one which locates values in timeless scriptures, inviolate laws, and unchanging mores, the other which sees in the expansion of scientific knowledge a technological transformation of society that pluralizes options both for learning and for living."[84] While there are examples of those who reject modern technology altogether, the bigger problem is usually with the underlying philosophy of the modern world. Among extreme fanatics, there are even many who understand advanced technology well and seek to harness it in support of their religious ideology.

There are countless ways that the modern world has upset traditional values, politics, and social arrangements. Sudhir Kakar is a psychoanalyst who has spent much of his life studying the Hindu-Muslim conflict in India. He believes that the mass killings in the subcontinent can be explained as an outgrowth of new group identities that have been forged among many Hindus and Muslims, and that these identities are themselves a consequence of threats arising out of modernization, globalization, and perceived discrimination from the state. In the modern world, many of the old-time values and ideals of one's traditional culture—whatever it is—start to seem hopelessly outmoded and obsolete. Simultaneously, for many, crafts and work skills become irrelevant, and people lose yet another component of who they thought they were. And, in many parts of the world, including India, large groups also lose their geographic turf. When political authorities deal insensitively—as they often have—with the symbols of culture and religion, identity threats became, for many, intolerable.[85]

Religions began reconciling themselves to the modern age centuries ago. Most of the changes from modernization occurred earliest in the West, and perhaps that is why Protestant fundamentalism appeared first in the United States. Religious institutions in the modern world have lost influence, and science has—at least in some areas—supplanted theology. But equally important, political and economic forces have resulted in a reorganization of power and status. The modern storm has left many feeling alienated, and these people have been most apt to seek new identities, sometimes based on religion and ethnicity. The risk of fanaticism is probably greatest when ethnic and religious identities are merged together.[86]

Across the globe, there has been during the past half century a rise in violent religious extremism and also in the generally less extreme variants of fundamentalism. These developments are, in some sense, a reaction to changes first unleashed by the Enlightenment. However, it is apparent that forces that unleashed these late-twentieth-century developments are also more recent.

Some Christians in the United States and, to a lesser extent, around the Western world, grew disoriented, alienated, and discontented as a result of the decline in traditional values in the 1960s. In particular, they reacted to school prayer under attack, freer sexual mores, the advent of legalized abortion, greater rights for homosexuals, a reduction in the visibility of religious symbols in the public square, and—more generally—to the rise in relativistic systems of values.

Some of these same issues played a part in the rise of Jewish fanaticism in Israel. But there, Israel's international predicament was probably a more important precipitating factor. The Jewish state had been under attack from hostile neighbors since its birth and even before. But even after its spectacular victory in the Six Days' War, peaceful coexistence with the Arabs did not seem likely. Secular Israeli governments had made many offers to negotiate peace, but none seemed to make real progress. The world community and, especially the United Nations, seemed to have developed a particular hostility characterized by double standards toward Israel, even declaring the liberal nationalism of the state to be a form of racism. In the face of all this, a large segment of the Israeli public started to question the dominance of the left-leaning Labor government. And within this group, a small subset turned to religious extremism. They saw Israel's bad fortune as a consequence of too much faith in the principles of the liberal democratic world and too little faith in Jewish law and tradition. They also saw too much focus on compromise with an implacable foe, too much concern for politically correct niceties, and too little emphasis on outright military victory. In some ways, they started to view Israel's twentieth-century wars as a continuation of Jewish struggles in the Old Testament—a place where the Enlightenment was nowhere to be found.

In Christian America, Christian Europe, and Jewish Israel, however, the overwhelming majority of those who turned to revitalized but backward-looking forms of religion still found strong positive elements in their identification with mainstream society. Their belief systems and psychologies may have shared some commonalities with full-blown extremists, but they generally stopped short of advocating destructive behavior. Sometimes, as the in case of the Amish in Pennsylvania and most Jewish Hassidim across the globe, they did rebel against modernism, striving to preserve old-time traditions and a God-centered life. But they did so without traces of troubling antisocial behaviors. They became separate from mainstream society but without an agenda to harm others in any way.

Generally, cultures and those parts of cultures that have benefited from modernization and modernity may contain extremist elements, but the fanatic groups will not attain a dominant position. The greatest risk of religious extremism will be among nations, cultures, and other groupings that have been losers in the process.

While America and Europe modernized first and some Asian nations caught up rapidly, many parts of the world lagged behind. As one student of the Islamic world has noted, "There are tremendous penalties for latecomers to the modernization sweepstakes. . . . [T]his reality is painful, and the pain often is felt most keenly not by the poorest, but by those who have progressed a little and are frustrated in their aspirations to go further."[87] People in the places that modernized late perceive the obvious logic in adoption of ways that are not their own. They also see everywhere the equally apparent evidence of the failure of traditional ways. Though the benefits of the applied sciences at first seem hardest to reap, in the long run they travel fairly well across cultural borders. But imported benefits constitute a challenge to collective esteem.[88]

With the advent of globalization in media, politics, and economy, the dream of acquiring Western science while retaining traditional values starts to seem illusory. Dangerous threats to traditional culture come in the form of greater sexual openness, equality for women, religious tolerance, free speech, and a host of other imports. The situation creates anger among the losers and temptations for the winners. When people succumb, as they often do, to the logic of the new ways, there is sometimes a surge in guilt.

Precisely at the moment when one's culture seems under unremitting attack, one feels the greatest need for a reassertion of self-esteem based on the traditional identity. And this becomes the engine that fuels much fanaticism. It plays a role whenever modern imports seem to be chasing traditional values off the scene. But the Muslim world seems especially vulnerable to this type of problem because so much of the collective esteem in this culture rests on a memory of a highly successful religious civilization.

There are several other reasons why religious extremism has been so prominent in the Muslim world:

- Widespread rules prohibit criticism of Islam, leaving it the only untarnished symbol in societies that have failed in many ways.[89]

- Some Muslim countries permit and even sponsor extremist education and socialization.[90]
- Most Muslim countries lack meaningful constitutional protections for religious diversity.
- Some Arab and Muslim cultures seem to place a premium on pride and the need to avenge challenges to honor.[91]
- There is a strong religious tradition of battle in the name of the faith.
- Early extremist actions are widely perceived to have succeeded in their efforts to challenge non-Islamic religions and secular authorities in Muslim countries.

Though many analysts have attributed the rise in Islamic extremism to particular policies of the United States, such interpretations are missing the big picture. No nation's policies are flawless, and some American policies—good ones and bad ones—contribute to the waxing and waning of the nation's popularity in the Muslim world.

But religious extremism develops mainly in response to identity threats. Such threats, in turn, emerge from a lack of viability in one's personal life, culture, and worldview. Most often, such matters lie far beyond the influence of a particular American policy or set of policies. Even when America's deeds enrage the extremists, this is not necessarily because the policies were morally objectionable. Thus, one can make strong moral cases for America's historical support for women's rights, freedom of the press, rights of religious minorities, moderate Arab leaders, making peace with Israel, and defense of Kuwait and Saudi Arabia against Iraqi aggression. Yet all of these things are cited as a basis for anti-Americanism by extremists.

In sum, many people turn to religion to help address the existential concerns we all face. They seek, above all, a way of managing the fear of death. But they also desire a group to which they can belong, an experience of meaning in life, a sense of self-worth, and a coherent worldview. Most of the time, religious people can satisfy these needs without allowing their religion to become dangerous.

However, in some people, moderate religion fails and only an extremist vision can do the trick. Islam, Christianity, and Judaism all are equipped to provide the extremists with the theology they need to fuel their militant fires. Unfortunately, the fanatic faith they find comes at a high cost—for society and for the individual. By surrendering to their religion much of what it means to be human, these people may gain some real social and psychological benefits, but they also become resentful and driven to avoid open examination of their faith at any cost. Their religion draws them far afield from any constructive or humanistic approach to life. The danger is greatest when individuals and ideologies embrace four tendencies: (1) opposition to compromise with those who see things differently; (2) acceptance of religious ends as justification for any means; (3) willingness to assume the role of defender of God's honor by punishing all those who show disrespect; and (4) a drive to obtain heavenly rewards without regard for the earthly consequences of behavior.

Of course, a sensible religious tradition can reign in the worst tendencies of an individual who is psychologically prone to extremism. And a balanced, well-adjusted, and morally grounded person will often apply the brakes to a dangerous theology that attempts to drag him down its pathway of destruction.

Similarly, when the surrounding state or culture is basically sound, the worst extremists will typically be condemned and marginalized. Even a handful can wreak considerable havoc on the surrounding culture through acts of terror and violence. But strong social and political conventions can hold in check many of those whose religious ideology shares some elements with the extremists.

Sometimes, when controlling conventions are lacking, when destructive theology abounds, and when the surrounding state is a failure, the entire culture may run the risk of disintegration. Religion, under these conditions, will cease to work in the service of morality and social cooperation. It will become the tool of warped individuals and even large groups bent on destruction in the service of their theological and psychological agendas. This is what is now happening in large parts of the Muslim world.

Part Three

FIGHTING EXTREMISM SENSIBLY

CHAPTER 6

A Battle on Many Fronts

The Power and the Danger

A few years ago, French president Jacques Chirac chose a small bucolic town nestled in the hills of south-central France as the setting for a speech in which he condemned mounting intolerance, racism, and antisemitism in his country.[1] The choice of location—Le Chambon-sur-Lignon—was significant. During the Second World War, while that part of France was governed first by the collaborationist Vichy regime and, later, directly by the Nazis, the heroic residents of the town of about five thousand collectively hid between three thousand and five thousand Jews in their homes.[2] For four years, no one ever tipped off the authorities. Though often impoverished themselves, the Chambonnais generously provided food to their guests and assisted with forged identification cards. They also helped many Jews cross the border into the safe haven of Switzerland. Pierre Sauvage was a Jewish child born in the town during the wartime rescue operation; he is also the director of an award-winning documentary film about Le Chambon-sur-Lignon in which he describes the town's "unique conspiracy of goodness."[3]

President Chirac sought to capitalize on the heroism of these French men and women when he decided to issue his call for tolerance at this historic place. But his remarks irked Sauvage. In his speech, Chirac claimed that

> here, in adversity, the soul of the nation manifested itself. Here was the embodiment of our country's conscience. Le Chambon-sur-Lignon is a place of memory. A place of resistance. A place symbolizing a France true to her principles, faithful to her heritage, true to her genius. . . . On this high plateau, with its harsh winters, in solitude, sometimes in poverty, often in adversity, women and men have long upheld the values that unite us. . . . [T]hey chose courage, generosity and dignity. The chose tolerance, solidarity and fraternity. They chose the humanist principles that unite our national community, and serve as the basis of our collective destiny—the principles that make France what she is.

So what could have been Sauvage's complaint about this moving testament?

He explained that, in France today, "officials focus on upholding the militant French-style secularism. . . . In his speech in Le Chambon, Chirac made no reference to the Hebrew Bible or to the New Testament, to faith or the power of religious convictions. He touched only lightly on the Protestant Mountains once-determined particularism. He urged his compatriots always to carry [their national] heritage with pride. But had the people of Le Chambon not been motivated to resist the Holocaust by more than mere Frenchness?"[4]

Sauvage was raised by nominally Jewish but deeply antireligious parents; when he returned to Le Chambon-sur-Lignon, he maintains that he was not looking to uncover the religious roots of the wartime resistance movement. But that, at least in part, is what he found. The wartime rescue operation was sparked and fueled largely by two passionate but unconventional Protestant pastors, Andre Trocme and Edouard Theis. Both were strict pacifists who, prior to the war, had opposed fighting the Germans. Yet, after the fall of France, these religious leaders insisted with tremendous energy that the townspeople not collaborate with the Nazis. Indeed, the day after the sad armistice, the pastors had declared that "[t]he duty of Christians is to resist the violence that will be brought to bear on their consciences through the weapons of the spirit. We will resist whenever our adversaries will demand of us obedience contrary to the orders of the gospel. We will do so without fear but also without pride and without hate."[5] Apparently, this early declaration was widely influential and set the foundation for everything that was to follow, including participation in the resistance by some who did not attend the pastors' church.

One elderly woman recalled why she and her neighbors helped: "What happened had a lot to do with people still believing in something. . . . The Bible says to feed the hungry, to visit the sick. It's a normal thing to do."[6] Edouard Theis, assistant pastor during the war, explained decades later that one could summarize Christian faith, as Jesus did, in a single sentence: "Love the Lord your God with all your heart, your soul, your might and your neighbor as yourself. That's the summary. . . . It just had to be applied."

Another woman, described as a Christian fundamentalist, said that whether or not the Jews were observant of their religion, "for us they were the people of God." She added, "Your faith is in vain if works don't follow." One other important source of the soft-spoken heroism of the Chambonnais may lie in their own religious heritage. Most were descendants of Huguenots, French Protestants who centuries earlier had been severely persecuted for their beliefs. They had a tradition of resistance.

Psychologists and sociologists might be inclined not to take the townspeople's explanations at face value. And there are many valid questions one might raise about the motivation of the Chambonnais. For one thing, if Christian faith were so clearly and powerfully a motivator of unselfish benevolence, even in the face of danger, why did it manifest itself so prominently only in Le Chambon-sur-Lignon and a few other places? More often, Christianity in its various forms managed to coexist alongside a willingness to perpetrate atrocities and collaborate in Nazi crimes. Only very infrequently did it manage to jolt ordinary people from their predominant responses of doing nothing or looking away. One might also note that the same pacifistic Christianity that inspired Pastors Trocme and Theis to do great things during the occupation would have been entirely inappropriate were it implemented at high levels as a strategy during the prewar period. Finally, the Chambonnais Protestants were particularly open to helping Jews because their variety of faith included some Judaic elements and elevated the Jews to a particular position of honor. Would these townspeople have been equally willing to help some other group?

Social scientists might speculate that religion per se may have been less significant than the presence of a constructive, charismatic leadership. They might further suggest that peer pressure played an important part too; once a certain percentage of people began to participate in the resistance, it became publicly shameful not to join the effort. The somewhat isolated geographic location of Le Chambon-sur-Lignon may have contributed in two ways: first, by permitting a culture of independence to develop and, second, by allowing the rescue operation to proceed for some time without attracting much attention from the Vichy authorities. Finally, the Huguenot experience may have sensitized the Chambonnais to the cruelty of religious persecution, but this can be explained without any reference to religion itself. The experience of persecution may contribute to the development of a tolerant outlook.

Nonetheless, the study of religious evil should be tempered by the realization that religion has, at least on some occasions, provided a motivation to do tremendous good when secular and humanistic approaches did not, could not, or were not available. Religion, as the Chambonnais practiced it, may not in the final analysis prove alluring to outsiders and it certainly cannot be evaluated on the basis of its impact on one group of people in one aspect of their lives for one fairly brief period of time. But, at least in that context, it certainly commands our attention and respect.

Some see religion itself as the root cause of religious extremism. In a trivial sense, of course, if there were no religion, there could be no militancy carried out in its name. But there would, no doubt, be plenty of extremism derived from other ideologies. As we have seen, people turn to religion for many reasons, often to manage existential dilemmas, to feel connected to the past, to develop a sense of identity, to fulfill social needs, to regulate sexuality, and to aid in everyday psychological coping. For each of these needs, there are available numerous nonreligious alternatives that may have certain advantages, however.

A nonreligious person, for example, would not be saddled with problematic passages of scripture, antisocial religious traditions, and intellectually constraining outlooks. In addition, it seems that much of the constructive power of religion derives from the same sources as its destructive power, namely, the belief in the transcendence of some objects, rules, persons, or commandments. If religion trumps reason, it can readily become an energizing force for irrationality. If religion does not trump reason, it loses its special power to inspire, motivate, or effectively handle existential challenges. Numerous religious thinkers have acknowledged this problem, but most have concluded that—in some forms of faith—it is possible to get the good without the bad.[7] They may be wrong. Still, whatever systems or methods emerge to meet the needs of the nonreligious person must not be presumed to be perfect or necessarily better than the religious structures they replace.

Traditional religions may have some advantages of their own. Toward the end of the eighteenth century, two prominent thinkers of the day expressed opposing views on the early days of the revolution in France. Edmund Burke was an articulate, principled, sometimes reform-minded yet conservative member of the House of Commons in England. He accepted that "[a] state without the means of some change is without the means of its conservation."[8] But he also believed that "[t]he science of constructing a commonwealth, or renovating it, or reforming it, is, like every other experimental science, not to be taught *a priori*. Nor is it a short experience that can instruct us in that practical science. . . . It is with infinite caution that any man ought to venture upon pulling down an edifice, which has answered in any tolerable degree for ages the common purposes of society, or on building it up again, without having models and patterns of approved utility before his eyes."[9] One of the institutions Burke valued highly was the church establishment. He called this establishment "the first of our prejudices, not a prejudice destitute of reason, but involving in it a profound and extensive wisdom."[10] Unanchored reason, in short, was not up to the task of remaking the world and was insufficient to control the many base qualities apparent in human nature.

Thomas Paine disagreed strongly. He was known for his pamphlet *Common Sense*, which had inspired the American colonists to prosecute their war against England. He was also a prominent freethinker and an enthusiastic supporter of the revolutionaries in France. According to Paine, people could use reason to construct a better world, ridding themselves of the often unsuitable and unjust legacy of the past. He held that "[e]very age and generation must be free to act for itself *in all cases* as the ages and generations which preceded it. The vanity and presumption of governing beyond the grave is the most ridiculous and insolent of all tyrannies. . . . Every generation is, and must be, competent to all the purposes which its occasions require."[11] For Paine, the nefarious influence of organized religion was one of the most important things a reasonable society would have to control.

Burke was prescient in forecasting the disintegration of high-minded revolutionary dreams into the reign of the guillotine at the Place de la Concorde in Paris. But, in retrospect, we might also note that he defended many institutions that we now regard as outmoded and unjust. Still, there remains wisdom in Burke's advice about moving with caution when tearing down edifices without a clear sense of the consequences. Those who try to meet the needs addressed by religion in altogether novel ways may obtain unpredictable results. They may build something better, or they may not. Those who prefer more cautiously to modify existing religious structures certainly can make an argument that they are following Burke's advice. And this argument may appeal even to those who have no real faith in religion or God as supernatural entity.

Despite many studies, we don't really know whether religion, or some forms of religion, are, on balance, psychologically beneficial. It is also difficult to assess whether religion as a whole has a prosocial or antisocial effect. And top scientists continue to debate among themselves about whether religion can be reconciled with the latest scientific discoveries.[12] Some limit their uses of God to explain only those things that cannot be explained by science, a notion sometimes reflected in the concept of a "god of the gaps." Others endorse the view that religious and theistic outlooks are consistent with and even supportive of existing scientific evidence. Judgments on many religious matters must, therefore, be left to the individual, not only because this is a politically sound principle but also because no one is really in a position to provide meaningful and definitive guidance on the matter.

Religion in all its many manifestations is not an enemy that every reasonable person can or should oppose. We are able however to identify when religious beliefs become dangerous and, thereby, to highlight some forms of belief that are, quite clearly, the enemy of those who have come to enjoy and value the Western system of constitutional democracy.

A CONSUMER'S GUIDE TO RELIGIOUS BELIEF

Journalist Andrew Sullivan may have cut to the heart of something very troubling about Iranian president Mahmoud Ahmadinejad. Sullivan explains that "[i]t wasn't . . . [Ahmadinejad's] obvious intention to pursue nuclear technology and weaponry. It wasn't his denial of the Holocaust or even his eager anticipation of Armageddon. It was something else entirely. It was his smile. In every interview [during his 2006 visit to the United Nations], confronting every loaded question, his eyes seemed calm, his expression at ease, his face at peace. He seemed utterly serene."[13] Perhaps Sullivan makes too much out of a politician who knows how to put on a smile. But I don't think so.

Ahmadinejad is an evil man who does not seem plagued by doubt or distress. Sullivan does not attribute his smiley serenity to mental illness. Rather, he explains, Ahmadinejad "is smiling gently because for him, the most perplexing and troubling questions we all face every day have already been answered. He has placed his trust in the arms of God. . . . Complete calm comes with complete certainty. In today's unnerving, globalizing, sometimes terrifying world, such religious certainty is a balm more in demand than ever." Contentment in his case and that of many other religious militants may reveal that, despite horrible social consequences, extremism at some psychological level may work for him and others.

Generally, the support that a person gives to religion has little to do with its social or political efficacy—or its moral content. Instead, it comes from a sense that the faith is psychologically efficacious. To avoid extremism, people would have to attend more closely to the moral, social, and political consequences of their religions. Unfortunately, many believers see little reason to do this if a religion feels like it is working, especially with regard to matters of ultimate concern. Religious militancy is frequently a consequence of individuals choosing to pursue their personal "immortality projects" and "quests for meaning" by traveling down the wrong paths—wrong in the sense that they are socially and morally destructive.

Of course, one has only provided a partial answer when one says that extremists make bad choices. The reasons for these choices lie in aberrant individual psychologies, poor familial support systems, failed societies, dysfunctional political systems, distant historical events, antisocial religious traditions, and easy-to-abuse scriptures. Thus, efforts designed to persuade fanatics to discard their religious ideologies are not likely to get very far. When, for example, one is dealing with the likes of al Qaeda, Kahane Chai, or those who kill providers of abortion services in the name of Christian faith, one is apt to get nowhere.

Still, attempts to persuade the faithful may be a crucial part of the struggles against the various forms of religious extremism. Sullivan endorses this approach, saying: "There is, however, a way out. And it will come from the only place it can come from—the minds and souls of people of faith. It will come from the much derided moderate Muslims, tolerant Jews and humble Christians. The alternative to the secular-fundamentalist death spiral is something called spiritual humility and sincere religious doubt. Fundamentalism is not the only valid form of faith, and to say it is, is the great lie of our time."[14] Many others, especially from the ranks of liberal theologians, have suggested that it is up to the religious to avoid taking the steps that might lead to militancy in themselves, fellow congregants, and coreligionists across the globe.

Believers must begin to see their religions through entirely different lenses, which they may well be reluctant to do. As Reverend Kimball puts it, "Men and women of faith can and should be at the forefront of the long overdue struggle to stop religion from being used as a vehicle to oppress and dehumanize groups of people."[15] To do so, the religious must, on their own accord, start to assess not only the spiritual and psychological experience of their faith but also its social, political, and ethical consequences, especially with regard to nonbelievers.

This approach might work best where religious beliefs are contradictory and conflicted, with constructive beliefs existing alongside destructive ones. Psychologists have long known that people strive to achieve a degree of consistency among their ideas, especially when inconsistency might reflect poorly on their self-concept. The more a person is forced to confront these inconsistencies, the more disturbed he will become and, hence, the greater the potential for change.[16]

In any event, the whole process would need to start with the recognition that all religions are not equal, though they may have been endowed with equal protection under the Constitution of the United States and other similar documents. As Kimball explains, "If all religions are not the same, neither is it the case that all religious worldviews are equally valid. Those that have stood the test of time have clearly worked for most of the people who embraced them. This historical fact must be taken seriously, but it does not mean that all roads lead up the same mountain. Events in our world today suggest that value judgments are sorely needed. . . . Freedom of religion is a good thing. So is freedom from the religion others may wish to impose on those who differ."[17] The belief that all systems of faith are equally constructive is not a political principle of Western democracy but rather an unfortunate outgrowth of the doctrine of cultural relativism.

Psychiatrist Eli S. Chesen argued that "[r]eligion is actually a kind of consumer good that is without question potentially harmful to the user's mental health."[18] Like secondary smoke, it is also potentially harmful to others. A consumer might, in principle, be able to assess faiths in a manner not altogether different from the way *Consumer Reports* magazine assesses products. As established earlier, religions, denominations, sects, and cults that promote the following ideas are very dangerous:

- The faith, or the rule of the faithful, should be spread by violent means.
- Nonbelievers must obey the rules of the faith, even though there is no convincing nonreligious justification for such obedience.
- People cannot freely convert out of the faith.
- Certain geographical locations must be controlled by believers, even though there is no convincing nonreligious basis for this control.
- God requires earthly punishment of, or discrimination against, those who make certain sexual or lifestyle choices, even though there is no convincing nonreligious foundation for such a judgment.
- Certain individuals have been anointed to carry out God's punishments on earth.
- All means are acceptable when one is doing God's work.
- Blasphemers must be punished in the here and now.

Several other religious notions are potentially dangerous, but possibly not quite as dangerous:

- All or some nonbelievers are hated by God or destined to be punished by God after they die.
- God prefers some races, ethnic groups, or nationalities to others.

- The government and laws ought to favor believers, though there should be some protection for nonbelievers too.
- God prefers to see women in a subjugated role.
- God disapproves of certain sexual and lifestyle choices, even though there is no convincing nonreligious basis for this disapproval.
- No one may blaspheme against God or the faithful, lest they be punished by God in the afterlife.
- Certain leaders have access to God's wishes via a channel that is not subject to accuracy checks by others, and these leaders are endowed by God with the power to make life decisions for other believers.
- People—or some people—are deeply sinful and in need of special cleansing in order to avoid terrible punishments now or in the world to come.

It is hard to see how religious laws and precepts embracing the above ideas can avoid sooner or later becoming a source of extremist behavior. To the extent that a believer wants a faith that is not part of the problem, he or she must either change the religion or change religions. Adaptation of age-old religious sources may proceed very slowly and in accordance with religious traditions, but, in the interim, lives may be damaged. The risk can be mitigated if leaders of the faith are people of goodwill, guided by moral sensibility. But, as the founding fathers of the United States made clear, the system that rests on the hope for good leadership rests on a shaky foundation indeed.

Once a religion has been stripped of dangerous beliefs, it may leave some people with the feeling that something is missing. After all, those beliefs exist, in part, because they met psychological needs—at least superficially. More reasonable and socially constructive forms of faith will perhaps leave fewer people sporting Ahmadinejad's serene grin. But in the final analysis, perhaps Kimball is correct that authentic forms of religion, to the extent that any may be called authentic, "engage . . . the intellect as people wrestle with the mystery of existence and the challenges of living in an imperfect world. Conversely, blind obedience is a sure sign of corrupt religion. Beware [he warns] of any religion that seeks to limit the intellectual freedom and individual integrity of its adherents."[19]

Once the destructive principles have been weeded out of a faith, there should be a broad latitude for doctrine, theology, and religious practice. For example, the brave and noteworthy Islamic reformer Irshad Manji suggests that, for her, "[r]eligion supplies a set of values, including discipline, that serve as a counterweight to the materialism of life in the West. I could have become a runaway materialist, a robotic mall rat who resorts to retail therapy in pursuit of fulfillment. I didn't. That's because religion introduces competing claims. It injects a tension that compels me to think and allows me to avoid fundamentalisms of my own."[20] There is certainly room to disagree with this assessment. One may not have problems with consumerism or one may strongly reject the notion that life in the West or secularism necessarily leads one to become a "mall rat." But Manji's viewpoint is an arguable one, and the world benefits from diverse perspectives on matters such as these.

Some may choose a religion based on love and others may not; the requirement is merely for tolerance. Some may wish to carry out many religious rituals, others may engage in few, and still others may develop an exotic and unusual metaphysics. Some may wish to live their lives in separate communities of like-minded souls, while others prefer to be part of mainstream society.

A religion may even be psychologically damaging to its believers, but this alone does not make a religion destructive to society. It is up to individual believers to choose whether to follow their faith, notwithstanding its impact on them. Chesen has suggested that, among other things:

- "Religion serves in many ways to impede the development of flexible thinking processes. This ultimately results in adult thinking that is rigid, confined and stereotyped."[21]

- "Rigid, confined, and stereotyped religious thinking patterns can be directly contributory to emotional instability."[22]
- "Profound lifelong religious indoctrination may assume the form of a punitive conscience in the adult. This serves to stifle the person's conscious recognition of normal drives; he is therefore unable to deal with them in times of stress."[23]

These contentions may be true, though no convincing empirical evidence exists for any of them. Even if there were such evidence, however, it would be up to the believer to decide whether the risk was worth taking and which psychological goals were worthy ends toward which a person should strive. There is, after all, no ethical imperative that one avoid psychologically risky beliefs.

Similarly, the religious themselves must decide whether their faith imposes on them too many requirements for acceptance of irrationalities. But for religion to be on the side of the angels, it is necessary that antisocial beliefs be removed or otherwise neutralized. In some systems of faith, religiously sanctioned methods exist to accomplish such change. But even when they do not, the offending beliefs can pose a tremendous problem for the rest of us.

MANAGING THE EXTREMIST THREAT

What should the rest of us do when people refuse to abandon or modify a religion that has become the motivation, ideology, and organization for hatred, intolerance, and violence? This is one of the most important policy questions confronting the world today. Unfortunately, many of the places one might look for strategies and answers have been hobbled by an unwillingness to think with an open mind and draw necessary distinctions.

Consider the efforts of the United Nations. Over the past decade, the world organization has issued many lengthy reports on religious intolerance, most coordinated by Abdelfattah Amor, the special rapporteur of the Commission on Human Rights on freedom of religion and belief. For example, one report issued in September 2000—a lengthy yet highly selective overview of religious discrimination across the globe—expressed "its deep concern that Islam is frequently and wrongly associated with human rights violations and with terrorism [and that] . . . negative stereotyping of religions in general is a matter of concern. The special rapporteur considers that religious extremism is an aberration to the extent that all religions are based fundamentally on the values of human rights, tolerance and non discrimination. Certain interpretations and certain manipulations of people on the basis of religion have distorted it and wrongly associated it with extremism."[24] This statement—in particular the notion that all religions are based fundamentally on human rights and tolerance—misrepresents the reality of much religion in the world today and in the past. The UN program might still have been rescued by a clear enunciation of principles that could be used to distinguish between real and distorted religion. But no such standards are provided. As it stands, this report and others working from the same assumptions merely provide a smokescreen behind which extremists can hide.

In keeping with the general anti-Israel orientation of the United Nations, the special rapporteur's reports omit any discussion of the rampant, faith-based hatred of Jews that is prevalent in large parts of the Muslim world. The reports do, admirably, encourage "the development of respect for human rights and fundamental freedoms and . . . the preparation of the child for a responsible life in a free society, in a spirit of understanding, peace, tolerance, gender equality and friendship among peoples, ethnic, national and religious groups, and persons of indigenous origin; and [urge states] to take all appropriate measures to prevent racist, discriminatory and xenophobic attitudes and behaviour, through education."[25] But by refusing to move, for the most part, beyond glittering generalities to specifics, the reports again render themselves useless.

One United Nations report on religious tolerance discusses "violations of the principle of nondiscrimination in matters of religion or belief, namely, policies, legislation and regulations, practices and acts that discriminate against certain communities." Then the special rapporteur lists several nations where such cases have caught his particular attention: Egypt, France, Islamic Republic of Iran, and the United States of America.[26] What a profound inability to draw meaningful distinctions!

From such analyses emerge empty strategies. For example, states should "take the opportunity to focus on the promotion of rights which make it possible to adopt an essentially preventive approach, attacking the root causes of extremism and intolerance rather than . . . their overt manifestations. . . . [A]ction in the area of education and culture is a requirement and a prerequisite for any effort to combat extremism and intolerance; to do otherwise would constitute a mere reactive response with no impact on the future."[27] Thus, the problem is diagnosed in general terms and portrayed as worldwide, without any situations needing more or less attention than any others.

The strategy aspires to be long-term and preventive, based largely on an unspecified form of "education" and cultural change. What is sadly lacking is a sense of *what* people should be taught and how, as well as which aspects of which cultures need which sorts of change. All of these issues are apparently deemed too hot to handle by the special rapporteur.

We have already specified some of the theological and religious sources of extremism. But, as previously discussed, if we are serious about addressing these underlying sources, we must think also about the political, social, and psychological underpinnings of religious militancy in its various manifestations.

The psychology is complex. Most likely, individuals drawn to carry out extremist behaviors in the name of religion experience threats to some central components of their identities and, hence, to their self-esteem. They are often preoccupied with questions of pride and may feel humiliated in some aspect of their personal lives. Or they may feel that their national, religious, or local group has somehow been humiliated. Along similar lines, they may be deeply frustrated people, consumed by thoughts that their lives have been spoiled or wasted. They may be racked by guilt for real or imagined wrongdoings. They may be especially likely to come from families lacking in normal love and support. And they are most at risk of turning to extremism in late adolescence and early adulthood.

Such extremism-prone individuals may be found in any culture and any religion. However, they are much more likely to come from times and places where events are unpredictable, unstable, confusing, and potentially dangerous. Modernization and globalization have unleashed destabilizing forces in many parts of the world, and the consequences have been most intense for latecomers to modernity. Failed societies are most at risk, where political and social systems deny basic gratifications to large segments of the population.[28]

Where schools, houses of worship, mass media, and other cultural institutions indoctrinate people with extremist propaganda and where the state sponsors such indoctrination, large numbers succumb to the pressures. When mainstream religious leaders fail to condemn the extremists unconditionally and without ambiguity, the soil in which militancy grows becomes very fertile.

The lack of protective constitutional provisions like freedom of religion, freedom of speech, freedom of the press, and a strong independent judiciary all increase the potential for religious extremism. And, perhaps most important of all, when the extremists are perceived to have succeeded in their early challenges to the mainstream, a militant movement can acquire locomotive force.

An individual is perhaps best protected against succumbing to the extremism when he has multiple identities. Thus, when a person values his national identity, occupational identity, linguistic identity, familial identity, and personal identity as well as the religious identity, the likelihood that he will permit the religious self to ride roughshod over the others is minimized. When, however, all the other identities are subordinated to the religious self, the risk is multiplied.

Thus, if one truly wishes to follow the United Nations' advice to address the long-term root causes of religious extremism, one might develop an educational program that identifies the theological components of "inauthentic" religion, referring specifically to the various sources of destructiveness that cut across faiths. Little can be done to slow the pace of modernization or to change antisocial elements in religious scriptures. But it is certainly possible to push for greater responsibility on the part of mainstream religious leaders and less ambiguity in the denunciation of extremists within their own faiths.

Religions that sponsor indoctrination for hatred under the guise of pious education should be exposed for what they are. Though it would be useful for such declarations to come from the United Nations, the world organization is unlikely to overcome its own political limitations. Still, to have a chance at success, programs that oppose religious extremism should delineate general principles applicable to all religions and then proceed to identify offenders within particular faiths. Thus, Pope Benedict XVI's not unreasonable September 2006 remarks about Islamic theology might have been more effectively offered in the context of an acknowledgment of related, if not identical, limitations within Catholicism.

Most important of all, however, those who wish to promote religious tolerance must realize that true extremists are not apt to be appeased successfully. And when militants are made to pay consistently for their deviance from common laws, others will be less likely to sign on to their program.

Democracy in itself is no protection against extremism. James Madison was fully aware of the need to control religious factions, especially when they were in the majority.[29] It is not democratic elections that provide the most significant protection against religious extremism. Such elections have empowered militants in some places and, no doubt, will continue to do so. Instead, it is the spread of constitutional protections embodied in the American Bill of Rights and the notion of a strong, independent judiciary that would prove most protective.

The battle against religious extremism is a battle on many fronts, each requiring its own strategy. Once does not minimize the need to deal with Jewish and Christian extremists by noting that the scope of the problem of extremist Islam requires an entirely different approach.

Containing Militant Islam

Five years after the September 11 attacks, one Islamic extremist Web site posted a disheartening poem:

> I'm against America even if it
> Turns this life into a paradise.
> I'm against America even if a mufti issues a fatwa in its favor from within the glorious Kaaba.
> I'm with Osama no matter where he might be, so long as he carries a banner on the battle front.
> I'm with Osama whether he gains a quick victory or attains the rank of the martyrs.[30]

Readers of this declaration can only conclude, along with Salman Rushdie, that the military aspect of the battle against Islamic terror needs to proceed and that "[t]here are people you have to defeat."[31] This point needs emphasis, because—as journalist David Brooks warns—"more and more people are falling for the Grand Delusion—the notion that if we just leave the extremists alone, they will leave us alone."[32] One day, they will be awakened by a nuclear, chemical, or biological surprise, courtesy of the extremists they chose to ignore.

And we will not win this war through persuasion and diplomacy alone. As Michael Mazarr, one of the most psychologically sophisticated policy analysts, notes: "What a social-psychological approach to the problem of extremist terrorism does *not* do is undermine the importance of toughness or deny the simple truth that the conflict (as it was against the Nazis, the Bolsheviks, the Japanese ultranationalists, and all their like) pits the modern world against some truly evil people. Those fully in the grip of a fantasy ideology are in many ways lost to the ideology."[33] Thus, Mazarr rightly concludes, "In a broader sense, proving the willingness of America and the West to stand up for themselves, to pay real prices and run real risks in their own defense, is an important element of any strategy for addressing the mindset of those who might be tempted to become terrorists."[34]

A few weeks after the five-year anniversary of September 11, American intelligence agencies produced a very disturbing assessment of efforts to reverse the tide of Islamic extremism. After a half-decade of a heavily funded, top-priority global war against terror with a committed American president at the helm, the report stated that "activists identifying themselves as jihadists, although a small percentage of Muslims, are increasing both in number and geographic dispersion. . . . If this trend continues, threats to U.S. interests at home and abroad will become more diverse, leading to increasing attacks worldwide. . . . We assess that the operational threat from self-radicalized cells will grow in importance to U.S. counterterrorism efforts, particularly abroad but also in the Homeland. . . . CBRN [chemical, biological, radiological, and nuclear weapons] capabilities will continue to be sought by jihadist groups."[35] The deteriorating war in Iraq, according to the nation's top intelligence analysts, was "shaping a new generation of terrorist leaders and operatives" and, if the jihadis came away with a perception of success, something that seemed likely, that perception "would inspire more fighters to continue the struggle elsewhere."[36] One terrorism expert summarized that "the overall conclusion you get from . . . [the document] is that we don't have enough bullets given all the enemies we are creating."[37] Whether we are creating them or they are creating themselves is a matter for debate.

But what is beyond debate is that the stakes are high in a battle that the West is not near winning. As former British prime minister Tony Blair explained:

> 9/11 in the US, 7/7 in the UK, 11/3 in Madrid, the countless terrorist attacks in countries as disparate as Indonesia or Algeria, what is now happening in Afghanistan and Indonesia, the continuing conflict in Lebanon and Palestine, it is all part of the same thing. What are the values that govern the future of the world? Are they those of toler-

> ance, freedom, respect for difference and diversity or those of reaction, division and hatred? . . . In fact, these acts of terrorism were not isolated incidents. They were part of a growing movement. A movement that believed Muslims had departed from their proper faith, were being taken over by Western culture, were being governed treacherously by Muslims complicit in this takeover, whereas the true way to recover not just the true faith, but Muslim confidence and self-esteem, was to take on the West and all its works.[38]

As we have seen, there is considerable sympathy for much Islamic extremism in large segments of the population in some Muslim countries. In Europe, too, many Muslims—though not a majority—sympathize with parts of the militants' program. Journalist Theodore Dalrymple notes that "if one survey is to be believed . . . 100,000 British Muslims approve of the suicide bombing of Britain, or at least are prepared to say that they do to people who ask them in confidence. It is difficult to believe that this is not a soil propitious to the growth of terrorism. And from the point of view of the rest of the population, is it more significant that 1.5 million Muslims don't approve of such bombing?"[39] Dalrymple also notes that "fully 70 percent of British Muslims (again, if a survey is to be believed) do not think that British Jews are a legitimate target. . . . [He asks] If you were a Jewish employer [in Britain], would you be happy to take on a Muslim employee secure in the knowledge that there is only a one in three chance of his believing that it is religiously permitted, perhaps even religiously required, to kill you?"[40] Such levels of overt sympathy are not at present apparent among Muslims in the United States, though that could, of course, change.[41]

So what is to be done? Nearly all mainstream policy analysts in the West have come to the same core conclusion about how to deal with the threat emanating from extremist Islam. The solution is usually four-pronged: (1) fight and defeat the incorrigibles; (2) strengthen the moderates; (3) address the underlying causes of the problem; and (4) take steps to keep the extremism found in Muslim nations from damaging the Western way of life. Yet this seeming uniformity of approach breaks down almost immediately when one pushes for answers to certain critical questions, including:

- Who are the incorrigibles? How many Muslims fall into this category?
- What means should be employed to defeat the incorrigibles?
- Who are the moderates? What standard is used to distinguish moderates from extremists?
- How moderate does one have to be in order to merit Western support?
- Which moves can the West make that will strengthen these moderates?
- How can Western or American assistance strengthen anyone in the Middle East when we are currently so hated?
- How will we know when we have been successful?
- What are the underlying causes of the problem and how can they be addressed?
- Which aspects of the Western way of life are endangered?
- How do you keep overseas problems from becoming domestic ones?

Though these questions cannot all be resolved here, it is possible to draw some conclusions about which policy directions are likely to prove most effective.[42]

Blair's August 2006 address gets some parameters of the struggle right. He starts by noting that

> it is almost incredible . . . that so much of Western opinion appears to buy the idea that the emergence of this global terrorism is somehow our fault. . . . It is directed at the United States and its allies, of course. But it is also directed at nations who could not conceivably be said to be allies of the West. It is also rubbish to suggest that it is the product of poverty. It is true that it will use the cause of poverty. But its fanatics are hardly the champions of economic development. It is based on religious extremism. That is the fact.

> And not any religious extremism; but a specifically Muslim version.[43]

Here, Blair is echoing remarks made by Abdul Rahman al-Rashed, director of the Dubai-based Al Arabiya satellite network, who said: "The danger specifically comes from the ideas and the preaching of violence in the name of religion. . . . I am more convinced there is a problem with the culture, the modern culture of radicalism, which people have to admit. Without recognizing that as fact number one, that statistically speaking most terrorists are Muslims, we won't be able to solve it."[44]

Blair rightly suggests the battle must not be portrayed or conceived as the West versus the Islamic world. He argues that this is not a battle against Islam but rather a battle about Islam. Blair says: "There is an arc of extremism now stretching across the Middle East and touching, with increasing definition, countries far outside that region. To defeat it will need an alliance of moderation, that paints a different future in which Muslim, Jew and Christian; Arab and Western; wealthy and developing nations can make progress in peace and harmony with each other. . . . We will not win the battle against this global extremism unless we win it at the level of values as much as force, unless we show we are even-handed, fair and just in our application of those values to the world."[45]

Blair then goes a step further, making the unconvincing argument that "[i]n Iraq, in Afghanistan, and of course in the Lebanon, any time that people are permitted a chance to embrace democracy, they do so. The lie—that democracy, rule of law, human rights are Western concepts, alien to Islam—has been exposed."[46] None of Blair's examples, at present, seem much like a showpiece democracy, much less an embodiment of critical constitutional protections. Moreover, none of the major Western religions were shaped to exist comfortably in modern constitutional democracies.[47] To the extent that various faiths have been able to exist happily in such states, they have had to adapt in meaningful ways. Islam is not, by nature, any less suited to make the necessary adaptations. But, to date, many Muslim leaders have been reluctant to move in that direction.

Empowering moderates would seem to be an unarguably winning strategy, but it has not been confidence inspiring in the short term. Blair's plan calls for strengthening moderates in four ways. First, support, nurture, and build strong alliances with all those in the Middle East who are on the modernizing path. Second, reenergize the Middle East peace process in a way that will produce a fair, lasting peace that does not put Israel's security at risk. Third, build a stable, nonsectarian, democratic state in Iraq. Finally, make clear to Syria and Iran that they must play by the same rules as the rest of us or be confronted (presumably, by economic or military force). Just how any of these interim goals could be achieved is not immediately apparent. It is, however, probably sensible for the West to follow Blair's overall strategy until conditions become right for success.

In truth, only Muslims can delegitimize and root out Muslim extremists in a lasting way. The struggle must come from within, and, despite the West's vast resources, good intentions, and occasionally important support, this must, ultimately, be a battle waged by Muslims for the heart of their culture. Still, however long it is going to take, support of moderate Muslims remains critical as they struggle to regain control of their faith and their culture. As the United States intelligence assessment of September 2006 emphasized: "The jihadists' greatest vulnerability is that their ultimate political solution—an ultraconservative interpretation of [sharia]-based governance spanning the Muslim world—is unpopular with the vast majority of Muslims. Exposing the religious and political straitjacket that is implied by the jihadists' propaganda would help divide them from the audiences they seek to persuade."[48]

Mazarr suggests that the West needs to "underwrite a growing set of alternative identity entrepreneurs."[49] Such people will make the case that Muslims can meet their spiritual and political needs through a "happy marriage of modernism and Islam."[50] But the moderates he endorses will not be deemed very moderate by most Western observers. He writes: "The tougher their message, the more suspicious of the West and the United States they might be (short of advocating or condoning violence), the better placed they will be to serve the psychological needs of their people."[51] The West must be prepared to "compromise in our rhetoric, attitudes, and policy."[52] And to strengthen these "moderates," the United States should bring its support for Israel more in line "with the larger requirements of our interests in making Western-tinged modernism palatable to the Arab and Islamic worlds."[53] Thus, Mazarr would throw Western resources behind Muslim leaders who hold back on their use of pro-violence rhetoric and, to further support these leaders, he would advocate substantial compromise of our principles. The question, however, is whether leaders empowered by such a strategy could be trusted to remain on our side or to be controlled, should the going get tough. Moreover, Mazarr's plan undermines his own recognition of the need for toughness in dealing with the extremists; many would take his approach as evidence of Western weakness and loss of resolve. On the other hand, Mazarr is probably right that the prospects are not good for genuine moderates, especially if they can so easily be discredited by virtue of their connection to the West.

What may truly be needed is a wholesale, indigenous reformation of Islam—something not now in the cards—or perhaps the expansion of some currently unpopular ideas that have already been expressed by Muslims showing signs of genuine moderation or impulses in that direction. For example, even in Iran, Hashem Aghajari suggested that Islam needs to be "a religion that respects the rights of all—a progressive religion, rather than a traditional religion that tramples people. . . . One must be a good person, a pure person. We must not say that if you are not with us, we can do whatever we want to you."[54] Also in Iran, Ayatollah Mohammed Kazemini Boroujerdi argued that "people are fed up with political religion and want traditional [presumably apolitical] religion to return."[55] In Bangladesh, Salah Uddin Shoaib Chowdury, a Muslim journalist, even had the courage to advocate ties with Israel.[56] Unfortunately, all of these moderates encountered serious trouble from the authorities. But in safer regions, it is possible to find many Muslim leaders who have expressed hopeful visions. They are rarely the dominant perspective, but they are clearly present.

Unfortunately, perhaps the best the West can do is make clear its values and hope that, sooner or later, a critical mass of Muslims will begin to see their merit. And each time the opportunity presents itself to support genuine moderates, we must take it. But we may not be able to *create* such opportunities. We must also use our influence cautiously lest we discredit those whom we are seeking to help. But until the strategy of empowering moderates begins to show signs of succeeding, the West will be forced to protect and defend its interests, militarily if necessary, and, on occasion, to make common ground with the best allies we can find.

We must also develop policies to limit the impact of the dangerous situation in the Muslim world on the Western way of life at home. Here, many difficult questions have arisen, all of which are now being discussed and debated in various Western countries, proof that the militants have already won some important battles and changed important aspects of the Western way of life:

- Should airport profiling be permitted on the basis of ethnicity or Muslim religion?
- Should Muslim religious leaders speaking in the West be permitted to speak freely in support of terrorism?
- Should immigration laws be written to limit or discourage immigrants from potentially hostile locations?
- Should prisoners have access to extremist religious leaders if they request them?
- Should law enforcement agencies pay disproportionate attention to Muslim suspects?
- Should law enforcement agencies monitor Muslim religious institutions to identify extremists?
- Should coercive interrogation techniques ever be used to obtain information about potentially dangerous Muslim extremists?

- Should Muslim workers ever be barred from jobs where they may pose a security risk?
- Should Muslim applicants undergo greater screening for some sensitive jobs?
- Should Muslims be permitted to contribute to charities that also support terrorism or illegal activities?
- Should the government sponsor schools for moderate imams?
- Should the government oversee or, at least, screen a selection of imams for prisons and the armed forces?

All of these matters run the risk of undermining the very system of civil liberties that has provided the Western democracies with the fairest way of regulating religious belief that the world has ever seen. But we must nonetheless address these decisions with speed and seriousness, as the consequences of not doing so may be to permit grave harm to come to our nations and ways of life.

Without doubt, merely asking such questions creates an immediate and unfair aura of suspicion around many Muslims in the West who have been deeply loyal to their adopted homelands. On the other hand, to avoid such questions is to deny the reality that, in Europe especially, Muslim extremists willing to engage in destructive action—though not a majority—can hardly be described as a handful. Western concerns arise not from a discriminatory impulse but rather from legitimate, significant, and immediate security concerns.

Each question, therefore, must be considered carefully, weighing the damage to our way of life from changing the way we do things against the damage that might ensue if we do nothing. In the United States, at least, some forms of the proposed policies are plainly illegal under current law. But most exist around the borders of legality and can be framed in a way that conforms to legal requirements. In some ways, the most important policy challenge is how to carry out necessary security measures without alienating the mass of the Muslim population that, at present, has little use for the extremists. There is no simple solution to this dilemma, though everything will be easier to the extent that Western Muslim populations support the war against extremist Islam and show sensitivity to the challenging nature of the policy questions that must be resolved.

A SYSTEM THAT WORKS FAIRLY WELL

Some leaders of the Christian right in the United States have been arguing for decades that America is a Christian nation. Although they have the support of a sizable minority of Americans—and there may even be a kernel of historical truth to the notion—the American political system shows few signs of moving in the direction of theocracy. The Supreme Court has taken some steps in recent years away from a strict interpretation of the doctrine of separation of church and state. And politicians have found it increasingly useful to broadcast religion credentials when they have them. Also, politicized Christians have influenced the outcome of elections and changed the character of some policy debates. Social liberals are usually less heartened by the impact of religion than social conservatives. However, when one considers the full range of religious involvement in policy discussions, it becomes apparent that religions surface across the spectrum of political ideology.

Despite all of this, it is hard to argue that the impact of religious groups in the aggregate has been greater, or even less constructive, than that of other interest groups in American politics. The nonsectarian foundation of the America political system seems as secure as ever. Although religious thinking often appears to fuel some secular positions, the terms of political discourse in the United States remain overwhelmingly secular. Indeed, Christian conservatives continue to rail against "the court's hostility toward religion and Christianity in particular."[57]

Two United States Supreme Court cases in 2004 tell us something about the relationship between religion and government in the United States.[58] In the first case, Joshua Davey, a member of the evangelical Assemblies of God denomination, sued the state of Washington because he had been denied a state-funded college tuition scholarship on grounds that he was going to use it to prepare for the ministry. Had he chosen another field of study, he would, everyone agrees, have been awarded the funds. Ultimately, the Supreme Court, in a split 7–2 decision, decided that Washington's decision was not a manifestation of prejudice against religion; instead, it reflected the state's long-standing interest in avoiding an "establishment" of religion. Davey, represented by a law firm affiliated with the Reverend Pat Robertson, had charged that Washington's law violated his rights to free exercise of religion, free speech, and equal protection. The Court held that his rights had not been violated. But it also ruled that Washington, had it wished to do so, could have given him the scholarship without violating the constitutional prohibition against an "establishment" of religion.

In the second case, Michael A. Newdow, an atheist, sought to have the words "under God" removed from the United States Pledge of Allegiance. He did not think his daughter should be asked to say the offending words in a public school. The words, he argued, were merely a Cold War addition to the original pledge and, in his opinion, turned the pledge into a profession of religious belief. From a secular standpoint, his point seems correct, though perhaps trivial. The Court seemed eager to avoid tackling the emotional issue and found a way out, ruling that Newdow did not have primary custody of his daughter and therefore lacked standing to bring the case. Newdow himself did not quit and found a new way to challenge the pledge. It remains unclear at this point how the issue will be decided.

The point about both these Supreme Court cases is that sensible, if imperfect, procedures have evolved to handle the ever-volatile clashes over religious matters that emerge in every society. In the United States, the questions the Court resolves are rarely matters that relate to the core of anyone's psychic, spiritual, or religious identity. They are far more peripheral matters. I, for instance, would like the words "under God" taken out of the Pledge of Allegiance and I prefer that government not sponsor the education of ministers, even if such a benefit would apply to clerical students of every persuasion. But, viewed in the context of the long history of religious conflict and discrimination, I would be only slightly dismayed by decisions that did not go in my preferred direction.

Forrest Church, the editor of an anthology of writings by the Founding Fathers on the separation of church and state, notes:

> The American Revolution was not driven by the antireligious pathos that powered the French Revolution a decade later. . . . As was true of the broader American struggle for freedom, the revolution that led to religious liberty was powered by two very different engines: one driven by eighteenth-century Enlightenment values, the other guided by Christian imperatives that grew out of the Great Awakening, a spiritual movement that spread like wildfire across the American colonies throughout the middle decades of that same century. The former movement, emphasizing freedom of conscience as both a political and a philosophical virtue, stressed freedom *from* the dictates of organized religion. The latter, stemming from a devout reading of the gospels (especially their proclamation of spiritual liberty from bondage to the world's principalities and powers), demanded freedom *for* religion.[59]

Despite continuing clashes over the next two centuries, the two impulses worked well to create the constitutional safeguards embodied in the First Amendment.

In the United States, the differences between the interests of religious believers and the interests of the heirs of Enlightenment secularism still do not involve these core protections. The religious right frequently attacks the godless Supreme Court, but this sort of attack is shortsighted. In recent years, the Court has moved from the doctrine of strict separation of church and state to one embodying equal treatment of religions. Though this latter approach does discriminate somewhat against those with no religion, it still provides protection against any one faith writing the rules for everyone else. Ultimately, this vital protection rests on the combination of legal doctrine, demographic diversity, and widespread public respect for freedom of religion as an American belief.

Problems typically arise, however, when legislators and the courts conceive of religion as an unmitigated good. As we have seen, this is hardly the case. After all, whatever thoughts prevail about one's own faith, there is nearly always the belief that some other faiths are entirely wrongheaded. Thus, cooperation among the faithful of different religions in support of recent pro-religious governmental initiatives is only a tactical alliance. It is essential for Americans—religious and otherwise—to stop basing policies on the "public's unexamined assumption that religion per se is, and always must be, a benign influence on society."[60]

For example, Americans generally support federal funding of faith-based organizations that provide social services. But they do not want the government to give money to groups that encourage conversions and they certainly do not want to underwrite any extremist groups. But as Susan Jacoby, a historian of secularism in the United States, has asked: "On what basis do we decide which religions—and which factions within religions—are 'moderate' enough to be eligible for tax money? That is precisely the question that the framers of the Constitution never wanted to fall within the authority of any government agency or official."[61]

Similarly, the state senate in Georgia passed a bill funding public high school classes on the Bible.[62] It is hard to imagine, however, that such a course will really meet the needs of the religious groups that endorsed it. The Bible will, indeed, become a school text, but it must be taught in the public schools in an objective and nondevotional manner. Would not the goals of the faithful be better met by leaving such matters to religious schools? And consider how religious holidays are currently treated in the public schools. Do members of religious groups really want their religious traditions taught and interpreted by a schoolteacher who no doubt possesses only the most superficial acquaintance with them? But these are all relatively minor concerns.

The interests of the religious and the secular in the United States are both served by the Constitution, whether interpreted as requiring strict separation or equal treatment. It is in the public interest, however, for political leaders to remind Americans on a regular basis just how these principles evolved and why.

Finally, religious beliefs—whether mainstream or otherwise, whether agreeable or distasteful—deserve protection. Society need not respect dysfunctional and destructive beliefs, but it must tolerate them. Religious *conduct*, on the other hand, may sometimes require limitation. As some legal scholars argue, "Religious entities have the capacity for great good and great evil, and society is not duty bound by any constitutional right to let them avoid duly enacted laws, especially where their actions can harm others."[63] When religion becomes evil, it must be treated as such.

Acknowledgments

Though I alone bear responsibility for the arguments and conclusions of this book, I have benefited greatly from the comments and advice of Dr. Mark Dillof, the Reverend Denise Haines, Dr. Elizabeth Haines, Dr. Tom Heinzen, Dr. Robbin Itzler, Professor Barry Silverstein, Dr. Miryam Wahrman, Steven Gorelick, and Adam Brodsky of the *New York Post*.

As always, my editor, Linda Greenspan Regan, and my agent, Susan Protter, have been extremely helpful and encouraging. My greatest thanks go to Dorit Kressel, my wife, partner, and collaborator on many projects.

NOTES

INTRODUCTION

1. Hassan Nasrallah, "Hizbullah Leader Nasrallah: Implementing Khomeini's Fatwa against Salman Rushdie Would Have Prevented Current Insults to Prophet Muhammad," excerpts from televised speech, trans. the Middle East Media Research Institute (MEMRI), MEMRI Special Dispatch no. 1088, February 7, 2006, http://www.memri.org/bin/articles.cgi?Page=archives&Area=sd&ID=SP108806 (accessed March 20, 2006). This speech was originally broadcast on February 2, 2006, on Al-Manar TV.

2. Ibid.

3. Yousef al-Qaradhawi, "Sheikh al-Qaradhawi Responds to Cartoons of Prophet Muhammad," excerpts from televised sermon, trans. MEMRI, MEMRI Special Dispatch no. 1089, February 9, 2006, http://www.memri.org/bin/articles.cgi?Page=archives&Area=sd&ID=SP108906 (accessed March 20, 2006). This sermon was originally broadcast on February 3, 2006, on Qatar TV.

4. Yaqoob Quereshi, as quoted in "Cartoon Controversy," *Hindustan Times* (New Delhi), February 20, 2006, http://www.lexisnexis.com/universe (accessed March 30, 2006). See also "Case against Minister Who Offered Bounty for Danish Cartoonist," *Indo-Asian News Service* (New Delhi), February 21, 2006, http://www.lexisnexis.com/universe (accessed March 30, 2006).

5. Yousaf Qureshi, as quoted by John Lancaster, "Pakistani Cleric Announces Bounty for Killing of Danish Cartoonists," *Washington Post*, February 18, 2006, http://www.lexisnexis.com/universe (accessed March 30, 2006).

6. Michael Slackman and Hassan M. Fattah, "Furor Over Cartoons Pits Muslim against Muslim," *New York Times*, February 22, 2006.

7. Dawood Wafa, "Fatwa Calls for Death of Cartoonists," *Daily Telegraph* (London), February 22, 2006, http://www.lexisnexis.com/universe (accessed March 30, 2006).

8. Ibid.

9. Salim Mansur, "Muslim World Not a Monolith," *Toronto Sun*, February 18, 2006, http://www.lexisnexis.com/universe (accessed May 19, 2006).

10. Mustafa Aykol, no title, *National Review*, February 7, 2006, http://www.lexisnexis.com/universe (accessed March 16, 2006).

11. See, for example, "Those Danish Cartoons," *New York Times*, February 7, 2006.

12. See, for example, cartoon, *New York Post*, October 16, 2001, http://www.nypost.com/delonas/delonas.htm?year=2001&month=10&day=16 (accessed May 19, 2006).

13. See, for example, Edward Morrissey, "Fear Factor," *Daily Standard*, February 7, 2006, http://www.lexisnexis.com/universe (accessed March 16, 2006).

14. Phil Miller, "In Hiding: But No Regrets," *Herald* (Glasgow), February 18, 2006, http://www.lexisnexis.com/universe (accessed March 30, 2006).

15. Doug Marlette, "I Was a Tool of Satan," *Columbia Journalism Review* (November/December 2003): 52, http://www.lexisnexis.com/universe (accessed March 16, 2006).

16. Ibid.

17. Ibid.

18. See Barbara Amiel, "A Twilight Zone of Insanity," *Maclean's*, February 13, 2006, http://www.lexisnexis.com/universe (accessed March 16, 2006); Hassan M. Fattah, "At Mecca Meeting, Cartoon Outrage Crystallized," *New York Times*, February 9, 2006; Ramesh Ratnesar, "Fanning the Flames," *Time*, February 20, 2006, p. 30, http://www.lexisnexis.com/universe (accessed March 16, 2006).

19. Jeff Jacoby, "When Fear Cows the Media," *Boston Globe*, February 19, 2006, p. 11, http://www.lexisnexis.com/universe (accessed March 16, 2006).

20. Said al-Ashmawy, as quoted by Slackman and Fattah, "Furor Over Cartoons." He is the author of *Against Islamic Extremism: The Writings of Muhammad Sa'id Al-'Ashmawy*, trans. Carolyn Fluehr-Lobban (Gainesville: University Press of Florida, 1999).

21. The words of the Jordanian Parliament are cited in Paul Marshall, "The Mohammed Cartoons," *Weekly Standard*, February 13, 2006, http://www.lexisnexis.com/universe (accessed March 16, 2006).

22. Akram Khan Durrani, as quoted in Salman Masood, "Pakistan's Violent Protests Over Cartoons Taking Political Turn," *New York Times*, February 16, 2006.

23. Lorenzo Vidino, "Tolerance Must Have Limits," *Boston Herald*, February 20, 2006, http://www.lexisnexis.com/universe (accessed March 16, 2006).

24. Paul Marshall, "Misrepresentations of Islam," *National Review*, February 13, 2006, http://www.lexisnexis.com/universe (accessed March 16, 2006).

25. Jonah Goldberg, "No Joke," *National Review*, February 8, 2006, http://www.lexisnexis.com/universe (accessed March 16, 2006).

26. Ann Coulter, "Beauty Pageants Can Be Murder," Free Republic Web site, November 27, 2002, http://www.freerepublic.com/focus/news/797176/posts (accessed November 29, 2006).

27. Sam Harris, *The End of Faith* (New York: Norton, 2005), p. 16.

28. Michael W. McConnell, "Religious Souls and the Body Politic," *Public Interest*, no. 185 (Spring 2004): 140.

29. George Washington as quoted in ibid., 133.

30. Though this quotation can be found in several anthologies, none that I have found cite the original source. The remark is in keeping with Chesterton's approach to religion, but it may be apocryphal.

31. William James, *The Varieties of Religious Experience* (New York: Simon & Schuster, 1997), p. 269. Originally published in 1902.

32. Ibid., p. 271.

33. Ibid., pp. 271–72.

34. Ibid., p. 272.

35. Ibid.

36. Ibid.

37. For two useful introductions to these theories, see James Forsyth, *Psychological Theories of Religion* (Upper Saddle River, NJ: Prentice-Hall,

2003); Andrew R. Fuller, *Psychology and Religion: Eight Points of View*, 3rd ed. (Boston: Rowman and Littlefield, 1994).

38. For an overview of this research, see Raymond F. Paloutzian, *Invitation to the Psychology of Religion*, 2nd ed. (Boston: Allyn and Bacon, 1996).

39. Charles Kimball, *When Religion Becomes Evil* (New York: HarperSanFrancisco, 2003), p. 39.

40. Ibid., p. 89.

41. Pew Research Center Poll, March 20, 2002, Public Opinion Online, Roper Center at the University of Connecticut, accession number 0400695, question number 52, http://www.lexis-nexis.com/universe (accessed November 29, 2006). But see also *Religion and Ethics News Weekly/U.S. News & World Report* Poll, April 13, 2004, Public Opinion Online, Roper Center at the University of Connecticut, accession number 0453263, question number 111, http://www.lexis-nexis.com/universe (accessed November 29, 2006).

42. Karen Armstrong, *The Battle for God* (New York: Ballantine, 2000); Kimball, *When Religion Becomes Evil*; Harris, *The End of Faith*; Ralph W. Hood Jr., Peter C. Hill, and W. Paul Williamson, *The Psychology of Religious Fundamentalism* (New York: Guilford, 2005).

43. Elie Wiesel, "When Passion Is Dangerous," *Parade*, April 19, 1992, p. 20.

44. Andrew M. Greeley, *Unsecular Man* (New York: Schocken, 1972), p. 241.

45. One of the earliest sources of this argument is Erich Fromm, *Psychoanalysis and Religion* (New Haven, CT: Yale University Press, 1950).

46. Charles S. Liebman, "Extremism as a Religious Norm," *Journal for the Scientific Study of Religion* 22, no. 1 (1983): 79.

47. Gilles Kepel, *The Revenge of God*, trans. Alan Braley (University Park: Pennsylvania State University Press, 1994); Armstrong, *The Battle for God*; Martin E. Marty and R. Scott Appleby, eds., *Fundamentalisms Observed* (Chicago: University of Chicago Press, 1991).

48. Abbas El-Zein, "The Tribes of War," *New York Times*, July 27, 2006.

49. Galileo Galilei, "Letter to the Grand Duchess Christina of Tuscany," 1615, *Modern History Sourcebook*, http://www.galilean-library.org/christina.html (accessed May 19, 2006).

CHAPTER 1

1. BBC, "New Muslim Centre Opens Its Doors," transcript of broadcast, June 12, 2004, http://news.bbc.co.uk/1/hi/uk/3796631.stm (accessed June 11, 2006). See also Tom Gross, "Living in a Bubble," *National Review*, June 18, 2004, http://lexis-nexis.com/universe (accessed June 11, 2006).

2. Al-Sudais, as quoted in Aluma Solnick, "Based on Koranic Verses, Interpretations, and Traditions, Muslim Clerics State: The Jews Are the Descendants of Apes, Pigs, and Other Animals," MEMRI Special Report #11, November 1, 2002, http://www.memri.org/bin/articles.cgi?Page=archives&Area=sr&ID=SR01102 (accessed November 25, 2006).

3. Gore, as quoted in David Remnick, "The Wilderness Campaign," *New Yorker*, September 13, 2004, http://www.lexis-nexis.com/universe (accessed July 31, 2006).

4. Thomas L. Friedman, "Two Nations Under God," *New York Times*, November 4, 2004.

5. Gregory Rummo, "Calling Christians 'Taliban' Is Slander," *Record* (North Jersey), February 21, 2002, http://www.lexis-nexis.com/universe (accessed June 11, 2006).

6. John Henry Newman, *Apologia pro Vita Sua*, ed. Wilfrid Ward, p. 247, http://www.newmanreader.org/works/apologia65/chapter5.html (accessed March 13, 2006). Originally published in 1865. The quotation is also found in Newman's *Difficulties of the Anglicans*, p. 240, http://www.newmanreader.org/works/anglicans/volume1/lecture8.html (accessed March 13, 2006).

7. LaHaye, as quoted in David D. Kirkpatrick, "In 12th Book of Best-Selling Series, Jesus Returns," *New York Times*, March 29, 2004.

8. Tim LaHaye and Jerry B. Jenkins, *Left Behind: A Novel of the Earth's Last Days* (Wheaton, IL: Tyndale House, 1995), p. 26.

9. Tim LaHaye and Jerry B. Jenkins, *Glorious Appearing* (Wheaton, IL: Tyndale House, 2004).

10. Nicholas D. Kristof, "Jesus and Jihad," *New York Times*, July 17, 2004.

11. See, for example, Carl E. Olson, "The 12th Coming of Less-Than-Glorious Fiction," *National Review*, April 2, 2004, http://www.lexis-nexis.com/universe (accessed August 17, 2004); Jane Lampman, "Apocalyptic—

and Atop the Bestseller Lists," *Christian Science Monitor*, August 29, 2002, http://www.csmonitor.com/2002/0829/p14s01-lire.html (accessed August 23, 2004); David Gates, David J. Jefferson, and Anne Underwood, "Religion: The Top Prophets," *Newsweek*, May 24, 2004, p. 44, http://www.lexis-nexis.com/universe (accessed August 17, 2004).

12. See, for example, Raymond Blanton, "*Left Behind*: One of Satan's Latest Wiles," *Perilous Times* (February/March 2001), and Biblical Discernment Ministries, "Book Review: The Left Behind Series," March 2004, http://www.raidnet.com/~jbeard/bdm/BookReviews/left.htm (accessed August 17, 2004).

13. Gene Edward Veith, "Judging the Judgment," *World Magazine* 19, no. 31 (August 2004), http://www.lexis-nexis.com/universe (accessed August 17, 2004).

14. Tim LaHaye, *Finding the Will of God in a Crazy, Mixed Up World* (Grand Rapids, MI: Zondervan, 1989).

15. Ibid., pp. 71–72.

16. Ibid., pp. 72–73.

17. Ibid., p. 73.

18. Ibid., p. 41.

19. Tim LaHaye, "The Prophetic Significance of Sept. 11, 2001," Tim LaHaye Ministries Home Page, http://www.timlahaye.com/about_ministry/index.php3?p=sept11_tlm (accessed August 23, 2004).

20. Ibid.

21. Ibid.

22. Ibid.

23. Graham, as quoted in Michael Wilson, "Evangelist Says Muslims Haven't Adequately Apologized for Sept. 11 Attacks," *New York Times*, August 15, 2002; Vines, as quoted in Susan Sachs, "Baptist Pastor Attacks Islam," *New York Times*, June 15, 2002; Falwell, as quoted in Maureen Dowd, "Rapture and Rupture," *New York Times*, October 6, 2002.

24. Boykin, as quoted in "And He's Head of Intelligence?" *Newsweek*, October 27, 2003, MSNBC Web site, October 19, 2003, http://www.msnbc.com/id/3225695/print/1/displaymode/1098/ (accessed August 11, 2004). See also Mark Thompson, "The Boykin Affair," CNN Web site, October 27, 2003, http://www.cnn.com/2003/ALLPOLITICS/10/27/timep.boykin.tm/ (accessed August 11, 2004).

25. Ibid.

26. See, for example, "General Explains Statements Criticized by Muslims," CNN Web site, October 17, 2003, http://www.cnn.com/2003/US/10/17/boykin.apology/index.html (accessed August 11, 2004).

27. LaHaye, *Finding the Will of God*, p. 39.

28. Ibid., p. 39.

29. Rummo, "Calling Christians 'Taliban' Is Slander."

30. Charles Kimball, *When Religion Becomes Evil* (San Francisco: HarperSanFrancisco, 2002), p. 27.

31. William James, *The Varieties of Religious Experience* (New York: Simon & Schuster, 1997), p. 34.

32. William Dalrymple, "Islamophobia," *New Statesman*, January 19, 2004, http://www.lexis-nexis.com/universe (accessed July 30, 2006).

33. Karen Armstrong, "Cries on Rage and Frustration," *New Statesman*, September 24, 2001, http://www.lexis-nexis.com/universe (accessed July 12, 2004).

34. Karen Armstrong, "The Gods Meet with Fire," *New Statesman*, December 16, 2002, http://www.lexis-nexis.com/universe (accessed July 12, 2004).

35. Ibid.

36. Al-Sudais, as quoted in Jeff Heinrich, "A Day Like No Other," *Gazette* (Montreal), September 11, 2002, http://www.lexis-nexis.com/universe (accessed September 15, 2004).

37. Al-Sudais, as quoted in Bess Twiston Davies, "Shaikh Dr. Abdur Rahman al-Sudais," *Times* (London), November 8, 2003, http://www.lexis-nexis.com/universe (accessed September 11, 2004).

38. Al-Sudais, as quoted in ibid.

39. BBC, "New Muslim Centre Opens Its Doors."

40. Ibid.

41. Thomas Wagner, "Saudi Imam Urges British Muslims to Promote Peace," Associated Press Worldstream, June 11, 2004, http://www.lexis-nexis.com/universe (accessed August 1, 2006).

42. Wikipedia, s.v. "Abdul Rahman al-Sudais," July 27, 2006, http://www.en.wikipedia.org/wiki/Abdul_Rahman_Al-Sudais (accessed July 31, 2006).

43. Al-Sudais, as quoted in Steven Stalinsky, "Kingdom Comes to North America," *National Review* Online, May 13, 2004, http://www.nationalreview.com/comment/stalinsky200405130846.asp (accessed July 31, 2006).

44. Al-Sudais, as quoted in Anthony Browne, "Anti-Jewish? Anti-Gay?

Welcome to Britain," *Times* (London), July 6, 2004, http://www.lexis-nexis.com/universe (accessed September 11, 2004).

45. Al-Sudais, as quoted in Stalinsky, "Kingdom Comes to North America."

46. Solnick, "Based on Koranic Verses."

47. Al-Sudais, as quoted in "Friday Sermon By Leading Saudi Imam al-Sudayyis in Mecca," MEMRI Special Dispatch #939, July 21, 2005, http://www.memri.org/bin/opener.cgi?Page=archives&ID=SP93905 (accessed July 31, 2006).

48. Al-Sudais, as quoted in "Saudi Eid Sermon Lashes Out at Israel and 'Occupiers in Iraq,'" Agence France-Presse (English), February 1, 2004, http://www.lexis-nexis.com/universe (accessed September 11, 2004).

49. Stalinsky, "Kingdom Comes to North America."

50. Al-Sudais, as quoted in ibid.

51. "Saudi Imam Riles at Reality TV Shows that 'Spread Vice,'" Agence France-Presse (English), April 2, 2004, http://www.lexis-nexis.com/universe (accessed September 11, 2004).

52. Al-Sudais, as quoted in Khaled Abu Toameh, "Not In Our House," *Jerusalem Post*, April 9, 2004, http://www.lexis-nexis.com/universe (accessed September 11, 2004).

53. Al-Sudais, as quoted in Eman Abdullah, "Imam Stresses Importance of Dialogue," *Gulf News*, November 6, 2001, http://www.lexis-nexis.com/universe (accessed September 11, 2004).

54. "Mecca's Imam Slams Riyadh Bombers as 'Cowards,'" Agence France-Presse (English), April 23, 2004, http://www.lexis-nexis.com/universe (accessed September 11, 2004).

55. Al-Sudais, as quoted in "Mecca Imam Urges Halt to Bloodshed in Iraq After 'Defeat,'" Agence France-Presse (English), April 11, 2003, http://www.lexis-nexis.com/universe (accessed September 11, 2004).

56. The incident is described and discussed in Solnick, "Based on Koranic Verses."

57. Ibid. See also Menahem Milson, "What Is Arab Antisemitism?" MEMRI Special Report #26, February 27, 2004, http://www.memri.org/bin/articles.cgi?Page=archives&Area=sr&ID=SR2604 (accessed September 20, 2004); "Syrian Deputy Minister of Religious Endowment 'Abd al-Sattar Calls for Jihad and States Jews Are the 'Descendants of Apes and Pigs,'" MEMRI Special Dispatch #1217, July 29, 2006, http://www.memri.org/bin/

articles.cgi?Page=archives&Area=sd&ID=SP121706 (accessed November 25, 2006).

58. Solnick, "Based on Koranic Verses."

59. See, among many, Gerald C. Davison and John M. Neale, *Abnormal Psychology*, 7th ed. (New York: Wiley, 1998), pp. 6–8.

60. Los Angeles Times Poll, April 1996, available from Public Opinion Online, Roper Center at the University of Connecticut, accession number 0261447, question number 10, http://www.lexis-nexis.com/universe (accessed February 24, 2006). A 2005 poll showed that 44 percent of American adults believed that the Bible was the "actual word of God." See Virginia Commonwealth University Life Sciences Poll, October 24, 2005, Public Opinion Online, Roper Center at the University of Connecticut, accession number 1636374, question number 623, http://www.lexis-nexis.com/universe (accessed February 24, 2006).

61. CNN–*USA Today* Poll, October 16, 2003, Public Opinion Online, Roper Center at the University of Connecticut, accession number 0439555, question number 7, http://www.lexis-nexis.com/universe (accessed February 24, 2006).

62. *Newsweek* Poll, December 4, 2004, Public Opinion Online, Roper Center at the University of Connecticut, accession number 1611782, question number 180, http://www.lexis-nexis.com/universe (accessed February 24, 2006).

63. *Newsweek* Poll, December 1998, Public Opinion Online, Roper Center at the University of Connecticut, accession number 0335728, question number 6, http://www.lexis-nexis.com/universe (accessed February 24, 2006).

64. Woman quoted in James, *The Varieties of Religious Experience*, p. 71. James drew the material from an interview conducted by E. D. Starbuck, an early psychologist of religion.

65. Ralph W. Hood Jr., Peter C. Hill, and W. Paul Williamson, *The Psychology of Religious Fundamentalism* (New York: Guilford, 2005), p. 13.

66. Ibid., p. 70.

67. Austin Cline, "Nature of Islamic Fundamentalism," March 16, 2006, http://www.atheism.about.com/b/a/250195.htm (accessed May 18, 2006).

68. Kenneth Minogue, "Fundamentalism Isn't the Problem," *New Criterion*, June 2004, pp. 17–18.

69. Ibid., p. 18.

70. Hood, Hill, and Williamson, *The Psychology of Religious Extremism*, p. 196.

71. Kimball, *When Religion Becomes Evil*, p. 39.

CHAPTER 2

1. Unless otherwise noted, all Koranic verses come from *An English Interpretation of the Holy Qur'an*, 3rd ed., trans. Abdullah Yusuf Ali (Lahore, Pakistan: Sh. Muhammad Ashraf, 1938).

2. The story of Salah Ghandour and his family (including all quotations) comes from a television program, *The Culture of Martyrdom*, aired on Al Arabiya TV on July 22, 2005. A partial transcript of this program is available as "TV Program on Martyrdom and Suicide Bombers on Al-Arabiya," MEMRI Special Dispatch #961, August 19, 2005, http://memri.org/bin/opener.cgi?Page=archives&ID=SP96105 (accessed May 2, 2006). The program can be viewed at http://www.memritv.org/search.asp?ACT=S9&P1=807 (accessed May 2, 2006).

3. Qaradhawi appears on the telecast. His views and those of several other Muslim scholars can be found in "Debating the Religious, Political and Moral Legitimacy of Suicide Bombings," MEMRI Inquiry and Analysis Series #53, May 2, 2001, http://www.memri.org/bin/opener.cgi?Page=archives&ID=IA5301 (accessed May 2, 2006).

4. Nasrallah appears on the telecast.

5. Sade, as quoted in "Chairman of Arab Psychiatrists Association Offers Diagnoses," MEMRI Special Dispatch #373, April 30, 2002, http://www.memri.org/bin/opener.cgi?Page=archives&ID=SP37302 (accessed May 2, 2006).

6. Unless otherwise noted, all survey findings in this section come from the Pew Global Attitudes Project, "17-Nation Pew Global Attitudes Survey," July 14, 2005, Washington, DC, http://www.pewglobal.org/reports/display.php?ReportID=248 (accessed August 1, 2006). See also Richard Bernstein, "Muslim Approval of Terrorism Declines, a Global Poll Finds," *New York Times*, July 15, 2005.

7. See also Neil J. Kressel, "The Urgent Need to Study Islamic Antisemitism," *Chronicle of Higher Education*, March 12, 2004, B14; Neil J.

Kressel, "Antisemitism and the Muslim and Arab World," *Judaism* 52, no. 3–4 (Summer/Fall 2003): 225–45; Neil J. Kressel, "Mass Hatred in the Muslim and Arab World: The Neglected Problem of Anti-Semitism," *International Journal of Applied Psychoanalytic Studies*, in press.

8. "17-Nation Pew Global Attitudes Survey," July 14, 2005.

9. Ibid.

10. Ibid.

11. Ibid.

12. Ibid.

13. All articles appeared in *New York Times*, May 10, 2006.

14. *Newsweek* Poll, August 5, 2005, Public Opinion Online, Roper Center at the University of Connecticut, accession number 1631425, question number 205, http://www.lexis-nexis.com/universe (accessed February 24, 2006).

15. *Newsweek* Poll, December 2001, Public Opinion Online, Roper Center at the University of Connecticut, accession number 0409109, question number 24, http://www.lexis-nexis.com/universe (accessed February 24, 2006).

16. Pew Research Center Poll, July 26, 2005, Public Opinion Online, Roper Center at the University of Connecticut, accession number 1630369, question number 36, http://www.lexis-nexis.com/universe (accessed February 24, 2006).

17. Meg Bortin, "Poll Finds Discord between the Muslim and Western Worlds," *New York Times*, June 23, 2006.

18. ABC News Poll, September 11, 2003, Public Opinion Online, Roper Center at the University of Connecticut, accession number 0437079, question number 3, http://www.lexis-nexis.com/universe (accessed February 24, 2006). In a similar poll, one year earlier in October 2002, 37 percent thought mainstream Islam taught respect for the beliefs of non-Muslims and 35 percent did not think so. See ABC News/Beliefnet Poll, October 15, 2002, Public Opinion Online, Roper Center at the University of Connecticut, accession number 0415188, question number 3, http://www.lexis-nexis.com/universe (accessed February 24, 2006).

19. *Religion and Ethics Newsweekly/U.S. News & World Report* Religion Survey, April 26, 2002, Public Opinion Online, Roper Center at the University of Connecticut, accession number 0403054, question number 40, http://www.lexis-nexis.com/universe (accessed February 24, 2006).

20. Pew Research Center poll, July 26, 2005, Public Opinion Online, Roper Center at the University of Connecticut, accession number 1630373, question number 39, http://www.lexis-nexis.com/universe (accessed May 12, 2006).

21. CBS News Poll, April 12, 2006, Public Opinion Online, Roper Center at the University of Connecticut, accession number 1649193, question number 189, http://www.lexis-nexis.com/universe (accessed May 12, 2006).

22. Fox News/Opinion Dynamics Poll, October 13, 2005, Public Opinion Online, Roper Center at the University of Connecticut, accession number 1635827, question number 607, http://www.lexis-nexis.com/universe (accessed February 24, 2006).

23. Pew Research Center Poll, July 24, 2003, Public Opinion Online, Roper Center at the University of Connecticut, accession number 0435890, question number 38, http://www.lexis-nexis.com/universe (accessed May 12, 2006). A more recent poll, with slightly different wording, indicates that 56 percent of the American public admit to knowing "not much" or "not at all" about the "opinions and beliefs of people who live in Muslim countries." Gallup Poll, March 23, 2006, Public Opinion Online, Roper Center at the University of Connecticut, accession number 1646604, question number 10, http://www.lexis-nexis.com/universe (accessed May 12, 2006).

24. CBS News Poll, April 12, 2006, Public Opinion Online, Roper Center at the University of Connecticut, accession number 1649194, question number 190, http://www.lexis-nexis.com/universe (accessed May 12, 2006); Pew Research Center Poll, July 26, 2005, Public Opinion Online, Roper Center at the University of Connecticut, accession number 1630377, question number 43, http://www.lexis-nexis.com/universe (accessed May 12, 2006).

25. Abu Muhammad al-Maqdisi (pseudonym for 'Asem Al-Burqawi), excerpts from Friday sermon, August 21, 2004, as quoted in Marie-Helene Boccara and Alex Greenberg, "Islamist Websites and Their Hosts," November 11, 2004, http://www.memri.org/bin/opener.cgi?Page=archives&ID=SR3504 (accessed May 16, 2006).

26. Al-Ansari, as quoted in "Contemporary Islamist Ideology Authorizing Genocidal Murder," MEMRI Special Report #25, http://www.memri.org/bin/articles.cgi?Page=archives&Area=sr&ID=SR2504 (accessed November 29, 2006).

27. Ibn Hamed, as quoted in ibid.

28. Asma Gull Hasan, *Why I Am a Muslim* (London: HarperCollins, 2004), p. xiii.

29. Ibid., p. xiv.

30. Ibid.

31. Ibid., p. 157.

32. Ibid., p. 166.

33. Feisal Abdul Rauf, *What's Right with Islam* (New York: HarperSanFrancisco, 2004). See also two useful reviews of this book: Tibor Krausz, "If Religion Is the Quality of Our Actions," *Jerusalem Report*, May 30, 2005, http://www.lexis-nexis.com/universe (accessed May 24, 2006); Chris Hedges, "A Muslim in the Middle Hopes against Hope," *New York Times*, June 23, 2004, http://www.lexis-nexis.com/universe (accessed May 24, 2006).

34. John L. Esposito, *What Everyone Needs to Know about Islam: Answers to Frequently Asked Questions from One of America's Leading Experts* (New York: Oxford University Press, 2002), p. 124.

35. Ibid., p. 129.

36. Ibid., p. 130.

37. Krausz, "If Religion Is the Quality of Our Actions."

38. Ibid.

39. Aluma Dankowitz, "Tariq Ramadan—Reformist or Islamist?" Inquiry and Analysis #266, February 17, 2006, http://www.memri.org/bin/opener.cgi?Page=archives&ID=IA26606 (accessed May 16, 2006).

40. "Welcome to Understanding Islam," http://www.understanding-islam.org/related/introduction.asp (accessed May 23, 2006).

41. "Punishment for Apostasy," December 6, 1998, http://www.understanding-islam.org/related/text.asp?type=question&qid=286 (accessed May 23, 2006).

42. Moiz Amjad, "Extremism and Islam—Why Do People Not Participate in Jihad?" October 19, 2001, http://www.understanding-islam.com/related/print.asp?type=question&qid=1128 (accessed May 15, 2006).

43. "Punishment for Apostasy," December 7, 1998, http://www.understanding-islam.org/related/print.asp?type=question&qid=286 (accessed May 23, 2006). Here, and elsewhere, I have deleted the letters "pbuh," sometimes used by believers to mean "praise be upon him."

44. Ibid.

45. Amjad, "A Narrative Regarding the Prophet's Directive to Kill an Apostate Woman," December 7, 2005, http://www.understanding-islam.org/related/print.asp?type=article&aid=247 (accessed May 15, 2006).

46. Amjad, "Extremism and Islam."

47. Asif Iftikhar, "Murder, Manslaughter and Terrorism: All in the Name of Allah," October 22, 2001, http://www.renaissance.com.pk/mapred97.html (accessed June 12, 2007).

48. Abdullah Rahim, "Clarification on 'Does Jerusalem Belong to the Muslims?'" March 19, 2006, http://www.understanding-islam.org/related/print.asp?type=discussion&did=588 (accessed May 23, 2006).

49. Ronnie Hassan, "The Most Hated People," April 10, 2005, http://www.understanding-islam.com/related/print.asp?type=question&qid=3337 (accessed May 15, 2006).

50. "The Punishment for *Zina* (Fornication)," October 26, 1998, http://www.understanding-islam.org/related/print.asp?type=question&qid=387 (accessed May 23, 2006).

51. Iftikhar, "Murder, Manslaughter & Terrorism."

52. Bernard Lewis, *What Went Wrong?* (New York: Oxford University Press, 2002). See also Lewis, *The Crisis of Islam* (New York: Modern Library, 2003).

53. Paul Berman, "The Philosopher of Islamic Terror," *New York Times Magazine*, March 23, 2003, p. 26.

54. Wikipedia, s.v. "Sayyid Qutb," May 16, 2006, http://www.en.wikipedia.org/w/index.php?title=Sayyid_Qutb&printable=yes (accessed May 18, 2006).

55. Sayyid Qutb, *Milestones* (1966), "Introduction," http://www.youngmuslims.ca/online%5Flibrary/books/milestones/hold/index_2.asp (accessed May 18, 2006).

56. Ibid., chapter 10, "Far-Reaching Changes."

57. Ibid.

58. Ibid.

59. Ibid., chapter 4, "Jihaad in the Cause of God."

60. Berman, "The Philosopher of Islamic Terror," p. 65.

61. Zafar Bangash, "Remembering Sayyid Qutb," September 1–15, 1999, http://www.youngmuslims.ca/online_library/books/milestones/remember.asp (accessed May 31, 2006).

62. This section is adapted from my earlier work, *Mass Hate: The Global Rise of Genocide and Terror*, 2nd ed. (New York: Perseus/Westview, 2002), p. 56.

63. Menahem Milson, "Reform and Islamism in the Arab World Today,"

Special Report #34, September 15, 2004, http://www.memri.org/bin/opener.cgi?Page=archives&ID=SR3404 (accessed May 16, 2006).

64. Ibid.

65. See Barry Rubin, *Paved with Good Intentions* (New York: Penguin, 1981).

66. See, for example, Fouad Ajami, *Dream Palace of the Arabs* (New York: Pantheon, 1998); Daniel Benjamin and Steven Simon, *The Age of Sacred Terror* (New York: Random House, 2002); Lewis, *The Crisis of Islam*; Lewis, *What Went Wrong?*; David Pryce-Jones, *The Closed Circle* (New York: HarperPerennial, 1991).

67. Lewis, *The Crisis of Islam*, p. 93.

68. Susan T. Fiske and Shelley E. Taylor, *Social Cognition*, 2nd ed. (New York: McGraw-Hill, 1991), pp. 78–82, 212–18.

69. Kressel, *Mass Hate*, pp. 214–15.

70. Ibid., pp. 181–212.

71. Shamlan Yousef Al-'Issa, as quoted in Y. Yehoshua, "The Public Debate on Kuwait's School Curricula: To Teach or Not to Teach Jihad," June 2, 2005, http://www.memri.org/bin/articles.cgi?Page=archives&Area=ia&ID=IA22405 (accessed May 16, 2006).

72. American Jewish Committee, *The West, Christians and Jews in Saudi Arabian Schoolbooks* (New York: American Jewish Committee, 2003), conclusion, http://www.ajc.org/IntheMedia/Publications.asp?did=750 (accessed August 5, 2003).

73. Rick Bragg, "Shaping Young Islamic Hearts and Hatreds," *New York Times*, October 14, 2001.

74. There is the special case of Israel, where the problem goes well beyond Islamic extremists and extends to most segments of society. People in the Muslim and Arab world have very few opportunities to assess the veracity of antisemitic and anti-Zionist beliefs. For one thing, as a result of mass expulsions in the late 1940s, past discrimination, and the Jews' own Zionist inclinations, very few Jews remain in Muslim or Arab countries. Thus, one is not forced to test preconceptions about Jews against perceptions originating in everyday encounters. Moreover, even in so-called moderate states, no open debate occurs on Israel and very little on any topics concerning Jews. An honest student would need to search diligently to find unbiased information. And if any political, religious, or intellectual leaders ever felt inclined to offer boldly pro-Israel sentiments, they could not do so

without endangering their careers and perhaps their safety. President Sadat of Egypt and Kings Hussein and Abdullah of Jordan showed a willingness to negotiate with Jews in Israel, albeit cautiously. Assassins ended the lives of Sadat and Abdullah, while Hussein was forced to live under constant threat of bodily harm. Not surprisingly, most other leaders—even otherwise reasonable ones—have been reluctant to break with the party line concerning Israel.

75. National Commission on Terrorist Attacks upon the United States, *The 9/11 Commission Report* (New York: Norton, 2004), pp. 160–61.

76. Benjamin and Simon, *The Age of Sacred Terror*, p. 165.

77. Lewis, *The Crisis of Islam*, p. 17.

Chapter 3

1. Cheryl Alkon, "Confessions of an Abortion Doctor," *Boston Magazine*, December 2004, http://www.lexis-nexis/universe (accessed June 5, 2006). The coauthor of this article, the physician who describes her experiences, is not named.

2. Ibid.

3. National Abortion Federation, "NAF Violence and Disruption Statistics," April 2006, http://www.prochoice.org/pubs_research/publications/downloads/about_abortion/violence_statistics.pdf (accessed June 12, 2006). For other sources of statistics on antiabortion violence, see Gregory deGiere, "Crimes against Reproductive Rights in California," January 2002, http://www.sen.ca.gov/sor/reports/REPORTS_BY_SUBJ/PUBLIC_SAFETY_JUDICIARY/REPROCRIMES.HTM (accessed June 5, 2006); B. A. Robinson, "Violence and Harassment at U.S. Abortion Clinics," November 9, 2004, http://www.religioustolerance.org/abo_viol.htm (accessed June 6, 2006).

4. Anna Quindlen, "The Terrorists Here at Home," *Newsweek*, December 17, 2001, p. 78.

5. "Why Did James Kopp Choose a Bench Trial?" Army of God Web site, http://www.armyofgod.com/JamesKopp2.html (accessed June 7, 2006).

6. Ibid.

7. Ibid.

8. Journal Sentinel Wire Reports, "Abortion Opponent Says He Meant

Only to Wound," *Milwaukee Journal Sentinel*, November 21, 2002, http://www.lexis-nexis/universe (accessed June 5, 2006).

9. For more details on this manual, see Jennifer Gonnerman, "The Terrorist Campaign against Abortion," *Village Voice* (New York), November 3–9, 1998, http://www.villagevoice.com/news/9845,gonnerman,1077,1.html (accessed November 26, 2006).

10. National Abortion Federation, "Anti-Abortion Extremists/James Kopp," National Abortion Rights Web site, http://www.prochoice.org/about_abortion/violence/james_kopp.html (accessed November 26, 2006). Much of the background information on Kopp comes from this report.

11. Frederick Clarkson, "Kopp Lays Groundwork to Justify Murdering Slepian," *Women's e-News*, November 25, 2002, http://www.womensenews.org/article.cfm/dyn/aid/1121/ (accessed June 13, 2006).

12. Joe Dejka, "Priest Faces Federal Charges in Incident," *Omaha World-Herald*, May 19, 2006, http://www.lexis-nexis.com/universe (accessed June 16, 2006).

13. Leonard A. Cole, *The Anthrax Letters* (Washington, DC: Joseph Henry Press, 2003), p. 184.

14. Waagner, as quoted in ibid., p. 161.

15. Waagner, as quoted in "Suspect Says Sept. 11 Changed His Mind on Killing Abortion Doctors," *Pittsburgh Post-Gazette*, December 15, 2001, http://www.lexis-nexis/universe (accessed June 5, 2006). See also "The Pro-life Assassin Who Took a Powder," *Pittsburgh Post-Gazette*, April 27, 2002, http://www.lexis-nexis/universe (accessed June 6, 2006); Frederick Clarkson, "The Quiet Fall of an American Terrorist," *Salon*, December 10, 2003, http://www.archive.salon.com/news/feature/2003/12/10/waagner/print.html (accessed June 13, 2006).

16. Clayton Waagner, *Fighting the American Holocaust* (Chesapeake, VA: Pro-Life Virginia). An excerpt of this book is available online at the Army of God Web site, http://www.armyofgod/ClaytonBook.html (accessed June 7, 2006).

17. Clayton Waagner, "Thus Saith the Lord," Army of God Web site, http://www.armyofgod.com/ClaytonProphecy.html (accessed June 7, 2006).

18. Ibid.

19. Cole, *The Anthrax Letters*, p. 181.

20. Alan Cooperman, "Is Terrorism Tied to Christian Sect?" *Washington Post*, June 2, 2003, http://www.lexis-nexis.com/universe (accessed June 6, 2006).

21. See Kenneth S. Stern, *A Force on the Plain* (New York: Simon & Schuster, 1996), p. 240; Robert L. Snow, *The Militia Threat* (New York: Plenum Trade, 1999), p. 35.

22. Cooperman, "Is Terrorism Tied to Christian Sect?"

23. Hill, as quoted in John Kennedy, "Do What I Did, Urges Killer of Doctor," *Advertiser*, September 4, 2003, http://www.lexis-nexis/universe (accessed June 5, 2006).

24. Hill, as quoted in ibid.

25. Hill, as quoted by Jacqui Goddard and Tim Reid, "'Pro-life' Killer Is Executed," *Australian*, September 5, 2003, http://www.lexis-nexis.com/universe (accessed June 5, 2006).

26. Paul Hill, *Mix My Blood with the Blood of the Unborn*, Army of God Web site, http://www.armyofgod.com/PhillbookIntro.html (accessed June 5, 2006).

27. Hill, "Defending the Defenseless," Army of God Web site, August 2003, http://www.armyofgod.com/PHIll_ShortShot.htm (accessed June 5, 2005).

28. Ibid.

29. Ibid.

30. Ibid.

31. "Homegrown Terrorists" (editorial), *Buffalo News*, November 16, 2001, http://www.lexis-nexis.com/universe (accessed June 6, 2006).

32. Arsalan Tariq Iftikhar, "In My Opinion: The Capture of Osama Bin Rudolph," *Oregonian*, June 4, 2003, http://www.lexis-nexis.com/universe (accessed June 6, 2006).

33. "Terror Bust" (editorial), *Toronto Sun*, June 6, 2006, http://www.lexis-nexis.com/universe (accessed June 14, 2006).

34. Najeeb, as quoted in Mark Johnson, "Defying Stereotype Through Outreach," *Milwaukee Journal Sentinel*, May 7, 2006, http://www.lexis-nexis.com/universe (accessed June 14, 2006).

35. Badawi, as quoted in Parvez Ahmed, "Can Islam Be Peaceful and Tolerant?" *Tampa Tribune*, April 9, 2005, http://www.lexis-nexis.com/universe (accessed June 14, 2006).

36. Quindlen, "The Terrorists Here at Home," p. 78.

37. Benham, as quoted in Michael A. Fletcher, "Sniper Kills Abortion Doctor Near Buffalo," *Washington Post*, October 25, 1998, http://www.washingtonpost.com/wp-srv/national/longterm/abortviolence/stories/sniper.htm (accessed June 5, 2006).

38. Mark Juergensmeyer, *Terror in the Mind of God* (Berkeley and Los Angeles: University of California Press, 2000), p. 21.

39. Michael Bray, *A Time to Kill* (Portland, OR: Advocates for Life, 1994).

40. The discussion of Bray's theology follows Juergensmeyer, *Terror in the Mind of God*, pp. 20–30.

41. Charles Kimball, *When Religion Becomes Evil* (New York: HarperSanFrancisco, 2002), p. 46.

42. Ibid., p. 45.

43. The Ethics and Religious Liberty Commission of the Southern Baptist Convention, "The Nashville Statement of Conscience: Why the Killing of Abortion Doctors Is Wrong," Army of God Web site, September 1994, http://www.armyofgod.com/PhillBookAppendixBwhysouthernBaptistsarewrong.html (accessed June 5, 2006).

44. Clarkson, "The Quiet Fall of an American Terrorist"; "Radical Abortion Opponents Said to Be Laying Low," *Women's e-News*, January 21, 2003, http://www.womensenews.org/article.cfm/dyn/aid/1190/context/archive (accessed June 15, 2006).

45. Gallup/*Newsweek* Poll, April 1989, Public Opinion Online, Roper Center at the University of Connecticut, accession number 0204581, question number 016, http://www.lexis-nexis.com/universe (accessed June 14, 2006).

46. CBS News/*New York Times* Poll, January 1985, Public Opinion Online, Roper Center at the University of Connecticut, accession number 0014056, question number 060, http://www.lexis-nexis.com/universe (accessed June 14, 2006).

47. Fox News/Opinion Dynamics Poll, March 7, 2006, Public Opinion Online, Roper Center at the University of Connecticut, accession number 1644513, question number 089, http://www.lexis-nexis.com/universe (accessed June 5, 2006).

48. CBS News Poll, April 9, 2006, Public Opinion Online, Roper Center at the University of Connecticut, accession number 1649404, question number 021, http://www.lexis-nexis.com/universe (accessed June 5, 2006).

49. National Constitution Center Poll conducted by the Public Agenda Foundation, September 2002, Public Opinion Online, Roper Center at the University of Connecticut, accession number 0425416, question number 051, http://www.lexis-nexis.com/universe (accessed June 14, 2006).

50. Kevin O'Brien, "On Our Worst Day, We're Not as Nutty as Our Ene-

mies," *Cleveland Plain Dealer*, February 8, 2006, http://www.lexis-nexis.com/universe (accessed June 14, 2006).

51. Ibid.

52. Barnett A. Slepian, "Free to Speak, Pro-Lifers Still Bear Responsibility," *Buffalo News*, August 13, 1994, http://www.buffalonews.com/newslibrary/ (accessed June 10, 2006).

53. Matt. 12.

54. Bertrand Russell, *Why I Am Not a Christian* (New York: Simon & Schuster, 1957), p. 36.

55. Paul Johnson, *A History of Christianity* (New York: Simon & Schuster, 1976), p. 306.

56. Will Durant, *The Reformation* (New York: Simon & Schuster, 1957), p. 205.

57. See, for example, the International Committee for the Canonization of Servant of God Queen Isabel the Catholic of Spain Web site, http://www.queenisabel.com (accessed June 26, 2006). This Web site actually includes a defense of the Spanish Inquisition. See also Jerome Socolovsky, "Canonization of Queen Isabella Moves Ahead Despite 'Jewish Lobby,'" Jewish Telegraphic Agency Web site (JTA), http://www.jta.org/story.asp?id=030425-isab (accessed June 26, 2006).

58. Johnson, *A History of Christianity*, p. 308.

59. Durant, *The Reformation*, p. 208.

60. Ibid.

61. Bernard Delicieux, as cited in Helen Ellerbe, *The Dark Side of Christian History* (Orlando, FL: Morningstar and Lark, 1995), p. 78.

62. Clyde L. Manschreck, *A History of Christianity in the World* (Englewood Cliffs, NJ: Prentice-Hall, 1974), p. 187.

63. Martin Luther, as quoted in Durant, *The Reformation*, p. 450.

64. Martin Luther, as quoted in ibid., p. 422.

65. Martin Luther, as quoted in ibid., p. 423.

66. Martin Luther, as quoted in ibid., p. 422.

67. Ibid., p. 474.

68. See, for example, Neil J. Kressel, *Mass Hate: The Global Rise of Genocide and Terror*, rev. ed. (New York: Perseus/Westview, 2002), pp. 11–40.

69. Raymond of Aguilers, as quoted in Ellerbe, *The Dark Side of Christian History*, p. 39.

70. Russell, *Why I Am Not a Christian*, p. 36.

71. James Q. Wilson, "The Reform Islam Needs," *City Journal* 12, no. 4 (Autumn 2002), http://www.city-journal.org/html/12_4_the_reform_islam.html (accessed November 29, 2006).

72. See, for example, ibid.

73. C. V. Wedgwood, as cited in ibid., p. 4.

74. Herbert Butterfield, as cited in ibid., p. 2.

75. Bernard Lewis, *The Crisis of Islam* (New York: Modern Library, 2003), pp. 16–17.

76. Ibid., p. 17.

77. Margot Dudkevitch, "Jewish Extremists a 'Volcano Waiting to Erupt,'" *Jerusalem Post*, January 13, 2006, http://www.lexis-nexis.com/universe (accessed July 7, 2006). The section heading comes from this article.

78. These quotations are cited in Jeff Jacoby, "On Condemning Terrorism," *Boston Globe*, August 11, 2005, http://www.lexis-nexis.com/universe (accessed July 7, 2006).

79. Ibid.

80. Moshe Meirsdorf, as quoted in Matthew Gutman, "Kfar Tapuah Weighs Ban on Kahane Chai Members after Shfaram Attack," *Jerusalem Post*, August 7, 2005, http://www.lexis-nexis.com/universe (accessed July 10, 2006).

81. These quotations are cited in Harvey Morris, "Sharon Condemns Israeli Who Shot Four Dead," *Financial Times*, August 5, 2005, http://www.lexis-nexis.com/universe (accessed July 5, 2006).

82. Eitam, as quoted in Herb Keinon and Gil Hoffman, "PM Condemns Shooting," *Jerusalem Post*, August 5, 2005, http://www.lexis-nexis.com/universe (accessed July 10, 2006).

83. Arieh O'Sullivan, "IDF Inquiry: Zada Wasn't Fit for Draft," *Jerusalem Post*, August 26, 2005, http://www.lexis-nexis.com/universe (accessed July 10, 2006).

84. Ben-Ya'acov, as quoted in Yaakov Katz et al., "Far-Right Soldier Slays 4 Arabs in Shfaram," *Jerusalem Post*, August 5, 2005, http://www.lexis-nexis.com/universe (accessed July 5, 2006).

85. David Margolis, "The Dangerous Allure of Theocracy," *Jerusalem Report*, February 10, 2003, http://www.lexis-nexis.com/universe (accessed July 7, 2006).

86. Ibid.

87. Teddy Preuss, "An Easy Excuse for Murder," *Jerusalem Post*, February 28, 1994, http://www.lexis-nexis.com/universe (accessed July 10, 2006).

88. Ibid.

89. Jacoby, "On Condemning Terrorism."

90. Pew Research Center Poll, March 16, 2006, Public Opinion Online, Roper Center at the University of Connecticut, accession number 1645928, question number 105, available from http://www.lexis-nexis.com/universe (accessed May 12, 2006). An additional 4 percent choose "none"; 17 percent didn't know or refused to answer the question.

91. See Yoram Peri, ed., *The Assassination of Yitzhak Rabin* (Stanford, CA: Stanford University Press, 2000); Neil J. Kressel, review of *The Assassination of Yitzhak Rabin*, ed. Yoram Peri, *Political Psychology* 23, no. 3 (September 2002): 636–39.

92. Ehud Sprinzak, "Israel's Radical Right and the Countdown to the Rabin Assassination," in Peri, *The Assassination of Yitzhak Rabin*, p. 125.

93. Ibid., p. 108.

94. Ibid., p. 124.

95. Ibid.

96. Ibid., p. 125.

97. Jeffrey Goldberg, "Protect Sharon from the Right," *New York Times*, August 5, 2004.

98. Ibid.

99. Ibid.

100. Sharon, as quoted in Ina Friedman, "Jews vs. Jews, Again," *Jerusalem Report*, August 9, 2004, http://www.lexis-nexis.com/universe (accessed October 22, 2004).

101. Goldstein, as quoted in Yaakov Katz, "Settlers Divided Over Anti-Sharon Campaign," *Jerusalem Post*, December 17, 2004, http://www.lexis-nexis.com/universe (accessed July 7, 2005).

102. "Dozens of Jewish Extremists Seeking Sharon's Death," Agence France-Presse (English), July 20, 2004, http://www.lexis-nexis.com/universe (accessed October 22, 2004).

103. Hanegbi, as quoted in Megan Goldin, "Sharon May Face Threat from Jewish Extremists," *Toronto Star*, July 8, 2004, http://www.lexis-nexis.com/universe (accessed July 5, 2006).

104. Friedman, "Jews vs. Jews, Again."

105. Edgar Lefkovits, "Temple Mount 'Missile Attack' Planners Had Changed Their Minds," *Jerusalem Post*, May 17, 2005, http://www.lexis-nexis.com/universe (accessed July 7, 2005).

106. Laurie Copans, "Chief Rabbis Prohibit Jews from Entering Temple Mount," *Jerusalem Post*, January 19, 2005, http://www.lexis-nexis.com/universe (accessed July 5, 2006).

107. Dicter, as quoted in Jeffrey Goldberg, "Among the Settlers," *New Yorker*, May 31, 2004, p. 48, http://www.lexis-nexis.com/universe (accessed July 11, 2006).

108. Gershom Gorenberg, *The End of Days: Fundamentalism and the Struggle for the Temple Mount* (New York: Oxford University Press, 2002), p. 6.

109. Gorenberg, as quoted in Missy Daniel, "Interview: Gershom Gorenberg on the Temple Mount," Religion and Ethics Newsweekly Web site, episode 416, December 15, 2000, http://www.pbs.org/wnet/religionandethics/week416/interview.html (accessed July 10, 2006).

110. Israel Shahak and Norton Mezvinsky, *Jewish Fundamentalism in Israel*, new ed. (London: Pluto Press, 2004).

111. Andrew E. Mathis, "The Interpretational Errors of Israel Shahak," June 8, 2000, http://andrew.mathis.net/shahak.html (accessed June 13, 2007).

112. See, for example, Rabbi Solomon Ganzfried, *Code of Jewish Law: Kitzur Schulchan Aruch*, annotated ed., trans. Hyman E. Goldin (New York: Hebrew Publishing, 1961). This point is not meant to imply that the rules contained in later compilations are sensible, reasonable, or innocuous, just that they do not provide the basis for extremism that Shahak and Mezvinsky insist they do. Some of the rules can cause considerable psychological harm to the believer. Consider, for example, the equation of masturbation with murder and the commentary that "[o]ccasionally, as a punishment for this sin, children die when young, God forbid." (vol. 4, p. 17).

113. Bezalel Stern, "Fundamentally Flawed," *Jerusalem Post*, September 15, 2004, http://www.lexis-nexis.com/universe (accessed July 7, 2006).

114. Eetta Prince-Gibson, "The Metro-Retro Divide," *Jerusalem Post*, November 15, 2005, http://www.lexis-nexis.com/universe (accessed July 5, 2005).

115. Peri, as quoted in ibid.

116. See, for example, Andrea Levin, "New Yorker Manipulations," Aish.com Web site, http://www.aish.com/jewishissues/mediaobjectivity/New_Yorker_Manipulations.asp (accessed November 29, 2006); Gary Rosenblatt, "Can Israel Be Criticized Fairly?" Middle East Information Center Web site, July 9, 2004, http://www.middleeastinfo.org/article.php?sid=4621 (accessed July 13, 2004).

117. Goldberg, "Among the Settlers."

118. See Samuel Peleg, *Zealotry and Vengeance* (Lanham, MD: Lexington Books, 2002); Yoram Peri, *The Assassination of Yitzhak Rabin*; Dov Waxman, review of *The Assassination of Yitzhak Rabin*, ed. Yoram Peri, *H-Net Reviews*, January 2004, http://www.h-net.msu.edu/reviews/showrev.cgi?path=317191078584063 (accessed June 1, 2006).

Chapter 4

1. Ralph W. Hood, Peter C. Hill, and W. Paul Williamson, *The Psychology of Religious Fundamentalism* (New York: Guilford, 2005), pp. 121–22.

2. Unidentified serpent handler recorded on Kingston Service Video, December 2, 1995, Hood-Williamson Research Archives, Archives on the Serpent Handlers of Southern Appalachia, Lupton Library, University of Tennessee, Chattanooga, as quoted in ibid., p. 115.

3. Ibid., p. 123.

4. Unidentified serpent handler as quoted in ibid., pp. 125–26.

5. Ibid., p. 127.

6. Bart D. Ehrman, *The New Testament: Course Guidebook* (Chantilly, VA: Teaching Company, 2000), pt. 1, p. 29. This book accompanies Professor Ehrman's audiotaped lectures on the New Testament. See also Morna Hooker, *The Message of Mark* (London: Epworth, 1983).

7. Hood, Hill, and Williamson, *The Psychology of Religious Fundamentalism*, p. 124.

8. Charles Kimball, *When Religion Becomes Evil* (New York: HarperSanFrancisco, 2002), p. 57.

9. Daniel Akaka, 2005 National Bible Week, *Congressional Record*, November 14, 2005, National Bible Association Web site, http://www.nationalbible.org/congressional.html (accessed July 26, 2006).

10. George W. Bush, 2005 National Bible Week Presidential Message, National Bible Association Web site, October 26, 2005, http://www.nationalbible.org/presidential.html (accessed July 26, 2006).

11. William Clinton, National Bible Week Presidential Message, National Bible Association Web site, November 20–27, 1994, http://www.ceai.org/fmembers/teaching_tips/tt_national_bible_week.htm (accessed July 26, 2006).

12. Ronald Reagan, Proclamation 5018, February 3, 1983, http://www.reagan.utexas.edu/archives/speeches/1983/20383b.htm (accessed July 26, 2006).

13. Ibid.

14. National Bible Association, "Celebrities Who Read the Bible," National Bible Association Web site, http://www.nationalbible.org/celebrities.html (accessed July 26, 2006); National Bible Association, "Historical Figures Who Read the Bible," National Bible Association Web site, http://www.nationalbible.org/historical.html (accessed July 26, 2006).

15. R. J. Rushdoony, *Institutes of Biblical Law* (Nutley, NJ: Presbyterian and Reformed Publishing Company/Craig Press, 1973); see also Frederick Clarkson, *Eternal Hostility* (Monroe, ME: Common Courage Press, 1994), pp. 78–81.

16. See, for example, Robert Goldenberg, "Talmud," in *Back to the Sources*, ed. Barry W. Holtz (New York: Simon & Schuster, 1986), pp. 129–76.

17. See, for example, Miryam Z. Wahrman, *Brave New Judaism* (Hanover, NH: Brandeis University Press, 2002) for an account of how different branches of Judaism have responded to challenges arising from new technologies.

18. Phil Zuckerman, *Invitation to the Sociology of Religion* (New York: Routledge, 2003), p. 37.

19. Ibid., p. 45. Zuckerman summarizes the work of numerous researchers.

20. Ibid., p. 51.

21. Orthodox Jews are most observant of the traditional Jewish law. The Reform movement arose in reaction to perceived conflicts between the modern world and the traditional religious system. Conservative Judaism is, in turn, a reaction against the abandonment of many traditions by the Reform Jews; it started—in essence—as a more traditionalist branch of the Reform movement. Reconstructionism focuses on Jews as a people or sociological

entity; it allows a great deal of latitude in religious belief and does not offer strict doctrines about the nature of God. In practice, Jews with a wide variety of beliefs and levels of observance can be found among the membership of most synagogues.

22. See, for example, Peter L. Bergen, *The Osama Bin Laden I Know* (New York: Free Press, 2006).

23. "Rape in the Bible," EvilBible.com Web site, http://www.evilbible.com/rape.htm (accessed July 28, 2006).

24. "Welcome to the EvilBible.com Web Site," EvilBible.com Web site, http://www.evilbible.com (accessed July 28, 2006).

25. See, for example, B. A. Robinson, "Bible Passages That Are Immoral by Today's Religious and Secular Standards," Religious Tolerance Web site, December 9, 2000, http://www.religioustolerance.org/imm.bibl.htm (accessed July 21, 2006); David Voas, *The Bad News Bible: The New Testament* (Amherst, NY: Prometheus Books, 1995); Walter C. Kaiser et al., *Hard Sayings of the Bible* (Westmont, IL: Intervarsity Press, 1996).

26. See Avi Sagi, "The Punishment of Amalek in Jewish Tradition," *Harvard Theological Review* 87, no. 3 (1994): 323–46; Gerald Cromer, "Amalek as Other, Other as Amalek," *Quantitative Sociology* 24, no. 2 (Summer 2001): 191–202; "Blotting Out Amalek: Theory and Practice," MSN Judaism FAQ's Web site, http://groups.msn.com/JudaismFAQs/blottingoutamalektheoryandpractice.msnw (accessed July 28, 2006).

27. Joseph Telushkin, *Jewish Literacy* (New York: William Morrow, 1991), p. 52.

28. Aron Moss, "Wipe Out Amalek, Today?" Chabad Web site, http://www.chabad.org/library/article.asp?print=true&AID=267677 (accessed July 28, 2006).

29. See, for example, Harvey K. McArthur, *Understanding the Sermon on the Mount* (London: Epworth, 1961), pp. 26–57; George H. Smith, *Atheism* (Amherst, NY: Prometheus Books, 1989), p. 317.

30. See, among many, Marvin Harris, *Cows Pigs Wars and Witches* (New York: Random House, 1974), pp. 155–206, for an interesting, if idiosyncratic, statement of this position.

31. Paul Johnson, *A History of Christianity* (New York: Touchstone, 1976), p. 241.

32. Bertrand Russell, *Why I Am Not a Christian* (New York: Touchstone, 1957), p. 17.

33. Ibid., p. 22.

34. Smith, *Atheism*, p. 308.

35. Ibid.

36. Stephens, as quoted in G. Seldes, *The Great Thoughts* (New York: Ballantine, 1985), p. 399.

37. Philip Greven, *Spare the Child* (New York: Vintage, 1990), p. 46.

38. Smith, *Atheism*, p. 313.

39. Ibid.

40. Greg Myre, "A Larger and More Powerful Rocket Hits Deeper in Israel, Adding a New Dimension," *New York Times*, July 29, 2006.

41. "Hizballah Rockets," GlobalSecurity.org Web site, July 30, 2006, http://www.globalsecurity.org/military/world/para/hizballah-rockets.htm (accessed August 2, 2006).

42. W. Montgomery Watt, *Muhammad* (New York: Oxford University Press, 1961), p. 130.

43. Ibid., pp. 171–72.

44. Ibid., pp. 173–74.

45. Hadith narrated by Abu Sa'id Al-Kudri, available from Wikipedia, s.v. "Banu Qurayza," July 26, 2006, http://www.en.wikipedia.org/w/index.php?title=Banu_Qurayza&printable=yes (accessed August 8, 2006). For sources and references, see also James M. Arlandson, "Muhammad's Atrocity against the Qurayza Jews," Answering Islam Web site, http://www.answering-Islam.org/Authors/Arlandson/qurayza_Jews.htm (accessed August 8, 2006); Andrew G. Bostom, "Muhammad, the Qurayza Massacre, and PBS," *FrontPageMagazine.com*, December 20, 2002, http://www.frontpagemag.com/Articles/Pritnable.asp?ID=5195 (accessed August 8, 2006).

46. Ibn Ishaq, as quoted in Wikipedia, s.v. "Banu Qurayza."

47. Yossef Bodansky, *Islamic Anti-Semitism as a Political Instrument* (Houston, TX: Freeman Center, 1999), p. 128.

48. Mir, as quoted in Bergen, *The Osama Bin Laden I Know*, p. 319.

49. This account comes from "Prophet's Companions: Safia bint Abdul Muttalib," *Islamic Voice* 16–03, no. 195 (March 2003), http://www.islamicvoice.com/march.2003/child.htm (accessed August 9, 2006).

50. Watt, *Muhammad*, p. 173.

51. Telushkin, *Jewish Literacy*, p. 509.

52. Nathan Katz, "How the Hindu-Jewish Encounter Reconfigures Interreligious Dialogue," Hindu Universe Web site, March 6, 1994, http://

www.hindunet.org/alt_hindu/1994/msg00109.html (accessed August 16, 2006).

53. Telushkin, *Jewish Literacy*, p. 552.

54. Yakov Malik, as quoted in ibid., p. 506.

55. Gershom Gorenberg, *The End of Days* (New York: Oxford University Press, 2000).

56. This quotation comes from a translation of a shorter and somewhat modified version of the Schulchan Aruch called the Kitzur Schulchan Aruch. Solomon Ganzfried, *Code of Jewish Law: Kitzur Schulchan Aruch*, annotated rev. ed., trans. Hyman E. Goldin. (New York: Hebrew Publishing Company, 1963), 4: 67. It should be noted that some Jewish authorities regard the Kitzur Schulchan Aruch as stricter, less authoritative, and less progressive than the original Schulchan Aruch.

57. Ibid., 4: 19.

58. Ibid., 4: 108–109.

59. Abraham J. Feldman, "Guiding Principles of Reform Judaism," in *The Life of the Torah*, ed. Jacob Neusner (Belmont, CA: Wadsworth, 1974), p. 173.

60. Ajith Fernando, "Other Religions Are False Paths That Mislead Their Followers," in *Enduring Issues in Religion*, ed. John Lyden (San Diego, CA: Greenhaven, 1995), p. 66.

61. Mahmut Aydin, "Modern Western Christian Theological Understandings of Muslims Since the Second Vatican Council," sect. 1.2, Council for Research in Values and Philosophy Web site, http://www.crvp.org/book/Series02/IIA-13/chapter_one (accessed August 16, 2006).

62. "Declaration on the Relationship of the Church to Non-Christian Religions," *The Documents of Vatican II* (New York: Guild, 1966), p. 662.

63. Ibid., pp. 662–63.

64. Karl Rahner, "Other Religions Are Implicit Forms of Our Own Religion," in Lyden, *Enduring Issues in Religion*, p. 72.

65. See, for example, John Hick, *An Interpretation of Religion* (New Haven, CT: Yale University Press, 1989); John B. Cobb Jr., "Beyond 'Pluralism,'" in *Christian Uniqueness Reconsidered*, ed. Gavin D'Costa (Maryknoll, NY: Orbis Books, 1990).

66. See Jon Meacham, "Pilgrim's Progress," *Newsweek*, August 14, 2006, p. 43.

67. See, among many, Marvin Perry and Frederick M. Schweitzer, *Anti-*

semitism: Myth and Hate from Antiquity to the Present (New York: Palgrave Macmillan, 2002), p. 17.

68. Aquinas, as quoted in ibid., p. 17.

69. Ibid., p. 18.

70. Marvin Harris, *Cows Pigs Wars and Witches*, p. 195. Harris writes: "A purely peaceful messiah became a practical necessity when the generals who had just defeated the Jewish messianic revolutionaries—Vespasian and Titus—became the rulers of the Roman Empire. . . . In the aftermath of the unsuccessful messianic war, it quickly became a practical necessity for Christians to deny that their cult had arisen out of the Jewish belief in a messiah who was going to topple the Roman Empire" (p. 195).

71. Bart D. Ehrman, "The New Testament," audiotaped lectures produced by the Great Courses, Lecture 6: Matthew. See Ehrman, *The New Testament: Course Guidebook* (Chantilly, VA: Teaching Company, 2000), pt. 1, p. 35.

72. Ibid., pt. 2, p. 48.

73. Perry and Schweitzer, *Antisemitism*, p. 42. They attribute the phrase to theologian and Holocaust survivor Eliezer Berkovits.

74. Unless otherwise noted, I rely on the A. Yusuf Ali translation.

75. Sam Harris, *The End of Faith* (New York: Norton, 2005), p. 123.

76. These two hadiths are cited in Bernard Lewis, *The Crisis of Islam* (New York: Modern Library, 2003), p. 32.

77. Harris relies on a translation that makes verses sound more inflammatory than some other translations. I use the A. Yusuf Ali translation.

78. Sam Harris, *The End of Faith*, p. 120.

79. Translation by A. Yusuf Ali, *The Holy Quran*, p. 166.

80. Dawood translation used here.

81. Dawood translation used here.

82. Dawood translation used here.

83. Bernard Lewis, *What Went Wrong?* (New York: Oxford University Press, 2002), p. 98. See also Lewis, *The Crisis of Islam*, p. 6.

84. M. H. Hart, *The 100: A Ranking of the Most Influential Persons in History* (Secaucus, NJ: Citadel, 1987), p. 40.

85. Menahem Milson, "Reform vs. Islamism in the Arab World Today," MEMRI Special Report #34, September 15, 2004, http://www.memri.org/bin/opener.cgi?Page=archives&ID=SR3404 (accessed August 15, 2004).

86. Lewis, *The Political Language of Islam* (Chicago: University of Chicago, 1988), p. 2.

87. See Fatima Mernissi, *Islam and Democracy* (New York: Addison-Wesley, 1992).

88. This section has been adapted from Neil J. Kressel, "Antisemitism, Social Science and the Muslim and Arab World," *Judaism* 52, nos. 3–4 (Summer–Fall 2003): 225–45. See, also, Neil J. Kressel, "Mass Hatred in the Muslim and Arab World: The Neglected Problem of Anti-Semitism," *International Journal of Applied Psychoanalytic Studies*, in press.

89. Bernard Lewis, *Semites and Anti-Semites* (New York: Norton, 1986), p. 132.

90. Lewis, *What Went Wrong?* p. 154.

91. Lewis, *Semites and Anti-Semites*, p. 121.

92. Dawood translation used here.

93. Lewis, *Semites and Antisemites*, pp. 117–39. Bat Ye'or, *The Dhimmi* (Madison, NJ: Fairleigh Dickinson University Press, 1985); Robert Spencer, *The Myth of Islamic Tolerance* (Amherst, NY: Prometheus Books, 2005).

94. Cited in Jacques Givet, *The Anti-Zionist Complex*, trans. Evelyn Abel and Norman Langford (Englewood, NJ: SBS Publishing, 1982), p. 72.

95. Cited in ibid.

96. Perry and Schweitzer, *Antisemitism*, pp. 1–42.

97. Neil J. Kressel, *Mass Hate: The Global Rise of Genocide and Terror*, rev. and updated ed. (Boulder, CO; Perseus/Westview, 2002), p. 18.

98. Mernissi, *Islam and Democracy*; Kressel, *Mass Hate*, p. 67.

99. Daniel Pipes, *Militant Islam Reaches America* (New York: Norton, 2002), pp. 1–14.

100. Pius X, as quoted in Ian Fisher, "Limbo, an Afterlife Tradition, May Be Doomed by the Vatican," *New York Times*, December 28, 2005.

101. Joseph Ratzinger, as quoted in ibid.

102. James J. O'Donnell, as quoted in ibid.

103. Harris, *The End of Faith*, pp. 18–19, Hood, Hill, and Williamson, *The Psychology of Religious Fundamentalism*, p. 27.

104. Harris, *The End of Faith*, p. 19.

105. James Hall, "Philosophy of Religion," audiotaped lectures produced by the Great Courses, lecture 33 (Chantilly, VA: Teaching Company, 2003). See also James Hall, *Philosophy of Religion: Course Guidebook* (Chantilly, VA: Teaching Company, 2003), pt. 3, p. 26.

106. Hood, Hill, and Williamson, *The Psychology of Religious Fundamentalism*, p. 26.

107. Lawrence M. Principe, "Science and Religion," audiotaped lectures produced by the Great Courses, lectures 1, 2, 11, 12 (Chantilly, VA: Teaching Company, 2006). See also Principe, *Science and Religion: Course Guidebook* (Chantilly, VA: Teaching Company, 2003), p. 42.

108. Jaroslav Pelikan, *Interpreting the Bible and the Constitution* (New Haven, CT: Yale University Press, 2005).

109. Alan M. Dershowitz, *Chutzpah* (New York: Simon & Schuster, 1991), p. 12.

110. See, for example, Sharon S. Brehm, Saul Kassin, and Steven Fein, *Social Psychology*, 6th ed. (New York: Houghton Mifflin, 2005), pp. 214–23.

111. Milson, "Reform vs. Islamism in the Arab World Today."

112. Pipes, *Militant Islam Reaches America*, p. 189.

113. Ibn Warraq, *Why I Am Not a Muslim* (Amherst, NY: Prometheus Books, 1995).

114. Aluma Dankowitz, "Accusing Muslim Intellectuals of Apostasy," MEMRI Inquiry and Analysis #208, February 18, 2005, http://www.memri.org/bin/opener.cgi?Page=archives&ID=IA20805 (accessed May 2, 2006).

115. Al-Qaradhawi, as quoted in ibid.

116. Al-Qimni, as quoted in ibid.

117. Al-Nabulsi, as quoted in ibid.

118. Al-Khuli, as quoted in ibid.

119. Jane Perlez, "Once Muslim, Now Christian and Caught in the Courts," *New York Times*, August 24, 2006.

120. Altemeyer and Hunsberger, as quoted in Raymond F. Paloutzian, *Invitation to the Psychology of Religion*, 2nd ed. (Boston: Allyn and Bacon, 1996), p. 230.

Chapter 5

1. El Aroud, as quoted in Peter L. Bergen, *The Osama Bin Laden I Know* (New York: Free Press, 2006), p. 259. Malika El Aroud's book is *Les Soldats de Lumière* (Brussels: Les Ailes de la Miséricorde, 2003). See, also, Jean-Francois Mayer, "*Les Soldats de Lumière*: Une Autre Image du Jihad," May 21, 2003, Terrorisme.net, http://www.terrorisme.net/p/printer_50.shtml (accessed December 15, 2006); "Appel Urgent Pour Aider Malika El Aroud

dans son Épreuve," La Voix des Opprimés, http://news.stcom.net/modules.php?name=News&file=print&sid=1377 (accessed December 15, 2006). (In Bergen's book, Malika El Aroud is referred to as Malika Malik. Abdessatar Dahmane is referred to as Dahmane Abdessatar in several sources.)

2. El Aroud, as quoted in Bergen, *The Osama Bin Laden I Know*, p. 258.

3. El Aroud, as quoted in ibid., p. 297.

4. El Aroud, as quoted in ibid., p. 298.

5. El Aroud, as quoted in ibid., p. 259.

6. W. W. Meissner, "The Pathology of Beliefs and the Beliefs of Pathology," in *Religion and the Clinical Practice of Psychology*, ed. Edward P. Shafranske (Washington, DC: American Psychological Association, 1996), p. 251.

7. M. Brewster Smith, Jerome S. Bruner, and Robert W. White, *Opinions and Personality* (New York: Wiley, 1956), p. 39.

8. Ibid., p. 41. See also Daniel Katz, "Functional Approach to the Study of Attitudes," *Public Opinion Quarterly* 24 (1960): 168–92. Katz offers an overlapping classification of the functions of attitudes. One difference is that he calls attention to a "value-expressive function," where holding certain opinions helps people to give positive expression to their central values and to establish an identity or sense of self.

9. Smith, Bruner, and White, *Opinions and Personality*, p. 42.

10. Neil J. Kressel, *Mass Hate: The Global Rise of Genocide and Terror*, rev. and updated ed. (Boulder, CO: Perseus/Westview, 2002), p. 121.

11. Eli S. Chesen, *Religion May Be Hazardous to Your Health* (New York: Peter H. Wyden, 1972), p. 94.

12. Roger Martin du Gard, *Jean Barois*, trans. Stuart Gilbert (Indianapolis, IN: Bobbs-Merrill, 1969), p. 252. The book was originally published in 1913.

13. Ibid., p. 253.

14. Ibid., pp. 254–55.

15. Ibid., p. 255.

16. Ibid.

17. Ibid., p. 256.

18. Ibid., p. 354.

19. Irene Smith, "Quotation of the Day," *New York Times*, September 11, 2006.

20. Kenneth I. Pargament, "Religious Methods of Coping," in Shafranske, *Religion and the Clinical Practice of Psychology*, p. 231.

21. See, among others, Raymond F. Paloutzian, *Invitation to the Psychology of Religion*, 2nd ed. (Boston: Allyn and Bacon, 1996), pp. 14–20. This classification comes from the work of Charles Y. Glock, "On the Study of Religious Commitment," Supplement to *Religious Education* 42 (July–August 1962): 98–110.

22. Andrew M. Greeley, *Unsecular Man* (New York: Schocken, 1972), p. 261.

23. Ibid., p. 153.

24. Sarah R. Taggart, *Living As If* (San Francisco: Jossey-Bass, 1994), p. 118.

25. Find source in Erich Fromm, *Psychoanalysis and Religion* (New Haven, CT: Yale University Press, 1950) p. 6.

26. Sigmund Freud, *The Future of an Illusion*, trans. and ed. James Strachey (New York: Norton, 1961), p. 71. This work was originally published in 1927. See also Neil J. Kressel, "The Freudian Interpretation of Religion," *American Atheist* (August 1977): 28–32.

27. Freud, *The Future of an Illusion*, p. 51.

28. Ibid., p. 23.

29. Ibid., p. 51.

30. Ibid., p. 66.

31. See, for example, Sam McFarland, "Communism as Religion," *International Journal for the Psychology of Religion* 8, no 1 (1998): 33–48.

32. See James Forsyth, *Psychological Theories of Religion* (Upper Saddle River, NJ: Prentice-Hall, 2003), p. 72. For example, Carl Jung—Freud's one-time disciple who later developed his own analytic theory—thought that many of our unconscious needs derived from inherited, shared images passed down through human history. Traces of these images remained in what he called our "collective unconscious." If people wanted the experience of becoming whole, they needed to incorporate these unconscious images into their conscious life. To the extent that religious symbols, rituals, and beliefs contributed to the process, they were important and psychologically "true." Western religion sometimes provided a means to transform oneself in a positive direction, but—for Jung, at least in his later years—better answers came from religions of the East.

33. Fromm, *Psychoanalysis and Religion*, pp. 24–25.

34. Viktor Frankl, *The Unconscious God* (New York: Simon & Schuster, 1975). See also *Man's Search for Meaning* (Boston: Beacon, 2006).

35. Abraham H. Maslow, *Religions Values and Peak Experiences* (New York: Viking, 1970), p. 19.

36. Forsyth, *Psychological Theories of Religion*, p. 208.

37. Ernest Becker, *The Denial of Death* (New York: Free Press, 1973), p. 26.

38. Ibid., p. 66.

39. Ibid., pp. 203–204. See also Daniel Liechty, "Reaction to Mortality," *Zygon* 33, no 1 (March 1998): 45–58; Eva Jonas and Peter Fischer, "Terror Management and Religion," *Journal of Personality and Social Psychology* 91, no. 3 (2006): 553–67. Jonas and Fischer conduct some experimental tests of terror management theory, a currently influential scientific restatement of some elements of Becker's approach to human nature. According to terror management theory, people unconsciously manage their terror of death through the adoption of a cultural worldview and the bolstering of self-esteem. Cultural worldviews, religious or otherwise, provide "literal or symbolic immortality (e.g., through concepts of soul, heaven, or nirvana with regard to literal immortality and lasting cultural achievements as a vehicle for symbolic immortality). Self-esteem is acquired by believing in the cultural worldview and living up to its standards. Together, these psychological structures constitute an anxiety buffer that helps people to cope with the problem of death" (p. 553). Jonas and Fischer's experiments convince them that people who are intrinsically religious—i.e., those who strive for meaning and value through their faith—derive some terror management benefits.

40. Liechty, "Reaction to Mortality," p. 55.

41. Forsyth, *Psychological Theories of Religion*, p. ix.

42. Ibid., p. x.

43. Albert Ellis, "The Case against Religion," *Cogitocrat*, http://www.geocities.com/bororissa/rel.html?20069, 2006 (accessed November 27). Ellis defines religion in a way that excludes some of its most progressive manifestations.

44. See Sam McFarland, "Psychology of Religion: A Call for a Broader Paradigm," *American Psychologist* 39, no. 3 (March 1984): 321–24, an intelligent but largely unheeded call to study a broader range of religious experiences using a wider array of methodologies.

45. Paloutzian, *Invitation to the Psychology of Religion*, p. 260. Another

psychologist of religion, Kenneth Pargament, seems to agree in his assessment of the research:

> Some [forms of religious coping] are helpful (spiritual support, collaborative religious coping, benevolent religious reframing, and congregational support), some are harmful (expressions of discontent with the congregation and God, and negative religious reframing), and some have mixed implications (religious rituals, self-directing and deferring religious coping, and religious conversion). Several other conclusions are also warranted: (1) Religious coping seems especially helpful to more religious people, (2) religion can moderate or deter the effects of life stress, or both, and 3) religious coping adds a unique dimension to the coping process.

Kenneth I. Pargament, *The Psychology of Religion and Coping* (New York: Guilford, 1997), p. 312. John Gartner has suggested that much of this literature can be explained by attending to the ways religiosity and mental well-being are measured. In his view, most negative associations have been found between religious commitment and hard-to-measure dimensions such as self-actualization, authoritarianism, dogmatism, tolerance of ambiguity, rigidity, and ambiguity. Most positive associations have been found between religion and "real-life" behavior events such as physical health, mortality, suicide, drug use, alcohol abuse, delinquency, and divorce. John Gartner, "Religious Commitment, Mental Health, and Prosocial Behavior: A Review of the Empirical Literature," in Shafranske, *Religion and the Clinical Practice of Psychology*, p. 201.

46. Rollo May, *Man's Search for Himself* (New York: Norton, 1953), p. 193.

47. Ibid., p. 194.

48. See also Allport's distinction between mature and immature religion. Gordon W. Allport, *The Individual and His Religion* (New York: Macmillan, 1950).

49. For a good explanation of Allport's complex theory, see the old text by his student Walter Houston Clark, *The Psychology of Religion* (New York: Macmillan, 1958), pp. 240–48.

50. Fromm, *Psychoanalysis and Religion*, pp. 21–64. See also David M. Wulff, *Psychology of Religion*, 2nd ed. (Hoboken, NJ: Wiley, 1997), pp. 597–98.

51. A. J. Ayer, "The Claims of Theology," in *Atheism*, ed. S. T. Joshi (Amherst, NY: Prometheus Books, 2000), p. 105.

52. M. E. Marty, *The Modern Schism* (New York: Harper & Row, 1969). See also Ralph W. Hood, Peter C. Hill, and W. Paul Williamson, *The Psychology of Religious Fundamentalism* (New York: Guilford, 2005), p. 52.

53. Erik Erikson, *Childhood and Society*, 2nd ed. (New York: Norton, 1963), p. 250. He wrote:

> All religions have in common the periodical childlike surrender to a Provider or providers who dispense earthly fortune as well as spiritual health; some demonstration of man's smallness by way of reduced posture and humble gesture; the admission in prayer and song of misdeeds, or misthoughts, and of evil intentions; fervent appeal for inner unification by divine guidance; and finally, the insight that individual trust must become a common faith, individual mistrust a commonly formulated evil, while the individual's restoration must become part of the ritual practice of many, and must become a sign of trustworthiness in the community.

While this description is accurate for most forms of Abrahamic faith, Erikson errs when he ascribes these elements to all religions.

54. Wulff, *Psychology of Religion*, pp. 371–73.

55. James W. Jones, *Terror and Transformation* (New York: Taylor and Francis, 2002), p. 65.

56. For the classic psychological work on this topic, see Milton Rokeach, *The Open and Closed Mind* (New York: Basic Books, 1960).

57. Derek Wright, *The Psychology of Moral Behaviour* (Baltimore, MD: Penguin, 1971), p. 192.

58. Ibid., pp. 192–93.

59. Ibid., p. 193.

60. Rokeach, *The Open and Closed Mind*, p. 254.

61. Pargament, *The Psychology of Religion and Coping*, pp. 332–33.

62. Mark Juergensmeyer, *Terror in the Mind of God* (Berkeley and Los Angeles: University of California Press, 2000), p. 224.

63. Roy F. Baumeister, *Evil* (New York: Freeman, 1997), p. 174.

64. William Barrett, as quoted in Michael J. Mazarr, "The Psychological Sources of Islamic Terrorism," *Policy Review* (June/July 2004): 43.

65. Mazarr, "The Psychological Sources of Islamic Terrorism," p. 43.

66. Ibid., p. 43. Psychoanalyst Matthias Beier arrives at a related conclusion—though heavily coated in psychoanalytic theory and terminology—in his study of violent Christian fundamentalists. They committed acts of violence to assure themselves that they mattered in an ultimate sense. See Matthias Beier, "On the Psychology of Violent Christian Fundamentalism: Fighting to Matter Ultimately," *Psychoanalytic Review* 93, no. 2 (April 2006): 301–27.

67. See Erich Fromm, *Escape from Freedom* (New York: Avon, 1969).

68. Charles Kimball, *When Religion Becomes Evil* (San Francisco: HarperSanFrancisco, 2002), p. 67.

69. See May, *Man's Search for Himself*, p. 198; Jones, *Terror and Transformation*, p. 66.

70. Goethe, as quoted in May, *Man's Search for Himself*, p. 201.

71. Meissner, "The Pathology of Beliefs and the Beliefs of Pathology," p. 252.

72. However, the lure of sexual transgression, and the reaction against this lure, may be especially powerful. If this is the case, it could be accounted for by Becker's denial of death theory. When sexuality overpowers one's higher self, the result is an unwanted encounter with one's animality, and hence one's mortality. To deny this mortality, believers—and others—struggle to keep such impulses under control.

73. Walter A. Davis, "Bible Says: The Psychology of Christian Fundamentalism," *Psychoanalytic Review* 93, no. 2 (April 2006): 293.

74. Ibid., p. 198.

75. Beier, "On the Psychology of Violent Christian Fundamentalism," p. 307, makes the argument that many violent antiabortion activists "either had contentious relationships with or absence of their fathers, or felt deprived of becoming fathers due to an abortion." His list includes Paul Hill, Neal Horsley, Clay Waagner, James Kopp, and Paul deParrie. Osama bin Laden fits the pattern, too. It is a plausible, but unproven, hypothesis that violent religious fanatics rarely come from loving families.

76. See Wulff, *Psychology of Religion*, p. 384; Roy F. Baumeister, "Esteem Threat, Self-Regulatory Breakdown, and Emotional Distress as Factors in Self-Defeating Behavior," *Review of General Psychology* 1, no. 2 (1997): 146; Mazarr, "The Psychological Sources of Terrorism," p. 43.

77. Hoffer, as quoted in Mazarr, "The Psychological Sources of Terrorism," p. 44.

78. Ibid.

79. Hadley Cantril, "The Invasion from Mars," http://www.uiowa.edu/~soccomm/cantril.htm (accessed October 13, 2004). This is a summary of results presented in greater detail in Hadley Cantril, Hazel Gaudet, and Herta Herzog, *The Invasion from Mars* (Princeton, NJ: Princeton University Press, 1940).

80. Ibid.

81. See, for example, Gilles Kepel, *The Revenge of God*, trans. Alan Braley (University Park: Pennsylvania State University Press, 1994); Bruce B. Lawrence, *Defenders of God* (New York: Harper & Row, 1989); Karen Armstrong, *The Battle for God* (New York: Ballantine, 2000); Martin E. Marty and R. Scott Appleby, eds., *Fundamentalisms Observed* (Chicago: University of Chicago Press, 1991).

82. Lawrence, *Defenders of God*, p. 8.

83. Ibid.

84. Ibid., p. 232. See also Tom Pyszczynski, Sheldon Solomon, and Jeff Greenberg, *In the Wake of 9/11* (Washington, DC: American Psychological Association, 2003), p. 158.

85. Sudhir Kakar, *The Colors of Violence* (Chicago: University of Chicago Press, 1996), p. 187. See also Neil J. Kressel, review of *The Colors of Violence*, by Sudhir Kakar, in *Political Psychology* 19, no. 4 (1998): 853. For a similar explanation grounded in Adlerian psychology, see Eldar Hasanov, "Religious and National Radicalism in Middle-Eastern Countries," *International Forum of Psychoanalysis* 14 (2005): 120–22. For a more general discussion of how threats to esteem can be found at the source of many forms of self-defeating behavior, see Baumeister, "Esteem Threat," pp. 145–74.

86. Jones, *Terror and Transformation*, p. 74.

87. Thomas Simons, *Islam in a Globalizing World* (Palo Alto, CA: Stanford University Press, 2003) as quoted in Mazarr, "The Psychological Sources of Islamic Terrorism," p. 48.

88. See Mazarr, "The Psychological Sources of Islamic Terrorism," p. 40.

89. See, for example, Simon Haddad, "The Origins of Popular Support for Lebanon's Hezbollah," *Studies in Conflict & Terrorism* 29, no. 1 (January–February 2006): 21–34. Haddad shows that dissatisfaction with the government in Lebanon is one of two predictors of support for the extremist Hezbollah organization. The other, more intense factor is personal religiosity.

90. See Kenneth R. Timmerman, *Preachers of Hate* (New York: Crown Forum, 2003); Neil J. Kressel, "Antisemitism, Social Science, and the Muslim and Arab World," *Judaism* 52, no. 3–4 (Summer/Fall 2003): 239.

91. David Pryce-Jones, *The Closed Circle* (New York: HarperPerennial, 1991), p. 34.

Chapter 6

1. "Chirac Calls for Severe Punishment for Anti-Semitic, Racist Acts," Agence France-Presse (English), July 8, 2004, http://www.lexis-nexis.com/universe (accessed November 15, 2006).

2. The story of Le Chambon-sur-Lignon is documented in Philip P. Hallie, *Lest Innocent Blood Be Shed* (New York: HarperPerennial, 1994). Le Chambon-sur-Lignon is one of two towns collectively honored at the Yad Vashem Holocaust memorial in Israel.

3. *Weapons of the Spirit*, 1987, documentary film written and directed by Pierre Sauvage.

4. Sauvage, "Le Chambon's Challenge Today," Chambon Foundation Home Page, 2004, http://www.chambon.org/challenge2.htm (accessed November 15, 2006).

5. Quoted in the film *Weapons of the Spirit*.

6. All the quotations in this paragraph are from the film *Weapons of the Spirit*.

7. See, for example, James W. Jones, *Terror and Transformation* (New York: Taylor and Francis, 2002), pp. 106–17.

8. Edmund Burke, "Reflections on the Revolution in France," in *The Great Political Theories*, ed. Michael Curtis, vol. 2, new ed. (New York: Avon, 1981), p. 52.

9. Ibid., p. 58.

10. Ibid., p. 60.

11. Thomas Paine, "The Rights of Man," in Curtis, *The Great Political Theories*, pp. 64–65.

12. For a review of seven recent books in this debate, see Cornelia Dean, "Faith, Reason, God and Other Imponderables," *New York Times*, July 25, 2006.

13. Andrew Sullivan," When Not Seeing Is Believing," *Time*, October 9, 2006, p. 58.

14. Ibid., p. 59.

15. Charles Kimball, *When Religion Becomes Evil* (San Francisco: HarperSanFrancisco, 2002), p. 143.

16. See, for example, Sharon S. Brehm, Saul Kassin, and Steven Fein, *Social Psychology*, 6th ed. (New York: Houghton Mifflin, 2005), pp. 214–20.

17. Kimball, *When Religion Becomes Evil*, p. 25.

18. Eli S. Chesen, *Religion May Be Hazardous to Your Health* (New York: Peter H. Wyden, 1972), p. 1.

19. Kimball, *When Religion Becomes Evil*, p. 72.

20. Irshad Manji, "Under the Cover of Islam," *New York Times*, November 18, 2004.

21. Chesen, *Religion May Be Hazardous to Your Health*, p. 8

22. Ibid., p. 27

23. Ibid., p. 34.

24. United Nations, General Assembly, *Elimination of All Forms of Religious Intolerance*, September 8, 2000, A/55/280, Item 116 (b) of the provisional agenda, para. 85, p. 21.

25. Ibid., para. 119, p. 126.

26. United Nations, Economic and Social Council, Commission on Human Rights, *Civil and Political Rights, Including Religious Intolerance: Report Submitted by Mr. Abdelfattah Amor, Special Rapporteur on Freedom of Religion or Belief*, January 16, 2004, E/CN.4/2004/63, Item 11 (e) of the provisional agenda, para. 115 (a), p. 23.

27. United Nations, General Assembly, *Elimination of All Forms of Religious Intolerance*, August 19, 2003, A/58/296, Item 119 (b) on the provisional agenda, para. 141, p. 23.

28. For standards against which one might judge the relative success of various political and social systems, see Hadley Cantril, "The Human Design," in *Political Psychology: Classic and Contemporary Readings*, ed. Neil J. Kressel (New York: Paragon House, 1993), pp. 75–82.

29. James Madison, "Federalist 10," in Alexander Hamilton, James Madison, and John Jay, *The Federalist Papers* (New York: New American Library, 1961), pp. 77–84.

30. Barnard Haykel and Saud al-Sarhan, "The Apocalypse Will Be Blogged," *New York Times*, September 12, 2006.

31. Salman Rushdie, as quoted in Edward Rothstein, "Faith Has Reasons of Which Reason Knows Nothing," *New York Times*, June 26, 2006. Rothstein notes, however, that Rushdie is no fan of American policy.

32. David Brooks, "The Grand Delusion," *New York Times*, September 28, 2006.

33. Michael J. Mazarr, "The Psychological Sources of Islamic Terrorism," *Policy Review* (June and July 2004): 54.

34. Ibid.

35. "Declassified Key Judgments of the National Intelligence Estimate on Global Terrorism," *New York Times*, September 27, 2006.

36. Ibid.

37. Bruce Hoffman, as quoted in David E. Sanger, "Waging the War on Terror: Report Belies Optimistic View," *New York Times*, September 27, 2006.

38. Blair, as quoted in "Blair Delivers Dramatic Address on Extremism, Israel and Global Values," *Jerusalem Post Online Edition*, August 2, 2006, http://www.jpost.com/servlet/Satellite?cid=1154525793541&pagename=Jpost%2FJPArticle%2FPrinter (accessed August 3, 2006).

39. Theodore Dalrymple, "Divided Hearts," *National Review*, September 11, 2006, p. 23. Dalrymple does not identify the survey upon which he bases his calculation, but several are generally consistent with his point. See Alexandra Frean and Rajeev Syal, "Community Divided on Terrorism and Security," *Times* (London), July 4, 2006, http://www.lexis-nexis.com/ universe (accessed November 29, 2006); Melanie Phillips, "Blame Our Establishment for Appeasing These Extremists," *Daily Mail* (London), July 5, 2006, p. 15, http://www.lexis-nexis.com/universe (accessed November 29, 2006); Josie Clarke, "More British Muslims 'Believe London Terror Bombings Are Justified,'" Press Association Newsfile, August 7, 2006, http://www.lexis-nexis.com/universe (accessed November 29, 2006); "Attitudes to Living in Britain—A Survey of Muslim Opinion," Gfk NOP Social Research Report, http://www.imaginate.uk.com/MCC01_SURVEY/Site%20Download.pdf (accessed November 29, 2006); *The Great Divide: How Westerners and Muslims View Each Other*, Pew Global Attitudes Project (Washington, DC: Pew Research Center, 2006).

40. Dalrymple, "Divided Hearts." See also Patrick E. Tyler and Don Van Natta Jr., "Militants in Europe Openly Call for Jihad and the Rule of Islam," *New York Times*, April 26, 2004; Mark Landler and Souad Mekhennet,

"Wider Network May Be Linked to Bomb Plot, Germans Say," *New York Times*, August 23, 2006. Mark Steyn's assessment of the worst-case scenario is alarmist but nonetheless awakening. See *America Alone: The End of the World as We Know It* (New York: Regnery, 2006).

41. See, for example, Adam Brodsky, "Terror's U.S. Breeding Ground," *New York Post*, March 23, 2006.

42. The weakest policy proposals come from the United Nations. The clearest conclusion of the special rapporteur is that the events of September 11 "unleashed a veritable Islamophobia, the extent of which cannot yet be estimated." The report warns that

> Islamophobia in this context could well convert the historic failure of Islam-based extremism into an unexpected victory. The desire to confine Islam in a pathological straitjacket and make it the axis of evil ultimately leads to conferring the stamp of legitimacy on forms of extremism for which Islam has been a pretext rather than a cause. . . . The Special Rapporteur expresses the hope that, in their fight against terrorism, States will not mistake their target and, while continuing to combat terrorist acts, they will refocus their efforts on the origins of terrorism and on the need to ensure protection and promotion of human rights without bias or selectivity.

United Nations, General Assembly, *Elimination of All Forms of Religious Intolerance*, paras. 152–53, p. 30. This is, in effect, a failure to engage the problem.

43. Blair, as quoted in "Blair Delivers Dramatic Address."

44. Al-Rashed, as quoted in Neil MacFarquhar, "Muslim Scholars Increasingly Debate Unholy War," *New York Times*, December 10, 2004.

45. Blair, as quoted in "Blair Delivers Dramatic Address."

46. Ibid.

47. See, for example, Douglas C. Minson, "Ordered Liberty Under God," *Intercollegiate Review* 38, no. 1 (Fall 2002): 52–55; Robert P. Kraynak, *Christian Faith and Modern Democracy* (Notre Dame, IN: University of Notre Dame Press, 2001); Hassan M. Fattah, "Arab Democracy, a U.S. Goal, Falters," *New York Times*, April 10, 2006; Noah Feldman, *After Jihad: America and the Struggle for Islamic Democracy* (New York: Farrar, Straus & Giroux, 2003).

48. "Declassified Key Judgments."

49. Mazarr, "Psychological Sources," p. 58.

50. Ibid., p. 59.

51. Ibid.

52. Ibid.

53. Ibid., p. 58.

54. Hashem Aghajari, as quoted in Thomas L. Friedman, "An Islamic Reformation," *New York Times*, December 4, 2002.

55. Mohammad Kazemini Boroujerdi, as quoted in Nazila Fathi, "Iran Arrests Outspoken Cleric Who Opposes Religious Rule," *New York Times*, October 9, 2006.

56. Michael Freund, "Pro-Israeli Editor Beaten in Bangladesh," *Jerusalem Post Online Edition*, October 17, 2006, http://www.jpost.com (accessed October 18, 2006).

57. David D. Kirkpatrick, "Christian Conservatives Will Take Aim at Supreme Court in New Telecast," *New York Times*, July 15, 2005.

58. Linda Greenhouse, "Court Says States Need Not Finance Divinity Studies," *New York Times*, February 26, 2004; "Excerpts from the Ruling on Religious Scholarships," *New York Times*, February 26, 2004; Linda Greenhouse, "Atheist Presents Case for Taking God from Pledge," *New York Times*, March 25, 2004; "Excerpts from Arguments on the Meaning of 'Under God' in the Pledge of Allegiance," *New York Times*, March 25, 2004; Claire Cooper, "Newdow Enlists Allies, Renews Fight Over Pledge," *Sacramento Bee*, January 5, 2005, http://www.lexis-nexis.com/universe (accessed November 15, 2006).

59. Forrest Church, *The Separation of Church and State* (Boston: Beacon, 2004), pp. ix–x.

60. Susan Jacoby, *Freethinkers* (New York: Henry Holt, 2004), p. 355.

61. Ibid, p. 358.

62. Brenda Goodman, "Teaching the Bible in Georgia's Public Schools," *New York Times*, March 29, 2006, p. 7.

63. Marci A. Hamilton, *God vs. the Gavel* (New York: Cambridge University Press, 2005), p. 7.

Index

Aaron, 156
'Abduh, Muhammad, 81
abortion clinic violence statistics, 92
Abraham, 154, 182
Abu Sufyan, 164
Achan, 154
Adam, 161
adjustive function of personality, 201
adultery, 68, 117, 171
Afghani, Jamal al-Din al-, 80
Afghanistan, 11, 61, 87, 199, 200, 253, 256
African Americans, 146
Agag, 156
Ahmadinejad, Mahmoud, 59, 241
Ains Shams University, 57
Akaka, Daniel, 142
Akhtab, Huyayy b., 165
Akyol, Mustafa, 11
Al-Arabiya TV, 56–57, 256
Al-Azhar University, 196
Alcoholics Anonymous, 217
Algeria, 253
Ali, 165, 166
Allport, Gordon W., 210, 214, 215
Al-Mawrid Institute, 69
  interpretation of Koran and *hadiths*, 69–73
aloneness, 221
al-Qaeda, 11, 64, 199
Altemeyer, Bob, 197
Amalek, 130, 131, 155–58
American policy as source of Islamic extremism, 230
American public opinion
  on Islamic extremism, 62–64
  on religion, 40
  on religious violence, 127
American religious beliefs according to survey, 50
"American Taliban" and religious rights, 34, 40

Amir, Yigal, 128
psychological profile, 129
Amish, 228
Amjad, Moiz, 69
Islamic philosophy of, 69–73
Amor, Abdelfattah, 247
"ancient animosities" explanations, 187
ancient imagery, 168
Angelou, Maya, 143
anger and religious extremism, 54
Ansari, Seif al-Din al-, 64
anthrax, 95
antiabortion extremism, 91–108
compared to Islamic extremism, 101–103
justifiable homicide argument and, 102
motivations, 101
public support for, 107
anti-Americanism, 79, 82, 83, 230, 252, 258
psychological origins of, 84–86
anti-American terrorism and Islamic public support for, 59
Antichrist, 36
anti-Christianity, Islamic, 58, 184–87
antisemitism, 58, 83, 248
Christian, 98, 112–16, 185
Islamic, 72, 84–86, 87, 163, 166, 168, 184–87, 254
Islamic and Christian compared, 186
apocalyptic Christianity, 35–42
apostasy, 195, 196, 197
Islam and, 68, 70
Judaism and, 174
Arabian Jews, 163
Arafat, Yassir, 128
Arena, John, 94
Armstrong, Karen, 28, 43
Army of God, 93, 99, 100, 105
Asad, Ka'b b., 165
Ashcroft, John, 107
Ashmawy, Said al-, 14
Atta, Mohammed, 88
psychological profile of, 89
Augsburg, Peace of, 119
Augustine, Saint, 159, 176
authoritarian faith, 214
author's background, 25–29, 148
auto da fé, 114
Avivim, 125
Ayer, A. J., 215
'Azzouz, Salim, 48

Badawi, Jamal, 101
Bana, Hassan al-, 82
Bangash, Zafar, 79
Banu Nadir, 164
Banu Qaynuda, 164
Banu Qurayza, 165, 166, 168
Battle of Khaibar, 163, 165
Battle of the Trench, 164, 167
Battle of Uhud, 167
Bat Yam, 125
BBC (British Broadcasting Corporation) depiction of al-Sudais, 33, 44
Becker, Ernest, 211–12, 220
Belgium, 199
belief systems, 200, 218, 222, 228, 252
Benedict XVI (pope), 188

Benham, Flip, 103
Benjamin, Daniel, 89
Benjamin, tribe of, 150
Berman, Paul, 79
bestiality, 171
Bible
  antiabortion extremism and, 97, 99, 105
  corporal punishment and, 162
  Deuteronomy, 155, 156, 171
  Esther, 99, 156
  Exodus, 156
  feminism and, 161
  hard passages of, 153, 154, 161
  Hebrews, 162
  interpretation of, 37, 50, 139–44, 152, 156, 237
  Job, 141
  Joshua, 155
  Judges, 149
  King James Version, 141
  Peter, 161
  Proverbs, 161
  rape and, 151
  as school text, 264
  slavery and, 161
  social issues and, 161
  Timothy, 161
biblical literalism, 154
  and serpent-handlers, 139–42
Bill of Rights, 119
bin Laden, Osama, 46, 75, 82, 149, 166, 199–201, 252
  Islamic public support for, 59
birthplace and religion, 146
Blair, Tony, 253, 255–56
blasphemy, 68, 117, 161, 171, 193–94
Bolsheviks, 252
Bonhoeffer, Dietrich, 104
Boniface VIII (pope), 176
Bono, 143
Boroujerdi, Mohammed Kazemini, 258
Bosnia, 117
Boston Globe, 14, 127
Boykin, William "Jerry," 39
Bray, Michael, 104–105
Brooks, David, 252
Bruner, Jerome S., 201
Buffalo News, 108
Burke, Edmund, 239–40
Bush, George W., 60
  religious views of, 19, 33, 39
  statement on Bible, 142

Calvin, John, 117
Canaan, conquest of, 155
Cantril, Hadley, 224–25
Caro, Joseph, 144
Catholicism, 188
  antiabortion extremism and, 95
  religious extremism and, 116
  salvation and, 176
  treatment of nonbelievers, 176
Chesen, Eli S., 204, 244
Chesterton, G. K., 21
Chirac, Jacques, 235–36
chosen people, interpretations of, 172
Chowdury, Salah Uddin Shoaib, 258
"Christian" counseling, 40
Christian evil
  decline of, 117–18
  sources of, 111

Christian extremists, 91–108
Christian fundamentalism, 190, 223, 237
  Muhammad and, 39
Christian Identity movement, 98
Christianity
  benevolence and, 237
  foundational narrative of, 159
  salvation and, 175
  treatment of nonbelievers, 175
Christian moderation, origins of, 118
Church, Forrest, 263
Church of God, 140
Clinton, William J., 142
close-mindedness, 218–19
cognitive dissonance, 192
Cold War, 61
colonialism, Muslim reaction to, 80–82
Columbus, Christopher, 143
combating religious extremism, 247–61
  addressing root causes, 250–52
  believers' responsibilities, 241–47
  Islamic, 73
Common Sense (Paine), 240
Communists, 79
conquest of Canaan, 155
Constantine, 182
Constantinople, fall of, 80
Constitution, 262, 264
constitutional interpretation, 191
constructive faith, 213–16
Consumer Reports, 244
controlled secularity, 215
conversion, 68, 193, 197
  Jewish attitude toward, 171
Conversos, 114
corporal punishment in Bible, 162
Coulter, Ann, 16–17
Crist, Charlie, 99
Crusades, 80, 118

Dahmane, Abdessatar, 199–204
Dalrymple, Theodore, 254
Dalrymple, William, 42
Darwin, Charles, 120
Davey, Joshua, 261
death, fear of, 204–207, 211–12, 215, 230
democracy
  Islam and, 256
  Orthodox Judaism and, 125
Denial of Death, The (Becker), 211–12
Dershowitz, Alan, 191
Der Sturmer, 184
destructive faith, 213–16
dhimmi, 68, 185–86
din rodef, 130–31
doctrinal change, 187–93
Dubai, 56
Durant, Will, 112
dysfunctional religion, 54

effects of religion, 212–13
Egypt, 14, 57, 60, 75, 78, 81, 154, 186
Ehrman, Bart D., 141, 178
Eitam, Effi, 122
El Aroud, Malika, 199–204
Ellis, Albert, 212
Elshafay, James, 60
empirical research on religion, 212–13

End of Faith, The. See Harris, Sam
Enlightenment, 194, 226, 227, 263
Erikson, Erik, 216–17
Esposito, John, 66
Europe, 254
Eve, 161
EvilBible.com, 152
existential concerns, 219, 230
exodus from Egypt, 154
expiation, 222
externalization function of personality, 202
Extra Ecclesiam Nulla Salus, 176
extreme religiosity vs. religious extremism, 51
Ezra, Gideon, 122

faith
  advantages of militant, 219–20
  authoritarian, 214
  bad, 213–16
  good, 213–16
  humanistic, 215
  mature, 214
faith-based relief efforts, 28
Fajr-5 rocket, 163
fallibility, human, 192
Falwell, Jerry, 39
families of extremists, 56
fascists, 79
fatwa, 60, 252
fear of death. *See* death, fear of
feminism, 68
  Bible and, 161
Ferdinand (king), 112
Fernando, Ajith, 175
Fieldston School, 61
First Amendment, 263
Five Pillars of Islam, 169
fleeces, 40
flogging, 72
flood, biblical, 154
Foreman, George, 143
foundational narrative
  Christianity, 159
  Islam, 163
  Judaism, 153
Founding Fathers, 263
France, 206, 235
  Jews during World War II in, 235–36
Frankl, Viktor, 210
freedom of conscience, 120. *See also* religious tolerance
freedom to choose, 221
freethinkers, 118
Freud, Sigmund, 208–209
Friedman, Thomas, 34
friendship with nonbelievers, 68
Fromm, Erich, 210, 214–15
frustration, 84
fundamentalism
  Christian, 190, 223, 227, 237, 261
  definition of, 51–53, 197
  meaning of, 28

Galileo, 29
Gaza, 48, 61, 121, 128
gemara, 144
genocide, 155
geographical origins of religious affiliation, 146–47
Georgia (state), 264
Germany, 88

Ghandour, Maha, 55–57
Ghandour, Salah, 55–57, 89
Gibson, Mel, 143
globalization, 226, 229
Goethe, Johann Wolfgang von, 221
Goldberg, Jeffrey, 130, 135
Goldberg, Jonah, 16
golden calf, 154
golden rule, 169
Goldstein, Baruch, 125
Goldstein, Shaul, 131
Gore, Al, 33
Gorenberg, Gershom, 133
Gospel message, 176
Gospels
  John, 175
  Mark, 141, 142
  Matthew, 160, 178
Graham, Franklin, 39
Grant, Ulysses S., 143
Great Awakening, 263
Greeley, Andrew, 26, 207
guilt, 202, 222
Gunn, David, 99

hadith, 68, 70, 81, 165, 180
halakha (Jewish law), 129
Haman, 156
Hamas, 60, 61, 81, 87, 123, 166
Hamed, Nasser ibn, 64
Hamilton, Alexander, 109
Hanegbi, Tsahi, 131
hard passages, 153–54
  Bible, 161
  Koran, 179–87
  New Testament, 160
Harris, Sam, 19, 180, 189
Hasan, Asma Gull, 65
Hassidim, 34, 228
Hebron massacre, 126
Hensley, George Went, 139–42
Hezbollah, 9, 61, 88, 123, 163, 166
Hill, Paul, 97, 98–100
Hill, Peter C., 51–53
Hinduism, 171
Hindu-Muslim conflict, 226
Hitler, Adolf, 125
Hoffer, Eric, 223–24
Holland, 14
Holocaust, 235
Holocaust denial, 241
Holyfield, Evander, 143
Holy Spirit, Christian notion of, 38
homosexuality, 68, 98, 171, 222
Hood, Ralph W., 51–53
Horsley, Neal, 98
hostility toward Israel, origins of, 85
hostility toward Jews. *See* antisemitism
Huguenots, 237, 238
human fallibility, 192
humanistic faith, 215
humiliation, 223
Hunsberger, Bruce, 197
Hur, 156
Hussein, Saddam, 39
Husseini, Hajj Amin al-, 81
Huyayy, Safiyya bint, 166

Id al-Adha, 60
Id al-Fitr, 60
identity threats, 221, 222–23, 226–27, 229, 257
idolatry, 171
Iftikhar, Arsalan Tariq, 101

Iftikhar, Asif, 73
immortality, desire for, 215
immortality projects, 220
impact of religion on functioning, 212–13
incest, 171
India, 10, 81, 226
Indonesia, 58, 59, 253
infallibility of pope, 50
infidels, treatment of, 169–87, 175, 193
  Koran, 179–87
inquisitions, 112–16
insanity, suicide bombers and, 89
Institutes of Biblical Law, The (Rushdoony), 144
interfaith relations, 174
In the Shade of the Koran. See Qutb, Sayyid
Iqbal, Muhammad, 81
Iran, 59, 83, 163, 257
Iraq, 230, 253, 256, 257
Iraq war, 46
Irfan, Maulana Mufti Abul, 11
irreligion, extremism associated with, 26
Isabella (queen), 112
Islam
  American perceptions of, 62
  defining moderate, 42–49
  foundational narrative, 163
  susceptibility to extremism, 28
Islamic antisemitism. *See* antisemitism, Islamic
Islamic extremism
  American public opinion and, 62–64
  central tenets of, 68
  combating, 73
  compared to antiabortion extremism, 101–103
  growth potential of, 253
  ideological origins of, 74–83
  Islamic public opinion toward, 58–59
  Koran and, 179–87
  Muslim popular support for, 254
  origins in failed societies of, 83–84
  perceived success of past extremism and, 87–88
  political roots of, 83–84
  poverty and, 255
  psychological roots of, 84–86
  reasons for strength of, 194–97, 229–30
  self-serving bias and, 86
  social roots, 229–30
  survey findings concerning, 58–59
  underestimation of, 28
  vulnerability of, 257
  Western public opinion and, 255
Islamic hostility toward Israel, origins of, 85
Islamic moderates, 195, 197
  difficulties facing, 258
  encouraging, 256
Islamic theology, American perceptions of, 62
Islamic threat and public opinion, 62–64
Israel, 40, 61, 82, 85, 121, 124, 163, 166, 172, 227–28, 230, 258
Israeli extremism, 121–36
  public opinion and, 132

Israeli-Hezbollah conflict, 163
Israeli moderation, sources of, 127
'Issa, Shamlan Yousef al-, 86

Jabesh-Gilead, 151
Jacoby, Jeff, 14, 127
jahiliyyah, 77
Jamaat-i-Islami, 81
James, William, 21–23, 42, 51, 53, 204, 208, 215
Japanese ultranationalists, 252
Jean Barois (Martin du Gard), 204–207
Jefferson, Thomas, 109
Jenkins, Jerry, 35–37
Jericho, 154
Jesus, 109–11, 139, 158–59, 161–62, 175, 183, 185, 237
Jewish ethics, 158
Jewish extremism, 121–36, 227
  motivation behind, 158
Jewish Fundamentalism in Israel (Shahak and Mezvinsky), 134
Jewish Literacy (Telushkin), 157
Jewish moderation, 127
Jews, Arabian, 163
Jibril (angel), 164
jihad, 68, 71–72, 78, 86, 180, 200, 253
  interpretation of, 46
Johnson, Paul, 111
Jones, James V., 217
Jordan, 14, 58
Joshua, 154
Joy, Lina, 197
Judaism, 154
  apostasy and, 174
  foundational narrative of, 153
  Orthodox, 174, 191
  Reconstructionism, 172
  social justice and, 174
  treatment of nonbelievers and, 173
  varieties of, 189
judaizing, 114
Juergensmeyer, Mark, 104
justifiable homicide argument and antiabortion extremism, 102
Jyllands-Posten. *See* Muhammad, Danish cartoons of

Kach movement, 123, 125, 126
Kahane, Chai, 126
Kahane, Meir, 123, 125, 126
Kakar, Sudhir, 226
Kaplan, Mordecai, 172
Kepel, Gilles, 28
Kfar Tapuah, 122, 123
Khaibar, Battle of. *See* Battle of Khaibar
Khaibar-1 rocket, 163, 166
Khamenei, Ali, 195
Khan, Sayyid Ahmad, 81
Khomeini, Ruhollah, 9, 61, 82–83, 87, 195
Khuli, Ibrahim al-, 196
Kimball, Charles, 23, 41, 53, 105, 106, 221, 243, 245
King, Martin Luther, Jr., 143
Klein, Joel, 60
knowledge of Islam, American, 63
Kook, Avraham, 136
Kook, Zvi Yehuda, 136
Kopp, James, 92–96
Koran
  hard passages of, 179–87

interpretation of, 11, 48, 64–65, 67, 69–73, 81, 179, 196
Islamic extremism and, 179–87
martyrdom and, 55
moderate verses in, 181
treatment of women in, 182
Kuwait, 86, 230

LaHaye, Tim, 35–41, 37
Lambs of Christ, 94
Lapid family, 125
Lebanon, 55–57, 58, 61, 186, 253, 256
Le Chambon-sur-Lignon, 235–38
Lee, Robert E., 143
Left Behind series (LaHaye and Jenkins). *See* LaHaye, Tim
Levi, tribe of, 149, 150
Lewis, Bernard, 74, 85, 90, 120, 182–84
liberal democracy, 61
liberal theologians, 243
Libya, 60
Lieberman, Bentzi, 122
Liebman, Charles, 27
limbo, 187, 188
literalism, biblical, 154, 190
Locke, John, 120
London, terrorism in, 61
Luther, Martin, 116, 143

Ma-alot, 125
McConnell, Michael W., 21
McVeigh, Timothy, 42, 98
Madhi (sheikh), 48
Madison, James, 109, 120
Maimonides, Moses, 144
Malaysia, 197
Manji, Irshad, 246
Mansur, Salim, 11
Maqdisi, Abu Muhammad al-, 64
Maranos, 114
Margolis, David, 124
Marlette, Doug, 13
Marshall, Paul, 15
Martin du Gard, Roger, 204–207
Marty, Martin E., 28
martyrdom, 45, 55, 76, 159
Koran and, 55
psychology of, 57
Marx, Karl, 109
Maslow, Abraham, 210
Massoud, Ahmed Shah, 199
Mathis, Andrew, 134
mature faith, 214
May, Rollo, 213–15
Mazarr, Michael J., 220, 252, 257–58
Mecca, 164, 196
Medina, 164
Meissner, W. W., 200, 222
MEMRI (Middle East Media Research Institute), 67
mental illness, definition of, 49
messianism, 135
metros, 134
Mezvinsky, Norton, 134
Middle East peace process, 257
Milestones. See Qutb, Sayyid
militant faith, advantages of, 219–20
Milson, Menahem, 183
Minogue, Kenneth, 52
Mir, Hamid, 167
Mishneh, 144
Mishneh Torah (Maimonides), 144
missionary impulse, 170

Mix My Blood with the Blood of the Unborn (Hill), 99
moderate religion, weaknesses of, 216–24
modernity, threat of, 226–29, 257
modernization, 46, 80, 226–29, 226
Mongols, 80
moral goodness, religion and, 235–38
Moral Majority, 39, 40
Morocco, 58, 59
moser, 129
Moses, 156, 182
Moussaioui, Zaccarias, 90
Mu'adh, Sa'd ibn, 165
Muhammad, 70, 71, 109, 163, 165–68, 182–83, 196
  Danish cartoons of, 9–17
Mullah Omar, 199
Muslim Brotherhood, 81, 87
Muslim extremism. *See* Islamic extremism
Muslim Woman Magazine, 47
Muttalib, Safia bint Abdul, 167

Nabulsi, Shaker al-, 196
Najeeb, Janan, 101
Nasrallah, Hassan, 9, 56, 163
National Bible Association, 142
National Bible Week, 142
National Review, 16
Nazis, 79, 235, 252
Newdow, Michael A., 262
Newman, John Henry, 34
New Testament
  hard passages of, 160
  interpretation of, 109–12, 139–44. *See also* Bible, interpretation of
  psychology of, 160, 161
New York, 60
New Yorker, 130–31, 135
New York Post, 12
New York Times, 16, 34, 59–61, 143
Nichols, Terry, 42
Nigeria, Miss World contest in, 16
Nightline, 99
Noah, 154
Noahide laws, 171
  Trinitarian conception of God and, 171
nonbelievers, treament of. *See* infidels, treatment of
Nostra Aetate, 176

O'Donnell, James J., 188
Oklahoma City bombing, 42
Old Testament, 144
Omar, Mullah, 199
Onan, 154
Operation Rescue, 94, 103
Opinions and Personality (Smith, Bruner, and White), 201
Orthodox Judaism, 125, 144, 154, 191. *See also* Judaism
  democracy and, 125
Orthodox Union, 122
Oslo Accords, 128
Ottoman Empire, 80

Paine, Thomas, 240
Pakistan, 10, 14, 58, 59, 69, 194
Palestine, 253
Palestinians, 60, 64
  suicide bombers, 33, 45, 46
Paloutzian, Raymond, 213

Pargament, Kenneth I., 206
Parton, Dolly, 143
Paul, 159
Peace of Westphalia, 194
peoples of the book. *See dhimmi*
Peri, Yoram, 134
Perry, Marvin, 179
Pharaoh, 154
Phil Donahue Show, 99
"pigs and apes," Islamic depiction of Jews as, 33, 45, 47, 48
Pius X (pope), 187
Pledge of Allegiance, 262
Popper, Ami, 125, 126
poverty, Islamic extremism and, 255
pragmatism. *See* James, William
premillennial school. *See* LaHaye, Tim
Presley, Elvis, 143
Preuss, Teddy, 125
Principe, Lawrence, 190
Protocols of the Elders of Zion, The, 134
psychiatric diagnosis, 49
psychological impact of religion, 246–47
psychological interpretation, New Testament, 160, 161
psychological origins
  of Islamic extremism, 84–86
  of religion, 207, 216–24
  of serpent-handlers, 141
psychological profiles
  of Eden Natan Zada, 122
  of Mahmoud Ahmadinejad, 242
  of religious extremists, 223
  of suicide bombers, 88
  of Yigal Amir, 129

Qaradhawi, Yousef al-, 10, 56, 195
Qassam, 'Izz al-Din al-, 81
Qassam missiles, 81
Qimni, Sayyed al-, 195
Quereshi, Yaqoob, 10
Quindlen, Anna, 102
Qutb, Sayyid, 75–79, 82–83, 88, 90, 191

Rabbinical Assembly of Conservative Judaism, 122
Rabbinic period, 156
Rabin, Yitzhak, 128
Rahner, Karl, 177
Ramadan, Tariq, 67
rape, in Bible, 151
Rapp, Helena, 125
Rapture. *See* LaHaye, Tim
Rashed, Abdul Rahman al-, 256
Rational-Emotive Behavioral Therapy (REBT), 212
rattlesnakes, 139
Rauf, Feisal Abdul, 66
Rayhana, 165
Raziq, 'Ali 'Abd al-, 81
Reagan, Ronald, 142
Reconstruction Theology, 104, 105
Reformation, 194
relativistic systems of values, 227
religion and science, 190
religious belief
  comparing and assessing, 241–47
  psychological roots of, 204–207
  psychology of, 216–24
religious extremism
  anger and, 45
  appeal of, 50

Catholicism and, 116–17
combating, 247–61
core beliefs, 193, 195, 216–17, 244–45
definition of, 33–54
Islamic public support for, 58–59
motivation behind, 199–204
Protestantism and, 116–17
psychology of, 199–204, 223
root causes, 250–52
social and political roots, 224–31
religious moderation, 27
weaknesses of, 224–31
religious toleration, 119
Renaissance, 194
responsa, 144
Resurrection of Christ, 50
retros, 134
Ridha, Rashid, 81
Right-to-Life movement, 100
Robertson, Pat, 262
rodef, 129
Roe v. Wade, 103
Rokeach, Milton, 218
Roosevelt, Theodore, 143
Rudolph, Eric Robert, 98
Rummo, Gregory, 34, 41
Rushdie, Salman, 9, 195, 252
Rushdoony, Rousas John, 144
Russell, Bertrand, 111, 118, 160

sacred texts. *See also* Bible, Koran
abandonment of, 198
interpretation of, 28, 145, 152, 162, 187–93, 190
Sadat, Anwar, 78
Sadeq, 'Adel, 57
Safia, 167
Safire, William, 143
salvation, 175, 176
Sarwar, Malik Imtiaz, 197
Satanic Verses, The. See Rushdie, Salman
Sattar, Muhammad 'Abd al-, 48
Saud, Muhammad ibn, 82
Saudi Arabia, 46, 61, 64, 82, 87, 149, 230
Saul (king), 156
Sauvage, Pierre, 235
schizophrenia, 60
schools in Islamic world, 86–87
Schulchan Aruch (Caro), 144, 173
Schweitzer, Frederick, 179
science and religion, 190
scientific studies of religion, 212–13
Second Coming of Christ, 41
Second Temple, 158
Second Vatican Council, 176
self-serving bias, Islamic extremism and, 86
self-transcendence, 212
separation of church and state, 40, 68, 183, 194, 261–63
September 11, 2001, 88, 199, 200, 206, 220, 253
conspiracy theories about, 59
impact of, 18
reaction to, 37–38, 43, 61, 71, 73, 74, 88
Sermon on the Mount, 109–11, 115
serpent-handlers, 139–42
psychological explanations for, 141
Serrano, Andres, 12

sexuality, 222–23, 227
Shafi', Imam al-, 10
Shahada, 169
Shahak, Israel, 134
Shakespeare, William, 143
Shannon, Shelley, 94
sharia, 68, 78, 197, 257
Sharon, Ariel, 122–23, 131
Sharpton, Al, 12
Shema, 169
Shiite Islam, 60, 82, 166
Shin Bet security agency, 122
Simon, Steven, 89
Six Day War, 124
slavery, Bible and, 161
Slepian, Barnett, 92–96, 108
Smith, George H., 160, 162
Smith, Irene, 206
Smith, M. Brewster, 201
social adjustment function of personality, 202
social and political roots of religious extremism, 224–31
socialization and Islamic extremism, 86
socialization for hatred, 86, 230
social psychology, 192, 197, 201, 218, 238, 252
Southern Baptists, 107, 108
Soviet Union, 172
Spain, 253
Spanish Inquisition, 112–16
Sprinzak, Ehud, 129
Srebrenica, 42
Sri Lanka, 175
Star Academy reality show, 45
Stern, Bezalel, 134
Stevens, Alexander, 161
stoning, 72, 171
stories, religious, 190
Sudais, Abdur-Rahman al-, 33, 44
  views of, 44–48
Sudan, 60
suicide bombers, 140
  insanity and, 89
  motivation of, 220
  profiles of, 88
suicide bombings, 60
Sullivan, Andrew, 241–42
Sunnah, 68
Sunni Islam, 60
Supreme Court, 261–63
survey findings concerning
  American religious beliefs, 45
  antiabortion extremism, 107
  Islamic extremism, 58–59, 62–64
Syria, 48, 257

Taggart, Sarah, 207
Taliban, 82
  difference between fundamentalist Christians and, 41
Talmud, 156, 191
Tantawi (sheikh), 48
Technion (Israel Institute of Technology), 61
Telushkin, Joseph, 157
Temple Mount, 124, 132, 172
  plots against, 132–33
Teresa, Mother, 143
textbooks in the Muslim world, 86–87
Theis, Edouard, 236, 237, 238
theories of religion
  Allport, 210

Becker, 211–12
Chesen, 246–47
Ellis, 212
empirical evidence and, 212–13
Erikson, 216–17
Frankl, 210
Freud, 208, 209
Fromm, 210, 214
Maslow, 210
May, 213–14
Thirty Years' War, 119
Tiller, George, 94
Toleration Act, 119
Torah, 144, 157
interpretation of, 145, 158
Toronto Sun, 101
treatment of infidels. *See* infidels, treatment of
treatment of nonbelievers. *See also* infidels, treatment of
Catholicism, 176
Christianity, 175
Judaism, 173
treatment of women, 193
in Koran, 182
triacetone triperoxide, 61
tribe of Benjamin, 150
tribe of Levi, 149, 150
Trinitarian conception of God, Noahide laws and, 171
Trocme, Andre, 236, 238
True Believer, The (Hoffer), 223
Turkey, 58, 59

Umar, 166
Unam Sanctam, 176
"Understanding Islam" scholars, 69
United Kingdom, 253
United Nations, 228, 241, 247, 248
ineffectiveness of, 249
United Nations Human Rights Council, 60

Van Dyke, Dick, 143
Van Gogh, Theo, 14
Varieties of Religious Experience, The (James), 51
Vatican, 115, 188
Vatican Council II, 176, 194
Vichy regime, 235
Vidino, Lorenzo, 14
Vines, Jerry, 39
violence, Christian history and, 41–42
virgin birth, 50
vital lies, 211

Waagner, Clayton, 95–98, 95
Wahhab, Muhammad ibn 'Abd al-, 82
Warraq, Ibn, 195
Washington, George, 21
Watt, W. Montgomery, 168
Weisgan, Asher, 126
Welles, Orson, 224, 225
Weslin, Norman, 95
West Bank, 123, 128
Western public opinion and Islamic extremism, 255
What Everyone Needs to Know about Islam (Esposito), 66
When Religion Becomes Evil. See Kimball, Charles
White, Robert W., 201

Why I Am a Muslim (Hasan), 65
Wiesel, Elie, 26
Wilde, Oscar, 143
Williamson, W. Paul, 51–53
Wilson, James Q., 119
women, Islamic treatment of, 61
World War II, 235
Wright, Derek, 218

Ya'el, 168
Year of the Bible, 142
Yemen, 10
Yom Kippur War, 172, 186

Zada, Eden Natan, 121–23
  psychological profile of, 122
Zawahiri, Ayman al-, 75, 82
Zayd, Nasr Abu, 196
Ziglar, Zig, 143
Zuckerman, Phil, 146